PRESIDENTIAL CAMPAIGNS AND
PRESIDENTIAL ACCOUNTABILITY

DEMOCRACY, FREE ENTERPRISE,
AND THE RULE OF LAW

This series is devoted to the study
of democracy throughout the world,
of institutions that sustain and extend it,
and of forces that perpetually challenge
and endanger it.

Series Editor
Peter F. Nardulli, University of Illinois

Editorial Board
James Alt, Harvard University
Robert Bates, Harvard University
Henry Brady, University of California, Berkeley
Pradeep Chhibber, University of California, Berkeley
David Collier, University of California, Berkeley
John Freeman, University of Minnesota
G. Bingham Powell, University of Rochester
Beth Simmons, Harvard University
Paul Sniderman, Stanford University

MICHELE P. CLAIBOURN

Presidential Campaigns and Presidential Accountability

UNIVERSITY OF ILLINOIS PRESS
URBANA, CHICAGO, AND SPRINGFIELD

© 2011 by the Board of Trustees
of the University of Illinois
All rights reserved
Manufactured in the United States of America
1 2 3 4 5 C P 5 4 3 2 1
∞ This book is printed on acid-free paper.

Library of Congress Cataloging-in-Publication Data
Claibourn, Michele P., 1971–
Presidential campaigns and presidential accountability /
Michele P. Claibourn.
p. cm.
Includes bibliographical references and index.
ISBN-13: 978-0-252-03592-0 (hardcover : alk. paper)
ISBN-10: 0-252-03592-5 (hardcover : alk. paper)
ISBN-13: 978-0-252-07789-0 (pbk. : alk. paper)
ISBN-10: 0-252-07789-X (pbk. : alk. paper)
 1. Political campaigns—United States.
 2. Presidential candidates—United States.
 3. Government accountability—United States. I. Title.
JK2281.C58   2011
324.70973—dc22   2010040215

Contents

Illustrations vii

Acknowledgments ix

Introduction: Campaigning for Accountability 1

1. The Meaning of Presidential Accountability 9
2. Agenda Accountability in Action 25
3. Campaigning on Issues 41
4. Hearing the Campaign 56
5. Candidate Messages and Citizen Expectations 72
6. Campaign Connections and Presidential Evaluations 90
7. Beyond the Voting Booth: Clinton 1993 and Obama 2009 114
8. Campaign-Driven Accountability 148

Appendix A: Most Frequently Aired Ads in 2000 161

Appendix B: Estimated Models for Chapter 4 165

Appendix C: Estimated Models for Chapter 5 169

Notes 175

References 187

Index 201

Illustrations

FIGURES

1.1 First-Year Presidential Approval: Clinton, Bush, and Obama 3
3.1 Campaign Advertising Attention over Time 49
3.2 NBC Nightly News Campaign Coverage 53
4.1 Involvement with the Campaign 59
4.2 Hearing Candidate Issue Talk 63
4.3 Impact of Campaign Advertising Emphasis on Hearing Bush 65
4.4 Impact of Campaign Advertising Emphasis on Hearing Gore 66
5.1 Bush Issue Talk and Issue Priming 83
5.2 Gore Issue Talk and Issue Priming 84
6.1 Attention to Campaign Priorities: President Bush 96
6.2 Bush and Education 106
6.3 Bush and Taxes 107
6.4 Bush and Social Security 108
6.5 Bush and Prescription Drugs 110
7.1 Attention to Campaign Priorities: President Clinton 116
7.2 Clinton and Jobs/Economy 118

Illustrations

7.3 Clinton and the Budget Deficit *120*
7.4 Clinton and Taxes *122*
7.5 Clinton and Health Care *123*
7.6 Clinton and Trade *125*
7.7 Attention to Campaign Priorities: President Obama *131*
7.8 Obama and Jobs/Economy *132*
7.9 Obama and Taxes *134*
7.10 Obama and Health Care *136*
7.11 Obama and Energy *138*
7.12 Obama and the Financial Crisis *140*

TABLES

2.1 Agenda Priorities in Presidential Campaign Ads, 1992 *29*
2.2 Agenda Priorities in Presidential Campaign Ads, 2000 *34*
2.3 Agenda Priorities in Presidential Campaign Ads, 2008 *36*
5.1 Cumulative versus Recent Ads *82*
6.1 Agenda Outcomes *94*
6.2 Issue Approval, by Party Identification *104*
6.3 Comparison across Issues: President Bush *111*
7.1 Comparison across Issues: President Clinton *127*
7.2 Comparison across Issues: President Obama *143*
A.1 Bush/RNC Most Aired Ads *162*
A.2 Gore/DNC Most Aired Ads *163*
B.1 Hearing Education Talk *166*
B.2 Hearing Health Care Talk *166*
B.3 Hearing Social Security Talk *167*
B.4 Hearing Tax Talk *167*
C.1 Tax Priority and Candidate Evaluations *170*
C.2 Education Priority and Candidate Evaluations *171*
C.3 Health Care Priority and Candidate Evaluations *172*
C.4 Social Security Priority and Candidate Evaluations *173*

Acknowledgments

In the broadest sense, this book is about our ideas of democracy, ideas that have power over us as citizens, scholars, commentators, and leaders. Like all works, this one builds on the insights of generations of thinkers. I hope it honors these contributions by encouraging a more inclusive democracy. Like all empirical accounts, this one is far from definitive. My aim is to contribute to a useful conversation, to spark new questions about the links between our governors and those they govern, and the role of campaigns in creating these links.

This research was aided by multiple sources. I wish to acknowledge the support of the National Science Foundation through a dissertation improvement grant for helping to fund the 2000 election survey. The University of Wisconsin Survey Center provided in-kind support through countless hours of survey time as well. While writing this book, I was also fortunate to receive sabbatical support from the University of Virginia. The Miller Center of Public Affairs at the University of Virginia graciously provided a quiet place to work and an environment particularly conducive to thinking about presidents and our expectations of the presidency.

This work was improved immeasurably by the feedback of multiple colleagues. I would like to thank Paul Martin, David Klein, David Leblang, Paul Freedman, Chuck Jones, John Geer, Jamie Druckman, and several thoughtful reviewers for their suggestions on parts or all of the manuscript. In addition, the seed of this book was planted while writing my dissertation, and I wish to thank Charles Franklin, Gina Sapiro, and

John Coleman for, many years ago, pushing me to think more broadly about the interaction of citizens and democratic institutions.

My family has been invaluable in the completion of the manuscript. My mother, Joy, has been a tireless supporter. My partner, Paul Martin, a man of countless talents, has been an inestimable colleague, an honest editor, and the man who brings me treats. I could not have written this book without his patient listening, his careful reading of drafts, and his endless encouragement. And to Winifred, whose boundless joy and curiosity, combined with a three-year-old's impatience with this project, has helped me keep things in perspective, I dedicate this effort.

Introduction

CAMPAIGNING FOR ACCOUNTABILITY

> We made a series of what we felt were key statements on the American system, but I'm not sure how many really sank into the electorate. We couldn't tell if any made a difference. That's one reason why LBJ didn't feel particularly bound to follow through on everything. If we had been sure that an issue had been important, however, you can be sure of our reaction.
> —Aide to Lyndon Johnson (quoted in Light 1999)

Presidential election campaigns, and the electorate at which they are aimed, routinely come under fire from scholars, journalists, and pundits alike. Political analysts push candidates to clarify their policy differences. Scholars criticize campaigns for containing too little issue substance and specificity. And both shake their heads solemnly at voters who cannot correctly identify the policy positions of the candidates. Reading the critics, the presidential campaign hardly sounds like a successful process for choosing leaders, much less an effective link in democratic accountability.

In fact, presidential candidates are generally clear on at least one thing—their lists of problems and priorities. The public cares about these priorities and uses them in evaluating the contenders. What's more, in the long and repetitive campaign, citizens come to associate the candidates with their respective agenda priorities. The campaign establishes expectations about where a president will exert his effort once in office. Adherence to, or neglect of, these expectations goes some way in explaining presidential approval. And withdrawal of approval serves as an informal sanction against presidents who ignore the problems they campaigned on.

The fortunes of our most recent presidents early in their administrations serve as a useful illustration. Figure I.1 makes clear the very different patterns in the presidential approval of Bill Clinton, George W. Bush, and Barack Obama in the first year of each presidency.[1]

President Bill Clinton began well enough, with approval rates in the mid-50s. The trend line for Clinton's ratings, though, falls below 50 percent in mid-April 1993 and doesn't reach this midpoint again until early December 1993. Clinton's early tenure was rife with agenda distraction (gays in the military), agenda revision (concern for the economy shifted from unemployment and the fairness of the tax burden to the budget deficit and the response of the bond market), and agenda delay (health care, a signature priority, was put off until late October).

President George W. Bush, too, begins with approval ratings in the mid-50s. For Bush, though, the trend line in this early period never falls below 52 percent. While upticks and downturns are visible in Bush's pre–9/11 approval, they are modest compared to those for Clinton. Unquestionably Bush turned out to be a controversial president, but most of the controversy arose after the agenda-changing terrorist attacks. In the first eight months of office, he spent a great deal of energy on two of his campaign priorities, education and tax cuts, securing legislative victories on both before the year's end.

President Barack Obama's presidency started off in a remarkably strong position compared to his predecessors. The trend in Obama's approval begins in the mid-60s and only dips below 60 percent at the end of May 2009. His numbers decline steadily throughout the year, dropping below 55 percent at the end of July, and below the coveted 50 percent in December. Obama, true to his campaign emphasis, succeeded in securing the passage of the American Recovery and Reinvestment Act within his first month in office, allocating $787 billion for economic stimulus, with $237 billion targeted toward tax cuts aimed at the middle class, and the bulk of the sum aimed at saving and creating jobs. And as the year drew to a close, Obama seemed all but certain to enact comprehensive health-care reform.

Clinton's average approval in his first year is 48 percent; Bush's average approval prior to the attacks of September 11 is 55 percent; and Obama's average approval in his first year is 57 percent. Part of these differences, I maintain, arises from the degree to which each president attended to his campaign priorities.

This is not to say that citizens can tell you precisely what these

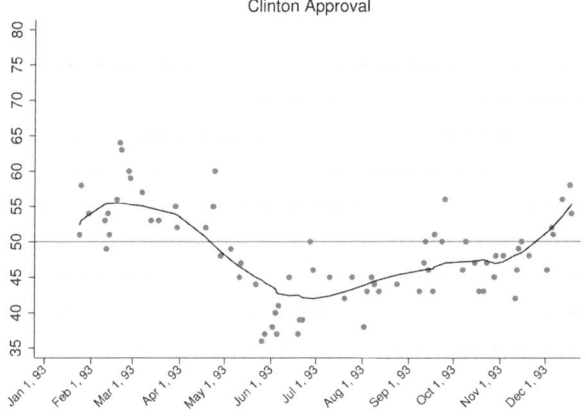

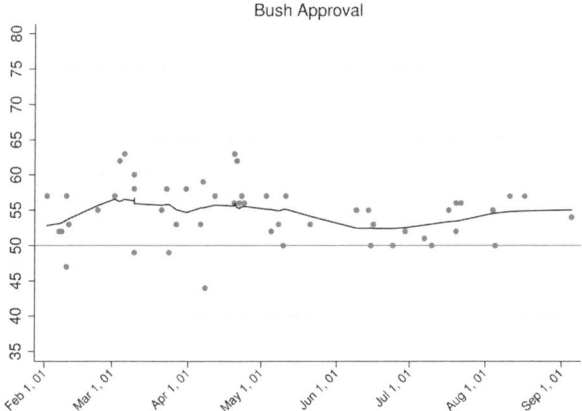

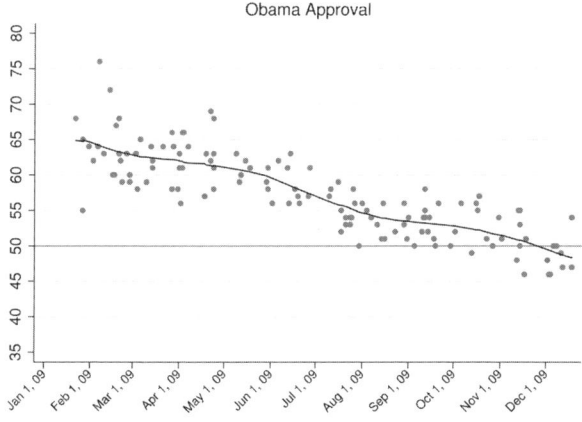

Figure 1.1 First-Year Presidential Approval: Clinton, Bush, Obama

presidents promised as candidates, their policy stands, or their campaign pledges. But the public does have some idea, developed during the campaign as a function of each candidate's issue emphasis, of what problems the public expects each president to tackle in office. The president's attention to those priorities, whether the wide-ranging agenda of candidate Obama or the more focused agenda of candidate Bush, is judged positively by the public. The president's distraction from those priorities, as Clinton learned, is judged poorly.

A Theory of Agenda Accountability

Contrary to the conventional wisdom about evasive candidates and incompetent voters, I argue that campaigns help citizens hold presidents accountable. Candidates clarify their issue priorities during campaigns, repeating them relentlessly, even as they remain artfully ambiguous on issue specifics. Citizens listen to the campaign agenda, connect the issue priorities to the candidates as a function of this repetition, and hold the president accountable for addressing his campaign-issue agenda afterwards. What matters in campaigns, for both candidates and voters, is the presence of clear issue emphases, not clear issue positions.

The theory of agenda accountability developed here tackles three key problems with how we currently think about and search for accountability in American democracy. First, it places presidential accountability into the framework of the American system of separate institutions competing for shares of power. Our theories of prospective and retrospective electoral accountability do not properly take the governing system into account, instead relying on the unsupported foundations of responsible parties or a presidency-dominated policy process. Theories of presidential accountability and our expectations of voting and campaigns that derive from these should conform to the presidency in a separated system, and not the reverse. The president is not chief lawmaker. He does not have the power to pass legislation unvarnished by congressional compromise or disruption. Nor does he have the power to improve economic conditions unilaterally. Consequently, the theories of voting that follow from current accountability models expect either too much from citizens, in the case of policy voting, or too little, in the case of economic voting. And they demand the wrong focus from presidential candidates.

What a president can do is designate and sequence the priorities he wishes Congress and the country to address. Thus it matters more that citizens come to understand the candidates' issue priorities in the campaign, the problems a potential president will focus on solving early in his administration, than that they correctly identify the specific issue positions of each candidate. For a pragmatic citizenry, one that cares more that particular problems are addressed than with the specific policy levers the government uses to address them, voting and later accountability should more reasonably depend on issue priorities, not issue positions.

Second, agenda accountability treats campaigns as a unique structuring institution with their own rhythms and rules, not simply another media event. Scholarship on campaigns has uncritically adopted theories from studies of the mass media without adapting these theories for the campaign environment. In particular, the idea that the news media "prime" the public, causing people to evaluate government on the basis of issues recently highlighted in the press, has been applied unconditionally to campaigns. This book introduces a new theory of priming—repetition priming—consistent with the structure of a modern presidential campaign emphasizing repetition of candidate priorities. Whereas media theories of priming, inappropriately applied to campaigns, suggest that campaigns undermine accountability by allowing new presidents to quickly change direction, to distract citizens with new issues and thereby evade citizen judgment, repetition priming, driven by the length of the campaign and the repetition of priorities throughout, ensures that the influence of the campaign is not a short-term priming event but a long-term understanding of presidential intent. Looking at campaigns from this perspective leads to different conclusions: Campaigns give citizens a voice in shaping the governing agenda and empower citizens to use candidate priorities to judge presidential performance in addressing the prioritized problems.

Finally, agenda accountability pushes us to examine campaigns by looking beyond the voting booth. Media professionals close their campaign coverage on election night and scholars have followed suit, missing how campaigns could relate to later governing or public opinion. This book argues that presidential accountability is an ongoing process that begins with, and relies crucially on, campaigns. Despite the popularity of *presidential* approval ratings in the press and in the public, we have not really considered how these are connected to the public's understanding of the *candidate* developed in the campaign. We've missed how approval ratings serve as an ongoing accountability judgment. And we know little about the enduring effect of the campaign on citizen expectations and evaluations, on presidential behavior and priorities, and on media coverage and expectations of performance. This book, in contrast, follows the dynamics of approval and priorities after the campaign.

These premises—the underlying assumption of a responsible party system or a presidency-dominated process, the conflation of media effects and campaign effects, and the neglect of the campaign after Election Day—have led to a fundamental misunderstanding of how accountability, and the campaigns on which they rely, could and should operate in the American system. And this misunderstanding is of consequence, shaping expectations about what candidates should be doing in campaigns, about how the media should be reporting on campaigns, and about how voters should be judging the candidates.

Plan of the Book

In the pages to come, I bridge scholarship on the presidency and on presidential approval with research on campaign effects and information processing to advance a theory of how campaigns endure in citizen psychology, shaping expectations and evaluations, and thereby affording citizens a means of holding presidents accountable long before the next election.

Chapter 1 reconsiders our understanding of accountability, focusing on the two dominant forms of prospective and retrospective accountability. I argue that our understanding of accountability is incomplete because we have not fully connected our ideas of accountability with the existing governmental system, and we have not fully connected work on candidate evaluation and vote choice to work on presidential approval. I more fully elaborate the theory of agenda accountability, offering it as an alternative form of democratic accountability, one that fits well in a system of separate institutions and weak parties, where presidential policy-making is concentrated around the setting and sequencing of agenda priorities.

Chapter 2 begins to draw the broad empirical picture, underscoring the ramifications of agenda priority adherence. After briefly reviewing prior explanations of presidential approval, I relay in more detail the contours of the 1992, 2000, and 2008 presidential campaigns referenced above, noting in particular the issue priorities that dominated the campaigns. I follow the first year of each of our last three presidents, noting the key presidential priorities and achievements and connecting these to the public's response via approval and perceptions of the presidents' promise-keeping efforts. Clinton, Bush, and Obama, together, usefully demonstrate the benefit of presidential follow-through and the pitfalls of presidential distraction from campaign priorities.

Chapter 3 narrows the focus to begin building the empirical case for the theory step by step, starting with the campaign. Since the president's legislative role is largely about setting priorities, holding a president accountable for addressing the problems he said he would address as a candidate serves as a reasonable standard of evaluation. A campaign that facilitates such accountability would reveal and clarify a potential leader's agenda priorities. Chapter 3 introduces the 2000 presidential campaign and assesses the degree to which the candidates paved the way for such accountability standards through the agendas outlined in the campaign advertising. I examine the extent to which the candidates talked about issues in 2000, how they talked about issues, and whether issue priorities are readily identifiable on the basis of the campaign rhetoric. In 2000, candidates George Bush and Al Gore converged on a set of key issues: education, tax cuts, saving Social Security, and distinct dimensions of health care.

Presidents, more than other elected leaders, have the resources to shape the agenda once in office; consequently, their proposed agenda priorities ought to be taken seriously by the public. Using the 2000 presidential campaign, chapter 4 assesses evidence for the next condition of agenda accountability: citizen learning of the campaign themes. Using an original rolling cross-section survey designed to measure citizens' understanding of candidate priorities over time combined with the campaign advertising data from chapter 3, I examine the characteristics of both individuals and candidates that promote accurate hearing. Citizens who live in places that saw more candidate advertising were more likely to report hearing the candidates talking about some, though not all, of the key issues. In addition, I consider the degree to which other cognitive processes (for example, projection, selective attention, heuristic thinking) seem to be operating or distorting the public's reception of the candidates' priorities.

Use of the standards promoted by candidates represents a consequential endorsement of the emphasized campaign themes. Chapter 5, relying again on the original survey data combined with the campaign advertising data, assesses two related questions: whether citizens base candidate evaluations on candidate messages, and whether they do so in ways that suggest developing expectations or a fleeting influence. This distinction is critical to understanding the implications of campaigns. Transitory effects offer presidents the opportunity to shirk on campaign themes; enduring effects, which become expectations, push citizens to hold presidents accountable for them. For the most part, I find that repeated issue emphasis matters more than recent issue emphasis in shaping the public's evaluations of the candidates. But not every key issue is strongly associated with evaluations of the candidate who emphasized it. The patterns across the multiple issues provide insight into the conditions promoting or inhibiting the development of candidate–issue connections.

Chapter 6 turns to the postcampaign period. I follow President Bush's attention and activity on the key issues in the campaign during the first year of his presidency. Bush's early term offers examples of agenda follow-through with education and tax cuts, and examples of agenda neglect with Social Security and Medicare reform. Importantly, only tax cuts and Social Security became tied to evaluations of Bush as a candidate. Drawing on presidential remarks, legislative histories, and public opinion polls, this chapter examines how activity on these four issues influenced and shaped evaluations of the president. Bush's first year provides consistent support for agenda accountability: The issues connected to him during the campaign are consistently more important in explaining approval of him in office, boosting his evaluations for issues on which he followed through and undermining his support for issues he neglected.

Chapter 7 follows the first year of the Clinton and Obama presidencies to examine the broader applicability of agenda accountability. Presidents Clinton and Obama provide additional examples of follow-through and neglect, as well as cases of agenda interruption—issues that became important in the administration despite their absence in the campaign. Again, I combine presidential remarks, legislative histories, and public opinion data to test the predictions of agenda accountability under different conditions—different issues, different policy outcomes. These presidencies suggest some qualifications but provide largely consistent support for the tendency of citizens to rely heavily on expectations of problem-solving emphasis developed during the campaign in judgments of presidential performance.

In the concluding chapter, I turn to a discussion of the broader consequences and implications of agenda accountability. Our ideas of accountability, and the definitions of good campaigns and competent citizens that derive from them, shape what we demand from candidates and leaders and from the media and voters. The emphasis on candidates' issue positions and differences promoted by our current theories of accountability has several unintended negative consequences for candidates, citizens, and governing. Agenda accountability, by legitimating the value of competing issue priorities and by making the tradeoffs among potential goals explicit, promotes a more realistic understanding of the governing process on the part of citizens and journalists. By recognizing the role of the president and tying the campaign more clearly to that role, it offers the prospect of better governance.

1 The Meaning of Presidential Accountability

Democratic accountability is at the heart of a functioning democracy. Our current understanding of accountability, though, does not fit comfortably with the American system of separate institutions competing for shares of power. Citizens, meanwhile, stubbornly refuse to strive for the standards laid out by democratic theorists. Behavioral scholars have long sought to save the citizens from irrelevancy by noting alternative ways the public can come to act "as if" they are exercising accountability. If, instead, we begin by placing the institutions in which leaders reside at the center of the equation, we come to a different understanding of accountability—one from which citizens (or campaigns) do not need quite so much saving.

Accountability, as a means of constraining power, requires three components: standards, information, and sanction (Grant and Keohane 2005). The accountability holders, citizens in this case, must recognize and endorse standards of evaluation, must have access to information about the behavior of power wielders, and must possess the means to sanction.

The concept of democratic accountability has shifted over time from a model of prospective accountability to the currently dominant model of retrospective accountability. In both forms, accountability is understood as a sanction imposed by citizens through elections.[1] Elections provide the only *formal* mechanism of sanction available to the mass public in the American system. Only during elections can citizens punish wayward leaders by voting them out of office. Leaders cannot be formally compelled by citizens to do anything in particular while in office, only sanctioned after the fact. Thus, incumbent leaders are expected, during the campaign, to "render an account" of their time in office; citizens are expected to judge their performance. Unfortunately, accountability is undermined by inherent informational asymmetries—politicians know more than do voters about their behavior in office. Further, since adoption of the Twenty-second Amendment to the U.S. Constitution, term-limited presidents, faced with no direct electoral accounting, must feel less concern for future electoral sanctions. Nonetheless, for democratic citizens to exercise formal accountability, elections are the only game in town. Disagreement arises, though, with respect to what we hold those in power accountable for.

Prospective Accountability

Prospective accountability follows from the responsible party model of representation. In this view, parties present citizens with alternatives along important policy dimensions and citizens signal their preferred policies by their choice of candidate (Manin, Przeworski, and Stokes 1999). After the election, strong, cohesive, and sincere parties enact policies congruent with their stated platforms. This is the party mandate model. Accountability derives most clearly from the "promissory representation" (Mansbridge 2003) embedded in this model, whereby citizens exercise a forward-looking power over leaders, exacting promises during the authorizing election that a leader will be obligated to perform in office and rewarding leaders in the next election for their faithfulness to those promises. In Jones' succinct description of this model: "We promise, you support, we deliver, you judge" (2000, 18).

Of course, in practice, it is hardly so simple. "Promises are partial, voters misunderstand or are unaware, delivery is indistinct, and judgments are incomplete" (Jones 2000, 18). Indeed, few explicitly advocate for responsible party government any longer. The failures of citizens and parties have become too well known, or, more charitably, the model simply asks too much. Citizens must have well-developed preferences and recognize which party best approximates those preferences. They must engage in "issue voting." Parties, for their part, must differentiate on important policy solutions and make these differences clear to the public. And government must be structured so that, once elected, parties can implement their programs.

Even a cursory reading of the work on political behavior is enough to dissuade most proponents that democratic citizens have well-defined preferences (Campbell et al. 1960; Converse 1964). Making matters worse, the public frequently cannot identify the issue positions of the leading presidential contenders or their parties, even after a long and loud campaign (Delli Carpini and Keeter 1997). Consequently, they cannot reasonably be expected to vote on the basis of future policy.[2] One of the enduring puzzles from the 2000 campaign is why Bush won, given a majority of voters agreed with Gore's positions on the issues. The average level of in-depth political information found among the citizenry is far too low to sustain a true prospective accountability.

Responsibility for this ignorance can hardly be placed entirely on the citizen's shoulders as candidates often work to obscure differences on some issues, possess little difference with respect to others, or simply talk past each other entirely. A key criticism of contemporary campaigns emphasizes how little campaigns do to educate the public about policy alternatives, running instead on broad goals. In his study of the 1960 campaign, Page (1978) found almost half of the candidates' statements were centered on the broad themes of goals, problems, and past performance; only a fifth involved any policy detail. More recently, Geer's (2006) detailed study of presidential advertising since 1960 finds similarly low levels of policy position talk. Beyond simply talking about issues, scholars have begun to examine how much dialogue occurs in campaigns (Kaplan, Park, and Ridout 2006; Sigelman and Buell 2004; Simon 2002). If candidates and parties aren't talking about the same issues, they can't very well be clarifying differences for the public. Work on issue convergence—the degree to which candidates in a race are talking about the same issues—has provided reassuring results.[3] Even so, talking about the same issues, while a prerequisite for dialogue, does not guarantee anything resembling debate. As Sides (2006) notes, when candidates of one party "trespass" onto the issue space of another party, they tend to simply endorse agreeable goals or frame the issue to emphasize a different policy dimension than their opponent. Little of this serves to clarify policy difference. News reports, which could provide a clearer contrast, instead focus on the horse race and candidate strategies (Farnsworth and Lichter 2002; Patterson 1993). Thus, in the first link of the accountability chain—the endorsement and recognition of standards of evaluation—the prospective accountability model falters.[4]

The second link in the accountability chain, acquiring information about the president's performance on his policy commitments, also poses a challenge. Ours is not, as Jones (2005) bluntly reminds us, a presidential system. Governmental power is separated, institutionally and electorally. In America's system of separated powers, presidents cannot easily enact programmatic change. The constitution puts presidents in a weaker policy-making position vis-à-vis Congress. The president cannot compel Congress to consider, much less pass, his legislative program. The failure of a particular president to implement policies outlined in the (ideal) campaign might not be a product of his own shortcomings but of his position atop separate institutions that must (grudgingly) share power. How are citizens to appropriately assign responsibility for failure when leaders can credibly blame one another for throwing a wrench into the wheels of policy making? To demand detailed policy commitments from a presidential candidate and to hold him individually accountable is, in the long run, unwise. It leaves him no leeway in a negotiated lawmaking process and it adds unnecessary weight to arguments for increased presidential power to meet such outsized expectations.

As Neustadt notes, "What the constitution separates our parties do not combine" (1990, 26). Ours is not a responsible party system. The president and his fellow partisans in Congress are elected by different voters at different times and, often, on different standards. Fellow partisans elected with a president will not be on the ballot with him in their next election.[5] And the divergent constituencies of representatives, senators, and presidents promote divergent perspectives in policy making. Electoral separation combined with a federal system works against collective party responsibility.[6]

The third accountability link, enacting sanctions, stands little chance in the rumble-tumble world of real politics. Given the lack of an endorsement of standards via widespread issue voting and the obstacles to acquiring the information necessary to make an informed evaluation about who is to blame if promises are unfulfilled, how can citizens reasonably vote on the basis of pledge fulfillment in the next election? This mandate view of elections and reliance on prospective accountability may work, if at all, only in a parliamentary system with clear lines of responsibility (Powell and Whitten 1993).

Retrospective Accountability

In response to the many ways that prospective accountability and the responsible party model did not conform to reality, the model of retrospective accountability gained ground.[7] This reward–punishment theory, most famously expounded by Key (1966), postulates only that citizens have some idea about political outcomes and vote the incumbents in or out according to their satisfaction with these. As Fiorina describes it in *Retrospective Voting* (1981, 5):

[Citizens] typically have one comparatively hard bit of data: they know what life has been like during the incumbent's administration. They need not know the precise economic or foreign policies of the incumbent administration in order to see or feel the results of those policies. . . . In order to ascertain whether the incumbents have performed poorly or well, citizens need only calculate the changes in their own welfare. If jobs have been lost in a recession, something is wrong. If sons have died in foreign rice paddies, something is wrong. If thugs make neighbourhoods unsafe, something is wrong. If polluters foul food, water, or air, something is wrong.

This retrospective accountability model relies on "anticipatory representation" (Mansbridge 2003). Elections are judgments about the outcomes produced by the current government. Voters sanction presidents by voting against them or their party when outcomes are unsatisfactory, not when policy promises are left unfulfilled. Citizen power, in this model, is backward-looking.[8]

The great advantage of retrospective accountability is the minimal information required by citizens to enact it, compared to prospective accountability. Citizens, in this view, care primarily about end states, not the policy instruments employed as the means to get there.[9] If citizens do not understand the policy positions of the competing candidates, no matter—they can still determine if life is better or worse at the end of the term and use this information in shaping a vote decision. Issue voting isn't expected and the vote decision signals no policy preference, much less a mandate. The complement of minimal informational demands for citizens, though, is enhanced elite power. While prospective accountability minimizes presidential leeway, retrospective accountability maximizes it. Leaders are free to identify and solve problems however they see fit.[10] Citizens are mostly left out of this process.

And yet, the retrospective model requires more information than the original formulations appreciated. The rapid growth of scholarship on retrospective judgment has begun to clarify these informational needs. Starting with an understanding of who, if anyone, in a complex and separated system is responsible for policies and ending with some understanding of how those polices follow a complex causal chain to produce outcomes (see, for example, Arnold 1990), the information necessary to enact a reasoned retrospective accountability is neither simple nor straightforward.

Leaders, for their part, hardly work to make this task easier, at least for the unsatisfactory outcomes that generate negative accountability judgments. As policy makers, they engage in a variety of blame-avoiding behaviors—hiding actions in broader omnibus bills, delaying costs, finding a scapegoat (Arnold 1990; Weaver 1986)—to obscure the traceability from action to outcome. As campaigners, they do not primarily emphasize retrospective appeals. A content analysis of the appeals made in the television advertising for presidential campaigns from 1960 to 2000 finds that for ads promoting the sponsor, only about 12 percent of the appeals were primarily retrospective in nature; for ads focusing on the opponent about 37 percent of the appeals were retrospective. More commonly, ads included both prospective and retrospective appeals (Geer 2006).

Citizens, too, appear to struggle with retrospective accountability. Presidential evaluations are generally only related to satisfaction with outcomes for citizens who believe the president is responsible for producing the outcome (Rudolph and Grant 2002). And responsibility is not automatically attributed to the president or governing party, as the most basic form of the reward–punishment model would have it (Key 1966).[11] Divided government and complex coalitions reduce the clarity of responsibility and make citizens less likely to hold any one leader or party responsible for ends (Nicholson and Segura 1999; Powell and Whitten 1993).[12] Party identifiers make self-serving attributions, holding a president of the opposing party responsible for negative outcomes and a president of their own party responsible for positive outcomes (Rudolph 2003; Tyler 1982). And politically sophisticated citizens, who might be expected to save us on the margins, tend to believe responsibility for outcomes is shared, making it harder to sanction any of those responsible (Rudolph 2003). Here, too, the absence of a collective, party responsibility inhibits citizen control.

Fiorina (1981), in his careful study of the practice of retrospective voting, provides one of the more nuanced treatments of retrospective accountability to date. He finds that retrospective judgment does matter but is not directly related to electoral choice, as Key's punishment–reward process asserts. Instead, retrospective considerations inform partisanship and, in some cases, future expectations. The influence of retrospective judgments, in his view, contains more policy content than the simpler reward–punishment model assumes. Much of this policy content, though, has to do with policy ends rather than policy means. Nevertheless, Fiorina is somewhat pessimistic about the ability of this version of retrospective voting to provide electoral accountability, since the foundation on which the *ex post* logic of accountability rests "presupposes meaningful parties" (1981, 202).[13] Still, Key's simpler formulation, and his greater optimism about the efficacy of accountability, has remained the dominant model of retrospective judgment.

Not all outcomes, though, are considered likely candidates for retrospective accountability. In particular, empirical studies of accountability tend to emphasize economic outcomes (see Anderson 2007 for a review). Though theorists talk about outcomes broadly, empiricists measure the influence of economic conditions. What begins as an observational dilemma—what outcomes can we reliably measure?—ineluctably influences our theoretical understanding and our normative expectations. Retrospective voting in theory becomes economic voting in practice. Citizens need only acquire information about how the economy is doing. This should prove a relatively easy task as information on economic growth is readily available in routinized news coverage of the economy, centered on the regular release of statistics from the government, from business, and from the stock market.

In this common understanding of retrospective accountability, the standards for evaluation are constant, not open to debate. Citizens have little say in desired ends. To the extent there are tradeoffs to be made between economic growth and other goals—environmental protection, social welfare—this model leaves no room for the public to care about or promote other priorities. Instead, citizens are assumed to naively administer electoral sanctions automatically. Citizens, in this view, are "myopic automatons" (Rudolph 2003), not reflective or deliberative parties to a democratic process. This, alone, poses a challenge to traditional understandings of accountability; the accountability-holders are never allowed to endorse standards. As Key himself notes, "Unless the mass views have some place in the shaping of policy, all the talk about democracy is nonsense" (1961, 7).[14]

In addition, despite the apparent objectivity of economic standards, there is some evidence that leaders can influence our perceptions of economic outcomes (Hetherington 1996; Nadeau et al. 1999). And scholars have long been concerned about the ability of leaders to manipulate actual economic outcomes at the margins for electoral advantage. The evidence of a "political business cycle" (Tufte 1978) has been mixed over the years, but recent work finds Republican presidents, in particular, able to produce more income growth in election years (Bartels 2008). Finally, the outcomes generally emphasized by research are aggregate numbers—income growth, growth in GDP, inflation, unemployment—whose rewards and benefits need not be distributed equally throughout society, yet citizens are presumed to respond to these performance measures in a uniform fashion.[15] Indeed, formal work suggests that unless citizens are responding to these outcomes uniformly and sociotropically, voter control through retrospective voting falters (Ferejohn 1986).

In short, the retrospective approach ignores the accountability-holders in the process of endorsing standards and adopts a standard that is, at least normatively, questionable.

To be fair, proponents of this view don't generally claim that economic voting constitutes an ideal form of accountability, instead emphasizing its attainability. There is much to commend such a model in practice—Page (1978, 221–22), for example, notes that a representative's anticipation of reward and punishment "orients government responsiveness toward fundamental needs and values of the people rather than toward ephemeral or weakly held policy preferences." Certainly the expectation that performance will be judged, and reelection won or lost, on the basis of economic achievements requires leaders to attend to how their policies will impact these substantively important indicators, and that is surely a plus. A healthy economy is often seen as a prerequisite for addressing many other national problems. Retrospective accountability, as a means of constraining presidential power, maximizes presidential leeway, leaving room for innovation and leadership. But the state of the economy, manipulation aside, is a beast over which presidents frequently have little control; and they must share what little statutory control they have with Congress (Arnold 1990; Keech 1995).

The extent of economic voting in practice has more recently come up for debate. Indeed, this reward–punishment theory of democracy, the existence of electoral accountability itself, has been called into question as an empirical reality because research on the practice of economic voting has provided "unstable" results (Lewis-Beck and Paldam 2000). Instead, scholars of economic voting talk about "contingent" accountability (Anderson 2007) or conclude, in the face of null findings, that elections do not induce accountability at all (Cheibub and Przeworski 1999).

Finally, as Mansbridge (2003) clarifies, while the promissory representation of prospective accountability focuses our attention on the relationship between the voters at Time 1 and the leader at Time 2, the anticipatory representation posited by theories of retrospective voting moves our attention to the relationship between a leader at Time 2 and some future voters at Time 3. This fundamentally changes the meaning of accountability. Rather than an agent accountable to his principals, a leader becomes an entrepreneur trying to attract future voters; rather than both moral and strategic incentives for responsiveness, leaders have only a strategic incentive (Mansbridge 2003). The first raises the specter of manipulation and transforms representation into a function of communication over behavior. The second lessens the normative burden of leaders.

Accountability Reconsidered

Recall the necessary steps for accountability: an understanding of the evaluative standards, access to relevant information about achievement of those standards, and a mechanism for sanctioning leaders (Grant and Keohane 2005). Accountability is democratic to the extent the public has some voice in these steps. This first component, standards, proves a weak link for both of the main theories of accountability. Prospective accountability asks too much; retrospective accountability allows too little. And neither model can be easily accommodated to the individualistic accountability promoted by a system of separate institutions and weak political parties.

A process of prospective accountability, long the civics text version of elections, fails to describe the actual, or even probable, behavior of citizens. The standards are admirably specific in theory, but the embedded conception of democracy is one of a responsible party system, which the American national government decidedly is not. Presidential candidates and parties do not generally offer clear and distinct programs; citizens do not extend a specific mandate in their vote choice. Presidents and parties rarely enact a coherent platform in office; citizens rarely vote, the next time around, on that basis. If citizens don't pick up information on party differences during the long and voluminous campaign, they aren't likely to pick up on the more complex information about government action after the campaign.[16] The likelihood of electoral sanction on the basis of candidate or party platforms is, as a consequence, low.

Retrospective accountability, the answer to these empirical shortcomings, leaves citizens out of this first step of accountability altogether. Instead, the model assumes a set of standards that in practice fall under the rubric of economic voting. These standards, clear on the surface, are frustratingly vague in practice, difficult for citizens to connect to decision makers in a complex policy environment, and leave a great deal of room for selective emphasis and perceptual manipulation. The outcomes, such as they are, may be more apparent, but the causes and consequences are not. Although there is variable evidence that citizens do sanction presidents for economic outcomes, this doesn't guarantee that they are doing it in a reasoned way.[17]

I want to reconsider this conception of how accountability is practiced by citizens in three ways: by taking ongoing presidential approval seriously as a mechanism of informal accountability; by recognizing that the standards for approval change over a president's term, beginning with a greater emphasis on the winning candidate's campaign priorities; and by appreciating the role of standards other than economic outcomes.

Elections are, of course, the only formal mechanism of sanction, the only point of citizen judgment that can impose the public will on leaders with any force or finality. It is appropriate that elections receive the bulk of research attention on accountability. It does not follow, however, that elections are the only point of judgment with which leaders are concerned and that can shape leader behavior. Citizens are "approving" or not of presidents almost daily, and these judgments are captured via opinion polls at least monthly. The measurement of job approval—"the new referendum" (Brace and Hinckley 1992)—has altered presidential behavior, power, and public relations. The modern plebiscitary president (Lowi 1985) is regularly relaying and justifying his actions, rendering accounts, as it were. Since 1948, when monthly measures of presidential approval began, citizens have had a means—visible and authoritatively ratified—of passing judgment on an ongoing presidency. These judgments are reliably related to the ultimate vote decision for citizens and to perceptions of presidential capability by other Washington elites. In short, elections are not the only time and place where citizens, as accountability holders, exercise their power.

The debate over whether accountability is forward-looking (based on a promissory relationship whereby citizens hold leaders to their promises) or backward-looking (based on an anticipatory relationship whereby citizens hold leaders accountable for anticipating their needs and preferences) applies to the ongoing referendum of presidential approval as well. Approval judgments, though, are repeated events that evolve over time. Therefore, there is more opportunity for both prospective and retrospective accountability. In particular, early in a president's administration, the standards of accountability revolve around adherence to a set of agenda priorities elaborated in the campaign. As time progresses and new problems arise, the standards adapt accordingly.

The time horizon of citizens is short. By the next election, they are not thinking primarily of the promises and priorities elaborated in the last election. At that point, and later in the president's administration more generally, they are looking to the more recent past (Bartels 2008).[18] Similarly, when making early performance assessments, citizens are looking to the recent past. What is salient from the recent past early in the administration is the president's campaign agenda and his actions taken on it to date. Citizens, as well, have some appreciation for the necessary evolution of the agenda in response to real events. The problems of today's campaign may not be the problems of tomorrow. Citizens, reasonably enough, are not clamoring for more direct democracy (Hibbing and Theiss-Morse 2002) but want their leaders to address new problems as they arise despite the absence of attention to these issues in the campaign preceding the authorizing election.

Leaders' time horizons also prompt an early attention to the campaign agenda when the incentives are to gain some early legislative successes and shore up political support. As the next election cycle draws near, leader incentives change, so that meeting previously unanticipated or unstated needs and interests becomes more important. Presidents hope to "hit the ground running" (Pfiffner 1996) because it won't take long before the continuing stream of the policy agenda sweeps away a president's time and energy.

This early agenda accountability, enacted through presidential approval, follows from an endorsement of standards. Candidates, in their campaigns, must offer agenda priorities; citizens must hear the campaign agendas and connect these to the candidates. Citizens, thus, are part of the conversation that establishes standards, choosing among competing priorities. The ongoing evaluation of a president allows for standards to change, initially in accord with the campaign emphasis and later in response to the emergence of new problems.

These changing standards of evaluation imply that criteria other than the trend in aggregate economic indicators, or in individual economic standing, will influence presidential performance evaluations. Early in the administration, the priorities emphasized by the winning candidate in his campaign will serve as a primary basis for citizen judgments about performance. This is a direct incorporation of the promissory perspective—that citizens will hold leaders accountable for their campaign pledges—but applied to presidential approval rather than the subsequent election, and with reference to agenda priorities rather than policy platforms. These standards will be heavily populated with valence issues, ends on which most of us can agree, such as economic growth,[19] but so too could these include improvements in education, reforms in health care, environmental protections, and the like.[20]

The expectation of variation in the standards of presidential approval is a real departure from current explanations of these performance ratings. Most work on presidential approval recognizes little to no role for presidential behavior. This view, in contrast, posits that the policies a president pursues are key to his evaluations. The argument follows from two key regularities: that citizens care more about problem solving than particular policy solutions and that agenda priorities rather than detailed policies are what candidates offer up in campaigns. Retrospective theories are explicit about this first regularity. The theory of issue ownership, a more prospective view, also begins with this premise. Most citizens are "pragmatic and instrumental, mostly interested in 'fixing' problems that voters want the government to address, not the policies the candidates promise to pursue" (Petrocik 1996, 830). Recognizing problems and understanding priorities among them are cognitively simpler tasks for the public. Citizens do not regularly apply ideological tests to policy options; indeed, many cannot do so (Converse 1964). The vote, in the aggregate and at the individual level, tracks with problem concerns—if citizens are concerned most about issues "owned" by Republicans, Republican presidential candidates fare better; if citizens are concerned more about issues "owned" by Democrats, Democratic presidential candidates fare better.[21] Issue-handling reputations, the likelihood of prioritizing a problem, are easier for citizens to incorporate into their understanding of the candidates; and they do so in relatively enduring ways. The theory of issue ownership emphasizes the stable partisan advantage of issues; I hypothesize that the campaign emphasis itself communicates to voters information about future presidential effort on the issue. Although party reputations matter, every representative of a party is not equally likely to focus on a particular issue in office.

Presidential candidates, for their part, have long been accused of avoiding the issues. In fact, modern presidential candidates talk a lot about issues, particularly as problems. What they generally fail to do with any consistency is talk in detail about policy solutions. This is the source of criticisms, or at least descriptions, of candidates as ambiguous, equivocal, or just plain vague (Page 1978; Shepsle 1972). If the candidates don't demarcate their policy alternatives clearly, they do convey issue differences by their choice of agendas. Even when both candidates include some attention to the same issues, they may differ markedly in the *amount* of attention they give to these issues. Some issues receive only token attention; other issues, the campaign priorities, are mentioned repeatedly. Campaign priorities signal to voters what a future president is more likely to focus on in office, a signal both important and substantive. In their choices about how to allocate their scarce time, candidates offer different agendas and provide the public an opportunity to choose between these.

The importance of agendas, as a precursor to policy positions, is not new. Schattschneider's well-known dictum—"the definition of the alternatives is the supreme instrument of power" (1960, 66)—highlights the interest elites have in deciding the issues and terms of debate. "Antagonists," Schattschneider elaborates, "can rarely agree on what the issues are because power is involved in the definition. He who determines what politics is about runs the country, because the definition of the alternatives is the choice of conflicts, and the choice of conflicts allocates power" (1960, 66).[22]

Kingdon (1995) usefully expands on this distinction between agendas and alternatives, between the problems and the policy proposals intended to solve them. Presidents, he concludes, have considerable influence over the creation of agenda issues but less in defining the alternatives. Problem recognition is critical to agenda setting, and presidential campaigns are central in assigning the status of problem (things we should do something about) to a few of the myriad potential conditions (things we put up with).

Increasingly, work on congressional representation has begun to define responsiveness in terms of agendas rather than positional policy congruence alone. It matters whether the issues about which the public is concerned are reflected in the government agenda, whether there is agenda congruence; there is (Jones and Baumgartner 2005). It matters whether winning legislators address the problems highlighted by their campaign challengers in office, whether issue uptake occurs; it does (Sulkin 2005). Representation, this perspective argues, is a problem-detection and prioritization device, and, importantly, the public is a "co-conspirator" in the agenda-setting process (Jones and Baumgartner 2005, 260).

Scholars have long understood that candidates spend more time talking about problems than policies. Candidates avoid too much specificity for fear of offending voters and to avoid constraining themselves from pursuing useful (or politically feasible) policies later. And work on the theory of issue ownership persuasively demonstrates that citizens vote on agendas, not policies. But we haven't yet considered what these empirical regularities mean for citizens, for leader behavior, and for accountability. Many of the ends emphasized by candidates are consensual in the abstract—peace, prosperity, welfare—and citizens themselves spend little time thinking about the various means to those ends. Nevertheless citizens desire, and deserve, some voice in the ranking of those ends. This is something candidates offer in their campaign rhetoric—a choice about which problems most urgently need solving. In fact, the competition over problems composes the bulk of the campaign discourse. Citizens want leaders who will carry the burden of thinking more carefully about means than do they, but want some voice in the ends. Indeed, this is a key benefit of representation over direct democracy. Agenda adherence, then, is one of the few means available for assessing accountability.

This view of ongoing accountability brings citizens back into the process of choosing standards—based on priorities rather than policies. Voters are more active in establishing standards and more active in holding leaders to them along the way, compared to the retrospective accountability model. But citizens needn't be the super-citizens implied by the prospective accountability model.[23] Certainly, more information becomes necessary to properly exercise a sanction. Citizens need information on presidential activity and attention on an ongoing basis and must generally rely on presidents themselves or surrogates like the media to provide it. The necessary information, though, need not be particularly detailed, and news reports of presidents tend to focus on what he's doing in ways that facilitate this knowledge. The increasingly routinized coverage of the first 100 days also fits nicely with this view, providing information on which of the policies and priorities from the campaign a president has achieved or is actively working on. In turn, ongoing accountability asks (at least some) citizens to render judgments on a regular basis—daily, weekly, monthly—which means some minimal attention to politics is necessary. The requirements of this model of accountability, though, are entirely achievable.

This view of agenda accountability also acknowledges the role of the president in governance, not as the chief lawmaker, but as the designator, certifier, and sequencer of priorities (Jones 2005). A presidency-centered perspective has distorted our understanding of accountability and of the relation between campaigns and accountability. Candidate ambiguity on issues isn't all about deceiving the public but can be crucial to retaining leeway in later policy making.[24] An emphasis by candidates on priorities, rather than policy details, is useful information for citizens. It provides the public a voice in future governance more in line with the public's true concerns and more in keeping with the presidents' powers.

Campaigning and Governing

The presidential campaign matters, I argue, for the future president's behavior, for policy making, and for the public's response. The claim that "campaigns matter" is almost a cliché. The claim that campaigns matter for the behavior of leaders or for policy making, while not new, is considerably less common. Though campaigns define the key interaction between would-be governors and those they would govern, we know surprisingly little about the impact this interaction has on either, outside of Election Day.[25]

The striking neglect of campaigns in governing and accountability is, in part, a function of the broad separation between research on institutions and on behavior. Some scholars focus on the presidency as an institution, others on the campaigns that precede a president's ascent to power.[26] Scholars of the presidency, attuned to the election results that put a president in office, have generally been skeptical that campaigns much mattered and so have largely ignored them. After all, a president must fit himself into an ongoing government with a preexisting stream of agenda items. His campaign agenda cannot be paramount.[27] Consequently, presidents are routinely advised to prioritize, to focus on only a handful of key issues. Why wouldn't these priorities in office be related to the priorities conveyed via the campaign?

On the behavioral side, political science has been more interested in voting than elections (Stimson 2004). Campaign scholars emphasize the short-term impact of campaigns because they are concerned, primarily, with vote choice. The vote choice is, no doubt, a key endpoint of the campaign. From the candidates' and citizens' points of view, the campaign is all about this essential decision. But that the key actors are focused on this day does not mean that the campaign has no impact outside of it. Campaigns do more, after all, than shape the vote decision and how it is made. Citizens learn about candidate priorities during campaigns and develop expectations for presidential attention via the campaign. The implications of voting behavior for later accountability, specifically how voters decide and the influence of campaigns in this process, needs explicit consideration.

Even within behavioral research there is a candidate–president divide. Some research focuses on voting behavior while other work focuses on other "public opinion" like presidential assessment. The vast work on presidential approval, in particular, takes little notice of campaigns and vote choice. Each president begins a new time series and is expected to follow a predictable path based on predictable considerations.

Finally, campaign scholars seldom consider the governing context when evaluating campaigns and instead seem to assume a much clearer governing environment than exists. Campaigns that encourage issue voting are preferred because these would seem to promote policy responsiveness. But presidents cannot unilaterally make policy. A key question we should ask is, do campaigns help citizens learn what they need to know to reasonably hold a president to account? The dominant theories of accountability do not adequately acknowledge the governmental system or the president's place in it. Prospective accountability calls for campaigns to clearly identify issues and differentiate the candidates on those issues. The model assumes a president sits atop his party, enjoys a unified party government, and can exert control over in-party legislators.[28] Retrospective accountability calls for campaigns that highlight the current state of society and how it has changed over the past four years. The model assumes a form of presidentialism, with the president sitting atop the government and controlling the policy levers.

This division of research comes at a cost. Inattention to these links between presidential behavior in campaigns and in office, between public judgments of candidates and presidents, means we miss important aspects of accountability, and we apply a set of standards to citizens and campaigns that do not make sense for the governing context. Presidents do sit atop government—but it is an ongoing government with a preexisting agenda. Presidents cannot substitute their own, new agenda but can help to designate priorities and to sequence policy making. What campaigns tell us, then, is which of the ongoing agenda items the new president is willing to expend his effort, his time, his resources on. And these priorities link the campaign to governance more than detailed policy papers. These priorities provide a foundation for a legitimate accountability. Our understanding of accountability is incomplete because we have not fully appreciated what campaigns do, and in particular, the role presidential campaigns play in sustaining accountability.

2 Agenda Accountability in Action

Presidential approval is the main mechanism for the public, en masse, to respond to presidential behavior outside of elections. Presidential approval, the percent of the public who "approve of the way [the incumbent] is handling his job as president," reflects the contemporary consent of the populace for the use of presidential authority. These familiar approval ratings have been called the "Dow Jones index for politics" (Brehm 1993) and a perpetual election (Hodgson 1980). Clearly, the idea of presidential popularity as a means of informal accountability is not new. Yet approval has not been directly tied to campaign evaluations or incorporated into our theories of democratic accountability.

Approval is consequential for a president. Although a decline in approval does not lead to immediate dismissal, it is politically meaningful. Approval levels influence the electoral calculations of potential opponents—low approval encourages the opposition—and the subsequent electoral success for both the president and his party in Congress (Gronke, Koch, and Wilson 2003). High levels of approval embolden the president (Light 1999), shape his legislative strategy (Canes-Wrone and Shotts 2004), and increase the likelihood of legislative success (Canes-Wrone and de Marchi 2002; Rivers and Rose 1985).

Though the president and the political world are fascinated with approval ratings, what they mean is not entirely certain. Neustadt early on pegged approval ratings as "unfocused," telling us "anything or nothing about what respondents meant by what they said" (1990, 81).[1] Despite the inherent ambiguity surrounding the reasons for approval ratings, they clearly reflect a withdrawal of contemporary public support, albeit an informal one. And presidents care immensely about their public support.

Even those who question the impact of presidential approval agree that presidents care about these ratings. Indeed, the president may well care too much (Heith 2004; Jacobs and Shapiro 1995). Jones (2005, 134), for instance, describes White House concern with approval ratings as a "near-obsession." Presidential approval ratings "are very widely read in Washington" and "widely taken to approximate reality" (Neustadt 1990, 81, n. 9). Political commentators presume that presidents with high job approval will succeed on Capitol Hill if they know how to wield this resource. These perceptions, by the White House and the larger political community, confer significance to presidential approval ratings regardless of their actual influence on subsequent presidential success.

What, then, shapes approval? After reviewing what scholars have previously concluded about presidential approval, I begin to build an empirical argument, based on the three most recent presidents, about the centrality of campaigns to understanding presidential approval in the early administration.

Understanding Presidential Approval

Perhaps surprisingly, the broad consensus among scholars is that there is little presidents can do to boost their numbers (Edwards 2003), at least once in office. Whether would-be presidents can influence their future standards of evaluation in the campaign, though, is a question we have not yet asked.

A vast literature on presidential approval exists, usually examining the over-time aggregate approval ratings, and most often underscoring the influence of economic conditions, war or related rally events, and the general passage of time on approval rates (Kernell 1978; MacKuen 1983; Mueller 1973; Ostrom and Smith 1992). Without a doubt, peace and prosperity are consistently related to presidential popularity. This understanding of presidential approval, though, rests on an assumption that the public does not care about what policies the government passes or what problems the president pursues.

Although most explanations of presidential popularity rely on individual-level theories, they are rarely tested at the individual level. And though presidents and political elites might well be most concerned with the aggregate numbers, there are good reasons to examine presidential approval at the level of the individual as well. First, presidential approval is most likely based on a wider variety of issues than those measured in the time-series models. Because over-time trends of public preferences on most issues are unavailable, they are left out of these explanations.[2] Policy outcomes other than economic conditions are also harder to measure, and thus, to include.

Second, the explanations of aggregate approval necessarily assume that all presidents are evaluated similarly, that is, that individuals have the same expectations and concerns regarding each president. Though the assumption is often left implicit, some scholars explicitly argue that people have enduring expectations of the president (for example, prosperity and peace) that "are etched into each person's integrated attitudinal schema" (Ostrom and Smith 1992, 130). Expectations, this perspective argues, derive from the office of the presidency itself (Brace and Hinckley 1992; Ostrom and Simon 1985). Such assumptions leave little room for variation in presidential ability to provoke or deflect criticism (Ostrom and Simon 1989) or to establish campaign-related expectations.[3] In this view, the distinctive campaigns that propel a candidate to office disappear into the void.

A new wave of research has begun to expand and test theories of presidential approval at the individual level. In an analysis of presidential approval from 1980 to 1996, Gronke (1999) finds, among other things, that retrospective economic assessments are more strongly related to presidential approval in presidential election years, suggesting that the link between economic growth or decline and the presidency is made salient by campaigns. Among policy measures, defense spending exerts the most influence on presidential approval in Gronke's analysis, but only after 1984, hinting at a more permanent change engendered by Reagan's emphasis on a strong international stance.

Other individual-level approaches to presidential approval suggest presidential evaluations are largely based on whatever issues are most salient at a given time (Edwards, Mitchell, and Welch 1995; Krosnick and Kinder 1990; Miller and Krosnick 1996). Indeed, in one of the earliest efforts to theorize presidential approval rather than predict it, Brody (1992) argues that the economy impacts presidential approval ratings via media attention. The citizen, as spectator, evaluates the president based on available information. The more government activity centers on a given policy area, like the economy, the more media attention it receives. Media attention signals problems to the public and thus helps to define the areas in which presidential performance is judged. This implies that the ingredients of presidential evaluation are not constant, and different presidents may be judged on different mixes of problems.[4]

Not all policy results or problems are equally important to the public, of course. Crises always take precedence, whether foreign or domestic. But approval is generally a function of problem solving. And though presidents may suffer for economic downturns or a prolonged and costly war, they do not enjoy a comparable benefit for their absence. Given peace and prosperity, then, other problems rise to the fore. This theory puts the policies the president tries to get passed at the heart of approval. In a president's early administration, the problems emphasized in the campaign will be key.

Three Recent Presidents

Presidents do exert some control over their evaluations. Their influence begins in the campaign, in the development of problem-solving expectations, and continues with their adherence to their campaign priorities. This is far from the only influence on approval ratings, but it is one we have neglected to date.[5]

The pattern of early approval across our three most recent presidents, provided in figure I.1, helps to demonstrate the point. Recall that President Clinton in 1993 and President Bush in 2001 began with similar levels of approval but experienced dramatically different fortunes in their public support. Bush, to be sure, enjoyed much more favorable economic conditions early on than did Clinton. This cannot be the whole explanation, as the economic conditions with which President Obama had to contend were, by any measure, more troublesome than those facing Clinton in year one. Yet the path of Obama's approval is far more positive than that of Clinton's. Part of these differences, I maintain, can be traced to what the candidates led the public to expect from their presidencies during their campaigns and the extent to which each followed through on those expectations, not in terms of policy outcomes but in terms of problem-solving emphasis.

BILL CLINTON: 1992–1993

The 1992 presidential election provided several noteworthy outcomes: the loss of the incumbent Republican president, George H. W. Bush, initially considered unbeatable after garnering record high approval rates in 1991 following the successful conclusion of the first Gulf War; the surprisingly high popular vote of independent candidate H. Ross Perot, who ran an unconventional campaign and dropped out of the race altogether in July only to reenter the fray in October; and the ultimate success of the Democratic governor from Arkansas, Bill Clinton, who earned the moniker "the Comeback Kid" due to his uncanny ability to survive charges of draft evasion and philandering.

Apart from the unlikely cast of characters, the 1992 campaign was not unusual. The campaign, pundits and scholars agree, was fundamentally about "the economy, stupid,"[6] a theme primarily associated with Clinton. Ross Perot's campaign is remembered for his folksy discussion of the budget deficit and the need for government reform. Bush, meanwhile, appeared to avoid the economy in favor of foreign policy, hoping to capitalize on his high performance ratings after the Persian Gulf War. The dominant themes in each candidate's television advertising during the general election reinforce these perceptions. Table 2.1 provides the issue content of the general election advertisements of Bush, Clinton, and Perot.[7]

Clinton's heaviest emphases were on jobs and unemployment and taxes, followed by the economy more generally, health care, and education. His economic rhetoric, apart from jobs and taxes, centered on public investments in education, worker training, child care, and other domestic initiatives to stimulate the economy. Bush most frequently mentioned foreign policy and taxes, followed by jobs, health care, and the budget deficit. While Clinton and Bush shared some focus on taxes, Bush primarily claimed taxes were too high overall while Clinton argued that the tax system was unfair to the middle class and promoted a middle-class tax cut. Perot emphasized jobs, usually with reference to what he called the "giant sucking sound" of jobs heading south that would follow from the North American Free Trade Agreement (NAFTA). He also talked about the budget deficit, the economy, and taxes prominently. The dominance of economic themes in the general election advertisements is clear.

Table 2.1 Agenda Priorities in Presidential Campaign Ads, 1992

	Percent of Ads Mentioning Issue		
	Clinton	Bush	Perot
Jobs/Unemployment	70.8	30.4	76.5
Taxes	62.5	47.8	29.4
Economy	33.3	26.1	41.2
Health Care	29.2	30.4	5.9
Education	29.2	17.4	5.9
Welfare	16.7	8.7	0
Budget Deficit	8.3	30.4	52.9
Tariffs/Trade	4.2	8.7	5.9
Race	0	0	11.8
Foreign Policy	0	69.5	17.7

Source: Just et al. (1996, 75)

Clinton's issue emphasis, though, resonated most clearly with the American public, who listed the most important problems in 1992 as unemployment (43 percent), the budget deficit (29 percent), the general economy (26 percent), health care (24 percent) and poverty and welfare (22 percent).[8] Clinton won a plurality of the popular vote, at 43 percent, and a comfortable 370 electoral votes to become the nation's forty-second president. Bush received 37 percent of the popular vote and the remaining 168 electoral votes. And Perot secured 19 percent of the popular vote, though this did not translate to any electoral votes. Given Perot's surprising showing and Clinton's win with less than a majority, the media generally viewed the outcome as "a relentless rejection of Mr. Bush's presidency" (Editorial 1992), not a clear mandate for Clinton.

Nonetheless, the nation would experience one-party government for the first time since the Carter administration. Democrats had maintained control of the House and Senate in the 1992 elections, albeit with a loss of 10 seats in the House and no gains in the Senate. In response, expectations for presidential achievement were especially high.

The Clinton team did little to lower expectations during the transition, instead recommitting to a dizzying series of priorities: deficit reduction, a new national health-care system, lobby reforms, and accessible college loans (Balz 1992); stimulating the economy with investment tax credits to create jobs and accelerating spending on highways and public works (Marcus 1992); a national service program (Balz and Pianin 1992); job training and reduced dependence on foreign oil (Drehle 1992); and fixing the "structural" problems in the economy—"lagging productivity, declining incomes and the nation's deteriorating industrial base" (Pearlstein 1992). Deficit reduction eventually took hold as the "top priority" during the transition, with budget chief Leon Panetta noting that, as a result, "administration officials no longer have much interest in short-term spending to boost the economy and have de-emphasized a middle-class tax cut" (Pianin 1993a).

A chief criticism of Clinton's early presidency was precisely this lack of focus or discipline. He promised to have his economic stimulus package ready to go at the beginning of his term; the economic stimulus package was not ready until mid-February. He pledged to introduce a health-care reform bill in his first 100 days; the health-care bill was not ready until the end of October. This lack of focus, a hesitancy in setting and sequencing priorities, left a void where others, allies and opponents alike, could insert their own. Clinton's most widely remembered misstep early on was over gays in the military. After reaffirming a campaign promise to allow homosexuals to serve openly in the military during a postelection interview, Clinton was caught off-guard by the ire of social conservatives and many military commanders. Three days before his inauguration, Clinton and his designee for Secretary of Defense Les Aspin, produced a compromise plan to slow the reversal of the military's ban, but with the military no longer asking about sexual orientation or discharging servicemen or -women found to be gay. On January 29, after several meetings with the Joint Chiefs of Staff and key senators, Clinton announced a new decision, widely seen as a reversal, deferring any final policy for six months while the Pentagon studied their options (Harris 2005).

Combined with his early executive actions regarding abortion—lifting the gag rule prohibiting abortion counseling in federally funded clinics, ending the Mexico City Policy prohibiting the use of U.S. funds for international family-planning efforts that included information on abortion, allowing privately funded abortions to be performed in military hospitals, and eliminating the ban on federally funded medical research on fetal tissue—the early attention to gays in the military identified Clinton with a more liberal agenda than the New Democrat campaign he ran on (Devroy 1993). Welfare reform, an issue that would have served to counter the idea of Clinton as a traditional liberal, did not make it onto the agenda in 1993.

In addition to his attention to a series of liberal issues not salient in his campaign, Clinton's top priority—the economy—became increasingly muddled. Creating jobs and increasing government investments, the key themes of his economic rhetoric, gave way to deficit cutting and monitoring the bond markets (Woodward 1994). The popular middle-class tax cuts were among the first priorities to be abandoned by the Clinton White House in response to the growing government deficits. Clinton outlined his economic plan in a televised address to a joint session of Congress on February 17, proposing an economic stimulus package dominated by deficit reduction. Unsurprisingly, Clinton's economic themes became increasingly identified with deficit reduction, not with economic growth as his political advisors urged (Woodward 1994). His campaign consultants viewed the direction of Clinton's economic policy with earnest objection, convinced that, as pollster Stanley Greenberg claimed, "the presidency has been hijacked" by deficit hawks (Woodward 1994, 94). Clinton, to their thinking, had betrayed his campaign priorities and persona. By April, the president himself noted ruefully of his economic policies: "We're Eisenhower Republicans here, and we are fighting with Reagan Republicans. We stand for lower deficits and free trade and the bond market. Isn't that great?" (Woodward 1994, 165).

The House and Senate passed budget resolutions in March that left Clinton's proposed budget largely intact (Pianin 1993b, 1993c).[9] The victory, though, was quickly overshadowed when Clinton's economic stimulus package was defeated by a Republican filibuster in April. The White House and allies worked to put a positive spin on the defeat. "The budget resolution is passed," said Senate Budget Committee chairman Jim Sasser (D-Tenn.). "Deficit reduction is still in there. Investments are still in there. And that's 95 percent of what the economic package is all about" (Mufson and Pianin 1993). The budget resolution, though, is only the blueprint. In early August, the Omnibus Budget Reconciliation Act narrowly passed both chambers, but only with Vice President Gore casting the tie-breaking vote in the Senate. The bill contained almost $500 billion in deficit savings over five years, but to win this much, Clinton had to give up much of his investment spending.

In the remainder of the year, Clinton would successfully implement his AmeriCorps initiative to help students pay for college in exchange for service (signed September 21); secure the passage of the bill implementing NAFTA in late November and sign the agreement into law (December 8); unveil his health-care plan in a nationally televised address before Congress (September 22) and send the draft of the bill to Congress a month later (October 27); and sign the National Defense Authorization Act for fiscal year 1994, codifying the controversial "Don't Ask, Don't Tell" policy with which he began the year (November 30).

President Clinton's approval ratings fell below the 50 percent mark in late April, after the defeat of his economic stimulus package, and reached their first-year nadir in late June, in the midst of the budget bill battles. In polls in February and again in July, when asked "Do you think that President Bill Clinton's economic plan is generally in line with what he said he would do as a candidate, or do you think it is considerably different from his promises during the campaign?", 53 percent of the public, in both months, thought his plan was considerably different.[10] By May, only 33 percent of those polled said Clinton was doing a "good job" of keeping his most important campaign promises (down from 46 percent in February); 55 percent felt he was doing a "poor job." When the question was next asked, in January 1994, the number saying "a good job" had only risen to 38 percent; half of respondents still answered "a poor job."[11] Similarly, in April of 1993, only 46 percent of those polled said that "keeping campaign promises" is a description that applies to President Clinton. This number dropped to 33 percent in August and rose slightly to 38 percent in November.[12] The public did not see Clinton's early presidency as consistent with his campaign. Though Clinton's ratings began increasing again in July, they did not pass the 50 percent mark until December, after Clinton's attention turned to health care.

Clinton's early fall in the polls is a function of many things, but one of them is assuredly his failure to promote the priorities he advocated during the campaign.

GEORGE W. BUSH: 2000–2001

The 2000 presidential election pitted Democratic Vice President Al Gore against the Republican governor of Texas, George W. Bush. Bush, of course, was also the son of the forty-first president, George. H. W. Bush. The campaign occurred at a moment when the country was feeling good about itself and its prosperity. Eight years of Clinton's presidency had seen record deficits turn into a budget surplus, opening the door to a broader dialogue about how best to use these new resources. Still, the sexual and impeachment fiascoes of Clinton's second term had left their marks, and the Gore campaign felt the need to distance the Democratic nominee from the man he hoped to succeed.

Despite widespread predictions of a Gore victory in early 2000 by scholars and pundits alike (Campbell 2001; Wlezien 2001), most polls consistently showed Gore starting behind Bush as the 2000 general election took shape. During most of the general election, the trial-heat polls were deadlocked, foreshadowing the popular vote.

In the campaign, the candidates followed remarkably similar scripts, with Bush promoting a "compassionate conservative" agenda that echoed traditional Democratic themes, such as education. Gore pushed health care and a middle-class tax cut, not unlike his predecessor. Table 2.2 details the issue emphasis in each candidate's television advertising campaign, based on the frequency of issue emphasis in the ads actually aired.

Bush's advertising campaign centered on education, where he pushed for accountability in educational outcomes, and Social Security, where he proposed adding personal investment accounts to the popular program. Bush also emphasized tax cuts and health care, the latter largely in response to Gore's promotion of the issue. In addition to health care, and in particular the need for a patient's bill of rights, Gore emphasized tax cuts for the middle class. Education generally topped the public's stated concerns in 2000, followed closely by the economy, health care, and Social Security. Both campaigns, then, adhered to an already evident public agenda.

The most notable part of the 2000 presidential election was the bitterly contested outcome. After five weeks of butterfly ballots, recounts, and court battles in Florida, the U.S. Supreme Court's 5–4 decision in *Bush v. Gore* effectively decided the election in Bush's favor. With Flor-

Table 2.2 Agenda Priorities in Presidential Campaign Ads, 2000

	Percent of Airings Mentioning Issue	
	Bush/RNC Ads	Gore/DNC Ads
Education	51.4	16.1
Social Security	36.4	14.4
Health Care	26.5	42.2
Taxes	22.3	26.4
Budget	19.2	11.8
Background	7.9	30.2
Environment	3.0	18.5

Source: Goldstein et al. (2002)

ida's electoral votes in his column, Bush won by a margin of 271–267. The popular vote was similarly close, but with Gore ahead by 540,000 votes. The outcome precluded an interpretation of the election as a repudiation of Clinton and denied Bush any clear claim of a mandate. At the beginning of his term, Bush enjoyed a Republican-controlled House, though the margin was a slim six seats; the Senate was evenly divided.

Despite the concern expressed at the time, Bush's presidency was not plagued by a lack of legitimacy early on. Indeed, in Bush's early presidency, he preceded to do largely what his campaign priorities signaled he would do: He started his legislative agenda with education and tax cuts. Unlike Clinton, Bush quickly became known for his message discipline and focus. Three days after taking office in January 2001, Bush announced No Child Left Behind, his framework for bipartisan education reform and his answer to the challenge of improving education highlighted by his campaign. Less than a year later, President Bush secured its passage despite the unprecedented challenges of leading the nation in the war on terrorism following the events of September 11. Three weeks into his term, Bush submitted his "Agenda for Tax Relief" to Congress. In June, he solidified his first major legislative victory when he signed into law the deepest tax cuts in two decades.

Bush's early presidency was not without missteps, but Bush's lower media profile and disciplined administration avoided small-scale controversies and the distractions they bring. The key campaign priority Bush essentially ignored in his first year was Social Security, which was sidelined with the appointment of a presidential task force. One of the bigger snafus of Bush's first year resulted in the defection of Republican Senator Jim Jeffords (Vt.), who was unhappy with both the lack of funding for special education and the size of the tax cuts. As an Independent, Jeffords would vote to turn control of the Senate over to Democrats. And, of course, the terrorist attacks of September 11, 2001, changed everybody's focus, effectively resetting the agenda for the remainder of Bush's first term.

As figure I.1 attests, Bush's approval ratings in his early presidency remained consistently strong and stable, compared to Clinton's. The trend in Bush's approval rating peaks at 57 in early March and bottoms out at 52 in mid-June. And public perceptions of Bush's promise-keeping were, not coincidentally, considerably more favorable than were Clinton's. In April 2001, 57 percent of polled respondents said that the characteristic "keeping his campaign promises" applies to Bush; in August, the number was 59 percent, a full 26 percent increase over Clinton's reputation.[13] When asked whether Bush was doing a good or poor job keeping his campaign promises in July 2002, 53 percent said he was doing a good job.[14]

Journalists and the public, alike, viewed the early Bush presidency as consistent with the Bush campaign. This perception helps account for his notably higher ratings in his first months in office compared to his predecessor.

BARACK OBAMA: 2008–2009

By the end of Bush's second term, public sentiment toward the ongoing Iraq War had turned decidedly south. In a poll right before the Democratic and Republican conventions, 66 percent of the public reported opposing the war in Iraq, double the percent who supported it.[15] Americans were not feeling good about the economy either, with 49 percent rating economic conditions poor, 35 percent rating them fair, and only 16 percent rating economic conditions excellent or good right before the conventions.[16] The deep dissatisfaction with the state of the country was reflected in Bush's poor approval ratings: Leading up to the conventions, Bush's approval was at 30 percent; his disapproval was at 68 percent.[17] The electoral forecasts for Republicans were dire.

In response, Republicans nominated Senator John McCain, a self-proclaimed maverick with an unusually centrist record, though not without reservations among conservatives.[18] Democrats, for their part, chose Barack Obama as their nominee, but only after a prolonged primary battle with Hillary Clinton. Obama, the first black man to run at the head of a major party ticket, was the only candidate in either party who had opposed the Iraq War from the beginning. He noted this repeatedly during the Democratic primaries and it granted greater credibility to his stated commitment to withdraw U.S. combat troops from Iraq by 2010.

Despite the fundamentals favorable to Democrats, the race was close heading into the conventions, with Obama leading on average by about 3.5 percent.[19] The conventions and the general election campaign that followed tightened the race even further; Obama's average lead during September dropped to 2.5 percent. The game changed in mid-September, though, with the onset of the Wall Street meltdown. The government seized control of Fannie Mae and Freddie Mac on September 7. Lehman Brothers declared bankruptcy on September 15. The government made an $85 billion emergency loan to rescue AIG on September 16. President Bush announced his $700 billion financial bailout plan on September 19, and on October 3, Bush signed the biggest U.S. bailout in history. In the midst of the meltdown, McCain suspended his campaign for several days and called, unsuccessfully, for the postponement of the first presidential debate. McCain's polling numbers dropped for the remainder of the campaign; during October, Obama's lead in the trial-heat polls averaged 8 percent, closely mirroring his 7 percent lead in the popular vote.

Obama's campaign is remembered for his emphasis on hope and change. The nature of the hoped-for change is clarified in his advertising strategy. Table 2.3 details the issue emphasis of Obama's and McCain's "air war," based on the frequency with which issues were mentioned in the television ads actually aired.

The ads aired in Obama's campaign most frequently mentioned taxes, followed by health-care reform and job creation. Obama's tax rhetoric emphasized two main themes: (1) that McCain voted for tax cuts for millionaires and big oil, while Obama supports tax cuts for the middle class; and (2) that McCain voted to retain tax breaks to companies that ship jobs overseas, while Obama supports ending these in favor of tax breaks for companies that create jobs at home. The second theme combined the goal of restructuring the tax system with the goal of job creation. Obama also combined his focus on jobs with a call for energy independence, cre-

Table 2.3 Agenda Priorities in Presidential Campaign Ads, 2008

	Percent of Airings Mentioning Issue	
	Obama/DNC Ads	McCain/RNC Ads
Taxes	61.0	56.0
Healthcare	36.4	1.6
Jobs	35.7	4.7
National Defense	15.8	13.5
Energy	13.2	34.0
Iraq	12.6	0.2
Gas Prices	11.2	23.2
Education	10.3	3.2
Government Spending	5.1	42.8
National Debt	3.3	14.2

Source: Goldstein et al. (unpublished)

ating green-energy jobs. And he referenced unemployment in several ads, connecting the current job losses to McCain's unfortunate declaration that "the fundamentals of the economy are strong." Some of Obama's references to health care were general calls to finally fix health care, but more of his health-care references occurred as attacks on McCain's health-care proposal—to provide tax credits to individuals to purchase health care paid for by taxing the current health benefits of workers and by cutting Medicare.[20]

Taxes were also the most frequently referenced issue in McCain's ads. McCain referenced taxes primarily to claim that Obama would raise them, though his ads sometimes relayed his commitment to lowering them. Similarly, McCain's references to the debt, his second most prominent issue theme, were generally contained in attacks on Obama who, McCain claimed, would increase government spending and dig us deeper into debt; some ads highlighted McCain's commitment to reducing spending and eliminating government waste. McCain's most prominent issue themes, then, were attacks on his "tax and spend" opponent. References to energy and gas prices generally occurred together in McCain's ads, emphasizing his commitment (and Obama's opposition) to more offshore drilling to reduce energy dependence and lower gas prices.

In an interview on October 31, days before the election, CNN's Wolf Blitzer asked Obama to name his top priority from among a list of issues. Obama answered: "[The] top priority may not be any of those five. It may be continuing to stabilize the financial system. . . . None of this can be accomplished if we continue to see a potential meltdown in the banking system and financial system. So that's priority No. 1: making sure the plumbing works." Obama followed with energy independence, tying this to national security and jobs (priority 2); health-care reform (priority 3); a middle-class tax cut and tax reform (priority 4); and education reform (priority 5). He followed up to note that tax cuts and a second stimulus package were part of priority No. 1, pledging that a stimulus package that includes tax cuts would be the first bill he introduced (Blitzer 2009). This conforms reasonably well to the priorities conveyed in his advertising campaign. Apart from education, the five most frequently mentioned issues in his ads are among his list of top priorities.

The 2008 election gave the United States her first African American president. Obama garnered 53 percent of the popular vote to McCain's 46 percent. Obama won 365 electoral votes, with 173 electoral votes awarded to McCain. The Democrats retained control of both houses of Congress, increasing their margins to 58 seats in the Senate[21] and 256 seats in the House. Despite the decisive victory, talk of a mandate among political observers was muted, with those on the left asserting a mandate for health-care reform and a redistribution of the tax burden from the middle class to the affluent (Krugman 2008; Shiller 2008). Obama, himself, generally only referenced his "mandate to move the country in a new direction" (Eggen and Fletcher 2008).

During the transition, Obama and his surrogates most frequently referenced economic stimulus and job creation as the top priority of the new president once in office (Connolly and Smith 2008). But the Obama team also mentioned managing the financial bailout (Montgomery 2008), securing a middle-class tax cut (Fletcher 2008), closing the detention facilities at Guantánamo Bay (Finn 2008), and clean energy and health-care reform (Connolly and Smith 2008). "Ambitious" was an adjective commonly used for Obama's agenda.

The ambition paid off with the passage of the American Recovery and Reinvestment Act (ARRA) on February 13, 2009, less than a month into Obama's presidency. The bill passed largely along party lines despite Obama's efforts to include provisions appealing to Republicans (for example, tax cuts for businesses). On February 17, a week before his first major address to Congress, President Obama signed the legislation allocating $787 billion over the next two years to stimulate the flagging economy with spending aimed at retaining and creating jobs and one of the largest two-year tax cuts in history.[22] Very early in his administration, Obama made significant progress on two of his major agenda items.

On January 22, Obama issued executive orders to create an interagency task force to define legal ways to handle terrorist suspects captured in the future, to bar the use of any interrogation methods not authorized in the Army field manual on *Human Intelligence Collector Operations*, and to close the detention center at Guantánamo Bay within a year (Bettelheim 2009).[23] Within days of taking the oath of office, President Obama made moves to fulfill several campaign promises. In addition, on February 27, Obama announced his plan to draw down U.S. military forces in Iraq by August 2010—a compromise between his campaign pledge of sixteen months and the military's preferred twenty-three months—leaving the timing of the precise withdrawals to General Odierno, the top U.S. commander in Iraq.

On April 29, Congress passed a budget resolution, with no Republican support, that included tax cuts for the middle class and language allowing health-care reform to move through a filibuster-proof reconciliation process in the Senate. Though the resolution capped discretionary spending at $1.088 trillion, $10 billion less than the administration had requested, the resolution incorporated an ambitious $3.6 trillion budget (Clarke 2009).

At the same time, Republican Senator Arlen Specter (Penn.) announced he was leaving the Republican Party to join the Democratic caucus, giving the Democrats fifty-nine seats in the Senate, within lobbing distance of the coveted 60 seats needed to forestall opposition filibusters.[24]

In June, the House approved a climate change bill intended to limit pollution by capping greenhouse gas emissions and pricing carbon. And despite the anticipated damage to health-care reform from the angry town halls of the summer of 2009, by December bills overhauling health care had passed both houses of Congress. In short, Obama's early administration was both productive and largely predicted by his campaign.[25] Given the very high expectations of Obama upon entering office and the severity of the problems he confronted, the first year may not have been productive enough.

There is no question that Obama's approval remained consistently higher than that of his immediate predecessors for at least his first eight months in office. The public expressed more early satisfaction with his record of promise keeping, as well, at least through April. In April, the first time such questions were asked of Obama, 61 percent of respondents agreed that Obama was fulfilling his campaign promises.[26] The Obama White House, too, seemed to believe that achieving some legislative progress on Obama's priorities was paramount and that the achievement more than the policy details would define the standard to which they expected to be held. "The only nonnegotiable principle here is success. Everything else is negotiable," claimed Rahm Emanual, Obama's chief of staff (Bai 2009).

By the end of the year, the severity and endurance of the economic crisis, however, appeared to drag his ratings down. Despite the truly stunning achievement in getting the ARRA through Congress, the economic stimulus was, by many accounts, simply not enough. Having built up expectations for resolving the unemployment crisis, in the face of rising unemployment numbers, Obama's efforts haven't kept pace. By October, the positive perceptions of Obama's promise keeping had dropped precipitously. Only 48 percent agreed that Obama had been keeping the promises he made in his campaign.[27] His reputation eroded further as the year ended. In January 2010, only 41 percent agreed that he was keeping his major campaign promises.[28]

Conclusion

These patterns of presidential approval are consistent with the idea that presidents, as candidates, establish expectations of their time in office via the goals and priorities conveyed in their campaigns. Presidents who appear to stand by these goals early on are judged favorably by the public; presidents who neglect these fare less well. Accountability, via approval, is plausibly tied to the campaign. Bush's early presidency is considered in more detail in chapter 6. Chapter 7 will present more evidence on the early presidencies of Clinton and Obama.

It is worth noting that the public appears neither unreasonable in their sanction nor entirely malleable in their standards. Both Clinton and Bush saw their priorities shift in office, Clinton in response to the growing budget deficit and Bush in response to the attacks of September 11. Bush's shift in focus was self-evidently justified. Clinton's shift was not. And Clinton did not make a compelling argument to the public to justify his change in focus. Clinton, as a consequence, was sanctioned. The public was not inflexible when conditions warranted flexibility, as was the case for Bush in September 2001. But equally, the public was not forgetful of Clinton's emphasis when he changed course.

The comparisons elaborated here motivate more attention to the microfoundations of this process. The next four chapters break the process of agenda accountability down to develop a firmer empirical basis for each of the steps: the clarity of candidate issue priorities, citizen's understanding of those priorities, citizen use of those priorities in evaluation, and the president's and public's response to those priorities in the new president's administration. The 2000 campaign and the early presidency of George W. Bush provide the data for the more detailed analyses that follow.

3 Campaigning on Issues

To promote accountability, candidates must talk about issues. Fortunately, presidential campaigns are filled with issue talk—in debates, in speeches, in television advertising. Given the quadrennial laments of political observers, this may be a surprising assertion, though it is one increasingly accepted by scholars of campaigns.

Take political advertisements, long considered the most debased form of campaign communication (Franz et al. 2007): In the 2000 presidential campaign, 69 percent of the ads aired on television focused on policy issues, and another 24 percent emphasized both policy and personal characteristics. Only 7 percent contained no issue information at all. And the 2000 campaign is not unusual in this regard. Geer (2006) finds, in an examination of presidential campaign ads from 1960 to 2000, that issue appeals make up 56 percent of all advertising appeals.[1] Certainly the focus on policy in contemporary campaigns far surpasses that of campaigns in the pre-media era. After all, if a candidate is going to speak directly to the people, he or she must have *something* to say.[2]

Consequently, campaigns contain ample issue discussion, though not, perhaps, ample issue debate. The emphasis is on problems and goals. Campaigns, particularly those of the opposition, are largely about calling attention to unfulfilled needs, highlighting problems left unaddressed or unsolved by the current president. In other words, campaigns often emphasize valence issues. Policy proposals are commonly released but not hyped by the candidates (or the media). The policy details and the campaign pledges are for coalition building, to appeal to segments within a party. They are not really intended for the voters at large except to signal seriousness about an issue. Policy specifics underscore a candidate's commitment. The issue priorities, the much maligned vague statement of goals, are aimed at the mass public. If citizens, broadly, are to have any role in accountability, it will be in evaluating performance on priorities, not fulfillment of detailed policy pledges.

Nevertheless, many observers are dissatisfied with *how* issues are talked about, particularly in campaign advertising, bemoaning the lack of specificity. Journalists decry the lack of controversial issues, what Stokes (1963) called position issues and Patterson (1980) called "clear-cut" issues. The focus on valence issues over controversial ones denies reporters a straightforward way to contrast the candidates. Campaign reformers, as well, wish to improve campaign discourse by making campaigns more informative and civil. Toward that end, reform proposals promote more debates, town meetings, and issue forums to clarify where the candidates stand on the issues (Maisel, West, and Clifton 2007). Political scientists, on the other hand, wish for more precision in the issue talk: for candidates to "state an intention; specify the time when action would be taken; chart the direction of action; and delimit the magnitude of action" (Page 1978, 163).[3] An analysis of the issue content of presidential candidates' position papers, speeches, and interviews finds issue rhetoric wanting. In the 1960 campaign between John F. Kennedy and Richard M. Nixon, for instance, Page finds that only 19 percent of the written and transcribed candidate statements talked about policy. More common, at 46 percent, was talk of goals, problems, and past performance (1978, 156).[4]

Given the criticisms of campaign advertising, we might expect the 30-second advertising spot to be particularly vapid. And yet, in his detailed content analysis of presidential television ads from 1960–2000, Geer (2006) breaks down the issue appeals, making up 56 percent of all appeals, into position appeals and valence appeals. He finds that 12 percent can be categorized as advocating some position, while 43 percent communicate the candidate's agreement with broadly consensual goals. The breakdown of rhetoric about policy, general goals, and broad values in presidential television ads is remarkably similar to the breakdown of these themes in the candidate speeches, statements, and papers analyzed by Page (1978).

The absence of issue specificity—stating the intention, timing, direction, and magnitude of policy preferences—is clearly not the same as the absence of issue talk. The nearly half of candidate remarks Page categorized as highlighting "goals, problems, and past performance" contain obvious issue relevance. It is just that candidates frequently prefer to emphasize their agenda priorities (goals and problems) rather than proposed policies. As Page notes (1978, 178), "[O]pinions differ on specific policy questions but . . . there is widespread consensus on general goals. . . . A candidate who takes a specific policy stand is bound to alienate those who disagree; but a candidate who promises peace, progress and prosperity . . . is likely to please almost everyone."

Identifying problems one intends to take on and goals one plans to achieve—in other words, emphasizing agenda priorities—is less controversial. That the goals are consensual, though, does not mean the American public agrees on the ranking of such priorities. For valence issues like improving education or reducing crime, which increasingly make up much of the campaign discourse, the key difference between candidates is how highly they prioritize the issue.

This defense of valence issues, of an emphasis on problems and goals, goes against the grain of most campaign research where position issues are generally judged as superior to valence concerns. A campaign in which issue positions play a prominent role is considered a more substantive campaign; such issue discussion serves to expose the grounds on which candidates agree (see Kelley 1960, for instance). Geer argues that "when a candidate, for example, favors 'economic growth,' that appeal is hardly going to help voters . . . sort out the differences between the nominees. On the other hand, specific information about the candidate's tax policy or willingness to increase the minimum wage would be useful and help voters make 'rational' choices" (2006, 46). Again, this presupposes that a presidential candidate can enact his or her stated policy preferences. I argue, in contrast, that issue talk, divorced from emphasis, doesn't tell voters how much energy a candidate is likely to devote toward a goal. Even if every Republican nominee proposed to cut taxes, not every nominee would prioritize this as highly.[5] Many of the issue positions that candidates state are boilerplate; the mere stating of the position, on its own, does not signal commitment, though it may reassure a candidate's base support. For a mass public concerned about results, *commitment* to addressing a problem matters.[6] And the mass public does, by and large, care about results. Brody (1992), in his trenchant examination of presidential approval, finds approval related to outcomes on valence issues more than proposals on position issues.

Campaign reformers overlook the value of issue priorities. In advocating for more substance and less negativity, reformers assume that what citizens need for an informed vote is to understand the policy positions of the candidates. They decry negative campaigns for failing to provide reasons to vote for one candidate, not just against another (Maisel, West, and Clifton 2007). Even attack ads, and certainly contrast ads, however, send implicit messages about what issues the sponsoring candidate thinks are important by pointing to issues and problems the opponent has failed, or would fail, to address.

An emphasis on goals and priorities is only problematic if it conveys no information at all. Contrary to much conventional wisdom, agenda priorities represent useful information for citizens. Candidates reveal their priorities through their campaign emphases, and these priorities signal what problems a future leader is likely to spend effort and resources on. Budge and Hofferbert show that the topics emphasized in a party's platform "constitute implicit commitments to greater effort in the area if elected" (1990, 114); budgets move in accord with these emphases, particularly for the party occupying the White House. These agenda-priority signals are not cheap talk.

Issue emphases in legislative campaigns, too, are linked to the amount of legislative activity on the part of the winner after the election, and this relationship does not depend on the specificity of claims made in issue appeals (Sulkin 2009). Candidate issue emphasis and the agenda priorities thereby declared are cues about candidates' revealed intensities, a way to predict their level of future effort toward a goal (Hall 1996). Consequently, if citizens hope to learn from campaigns the consequences of an election outcome, agenda priorities represent a reasonable prediction of what a candidate is likely to focus on once in office. This identification of what a candidate thinks the campaign is about—what issues are most important, what failures of the opposition are most serious—presents voters with a useful, substantive, and relatively straightforward basis for a vote decision. It also makes the tradeoffs in policy goals more explicit. The American public is regularly denounced for demanding contradictory ends from government—lower taxes and deficits and more government services, for example. The ends are contradictory to the extent that citizens rate them as equally important. But an emphasis on issue priorities acknowledges, and encourages citizens and candidates to acknowledge, that many valued ends must be ranked.

A majority of presidential campaign promises are kept, leading the handful of scholars who have analyzed pledge fulfillment to conclude that the campaign provides a "good indicator of future policy performance" (Krukones 1984, 127), a "reasonably meaningful indication" of intentions (Pomper 1980, 152), and "useful information about the broad contours of future presidential initiatives" (Fishel 1985, 49). Pomper finds that between 1944 and 1976 the party that won the White House accomplished about two thirds of its campaign-platform promises on average (1980). Fishel (1985), focusing on the years from 1960 to 1984, finds that presidents attempted to fulfill, at least partially, about 62 percent of the pledges made in speeches, interviews, and issue papers; and most of this effort was concentrated in the first two years in office.[7] Krukones (1984), examining fifteen elections from 1912 to 1976, produces an even more optimistic estimate of promise-keeping effort of about 75 percent.

These estimates are not without problems. Pledge-fulfillment studies weight all promises equally, though in fact some of the commitments are repeated by candidates more often than others. Consequently, some of the commitments matter more to the mass public than others. Further, Fishel and Krukones include presidential efforts at pledge fulfillment in addition to achievement. Effort, of course, does not guarantee fulfillment, though it is a necessary precursor. And the partial fulfillment highlighted by Fishel is meant to acknowledge that a president cannot get all he wants. It is precisely because a president cannot impose his policies on legislatures that we should care about his priorities, as these are indicators of which issues he is willing to expend his political capital on. Thus it is time to take the issue *priorities* of the candidates seriously, as relevant information about potential activity and policy commitments that both aids citizens in voting and directs attention and approval after the election. Indeed, given the prominence of valence issues in campaigns, agendas may well be the only available way to meaningfully assess future accountability.

The 2000 Campaign

There is no shortage of presidential campaign discourse in the months leading up to the general election. Political information becomes more readily available as the candidates and their emissaries send more messages to the public and as the news hole is increasingly filled with campaign coverage at the expense of noncampaign news. The 2000 campaign, the case under examination here, was no exception.

The 2000 campaign set new records in the amount spent on television advertising. The candidates themselves spent over $107 million; the parties spent another $81 million on behalf of Bush and Gore (Holman and McLoughlin 2001).[8] Overall, Bush and the Republican Party aired 146,320 television ads in the top seventy-five media markets over the course of the entire campaign. Gore's team aired 128,428 ads.

The 2000 campaign has been extensively deconstructed, with accounts calling it a referendum on Clinton (Pomper 2001), a campaign more about character than issues (Hershey 2001), and a campaign that left the public inattentive and uninterested (Patterson 2002). At first blush, then, we might question whether the 2000 campaign is a good candidate for testing a theory about the development of accountability mechanisms. A campaign that is perceived as less issue oriented, and to which the public paid less attention, ought to serve as a harder case for finding a persistent influence on presidential approval. If we see a consistent effect of issue priorities in this case, we can be more confident of the broader relevance.

Was the 2000 campaign unusually issue free? Geer's (2006) analysis of television advertising from 1960 to 2000 gives us no reason to suspect so. He finds, across this period, 56 percent of the appeals made in ads emphasized issues. In 2000, issue appeals made up over 70 percent of all appeals. Nor were citizens especially less interested in the 2000 presidential campaign. In 2000, 76 percent of respondents expressed being somewhat or very interested in the current campaign in the National Election Studies survey. The average for the period from 1960 to 2000 is 76.2 percent.[9] The number of citizens who care a good deal about who wins the presidential election has grown over time. In 2000, 76 percent of respondents to the National Election Studies survey said they cared a good deal. The average who answered similarly from 1960 to 2000 is 65.6 percent.

Was the 2000 campaign unusual in its issue concerns, by the public or the candidates? Certainly the economy did not play a strong role in 2000 owing to the relatively strong economy at the time. The economy, though, was only ranked as the most important problem among the public in five of the last eleven elections.[10] Similarly, in Geer's (2006) advertising data, the economy was the top issue in the winning candidate's advertising in five of the last eleven elections.[11] While the economy often is a dominant theme, its absence as the primary emphasis does not make the campaign unusual. In fact, that the campaign did not focus on the economy makes the 2000 race a better case for theory testing. Demonstrating that presidential approval responds to economic outcomes or efforts would not be especially convincing in building a case for the persistence of campaign priorities in public expectations given the prominent role the economy already plays in explanations of presidential approval.

Was the 2000 campaign unusual for the degree of "issue trespassing" by George W. Bush? In an examination of presidential campaign advertising appeals from 1952 to 2000, Petrocik, Benoit, and Hansen (2003) find a great deal of issue trespassing, that is, a candidate highlighting an issue his opponent's party is deemed better able to handle. Democrats, though, have generally engaged in more trespassing. While 63 percent of

Republican candidate appeals are on "Republican-owned" issues, only 51 percent of Democratic candidate appeals are on "Democratic-owned" issues. While trespassing is common, then, the 2000 campaign may be a little unusual for being fought more heavily on Democratic turf. This, too, might make 2000 a slightly harder case for the development of campaign-induced expectations, as it suggests citizens are hearing a slightly unexpected message.

One obvious limitation of the 2000 election and the administration that follows is that the first Bush presidency only provides us with eight months of crisis-free governing for observation. Crises can distort the normal workings of government (Jones 1999) as well as the normal structure of approval and accountability. Crises override the separation of institutions and the divide of partisanship, so we cannot fruitfully follow the administration and approval beyond September 11. On the other hand, it is the first year of the administration that is key for building a reputation with Congress, with the media, and with the public, so the shortened time frame is not as troublesome as it might at first appear.

There are, of course, always limitations to one case.[12] But delving deeply into this process in one campaign and administration, comparing across multiple candidates and issues, is a good place to start examining an otherwise neglected process. To begin that examination, I analyze the issue emphasis of the candidates' advertising during the campaign. Campaign issue talk in 2000 is measured with a data set of the presidential advertising campaign from the Campaign Media Analysis Group. This data set tracks television advertisements broadcast in the top seventy-five media markets across the nation, capturing information on what spot is aired, when, and where. The Wisconsin Advertising Project undertook extensive content analysis of these ads, including what issues, if any, are mentioned in each (Goldstein, Franz, and Ridout 2002). With these data, we can construct a reasonably faithful picture of the themes emphasized by each candidate.

In addition, I have analyzed the content of campaign coverage in *NBC Nightly News* (Monday through Friday) throughout the campaign to see if the issue priority messages conveyed through the media mirror or distort those conveyed by the candidates. *NBC Nightly News* was selected to reflect what the typical news viewer receives.[13]

To promote accountability, candidates need to signal their agenda priorities. Did Al Gore and George W. Bush do so in 2000? To what extent did the candidates actually talk about issues, and what issues did they talk about?

Issues and Agendas in the 2000 Campaign

Clearly campaigns inject a great many political messages into the public discourse. More than $187 million can buy a lot of communication. And the campaign fills an increasingly larger portion of available time and space in the media as the election draws near. In 2000, Bush and Gore and their national party committees most frequently mentioned education, health care, Social Security, taxes, the budget (deficits/surpluses, for example), and the environment (see table 2.2).

Bush and the Republican National Committee (RNC) most frequently mentioned education in the ads they aired; 51 percent of ad airings mentioned education, compared to 16 percent of Gore's ads. Gore and the Democratic National Committee (DNC) emphasized health care above other topics (42 percent, compared to 27 percent of Bush's ads). Mention of the top issue far outpaced any other issues for each of the candidates. Social Security and taxes were mentioned in 36 and 22 percent of the Bush ad airings, respectively, and in 14 and 26 percent of the Gore ad airings.[14] I will focus on these four.[15] These issues vary both in volume of attention during the campaign and with respect to party reputation, with Gore and the Democrats having a stronger claim on health care and education and Bush and the Republicans having a stronger claim on taxes. Social Security, long a protected issue in American politics, has historically leaned toward the Democrats but was a comparatively open issue by 2000. In 2000, the candidates engaged in strategies of issue ownership *and* issue trespassing.

Figure 3.1 portrays how emphases on these four issues fared over time in the advertising campaign. Though all issues receive more attention during the general election campaign, the figures highlight Bush's early attention to, and relative dominance on, education and Social Security in his campaign. Gore, on the other hand, leads off the attention to health care and, curiously, taxes in the general election, but Bush comes close to matching him, largely due to his more extensive advertising overall. This summary jibes fairly well with other accounts of the campaign that suggest no single issue dominated (McWilliams 2001; Quirk and Matheson 2001). Bush emphasized education and taxes, Gore emphasized health care, and the candidates do not diverge strongly in their issue emphases. In part, the candidates were responding to existing preferences in public opinion; in part, they were responding to one another.

What does Bush's attention to education look like? What does it mean that Gore emphasized health care? Did they focus primarily on "goals, problems, and past performance" or provide specifics? I consider

Campaigning on Issues 49

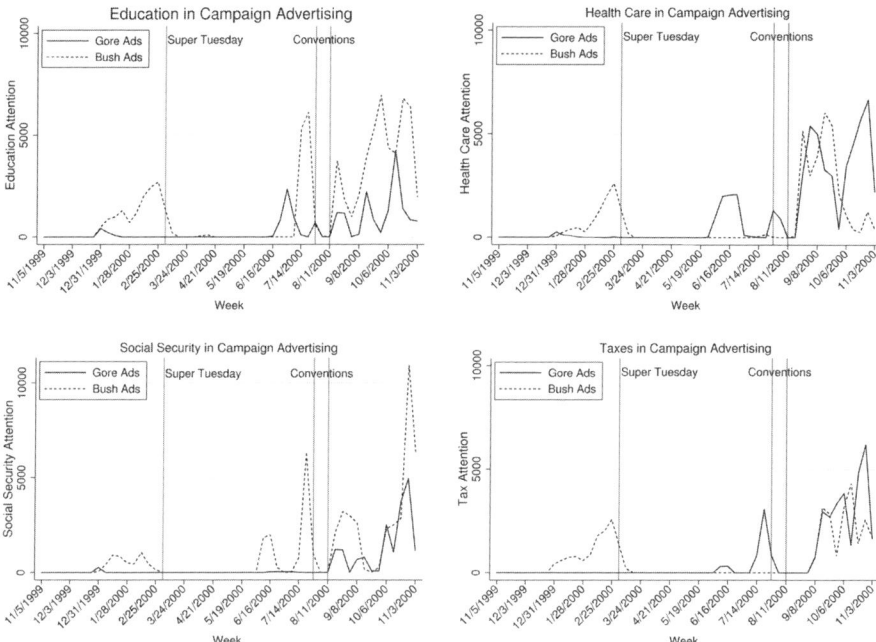

Figure 3.1 Campaign Advertising Attention over Time

the content of the most frequently aired ads (listed in appendix A) in more detail.[16]

Bush's focus on education was primarily positive in tone. Among the ads aired referencing education, 59 percent were coded as promotional by the Wisconsin Advertising Project; 38 percent were categorized as contrast ads—ads making an explicit comparison between the candidates—and only 3 percent were considered attack ads. Bush's emphasis on education in his advertising generally began by noting a problem—an unacceptable number of children can't read. In ads that mention multiple issues (for example, "Compare" and "Hard Things" in appendix A), that was the extent of the education emphasis, identifying this as a problem he intended to solve. In the ads that focused on education, Bush goes on to propose higher standards with more accountability and, sometimes, more local control of schools. The most frequently aired ad devoted to education, "Expect More," highlights Bush's record on education as the governor in Texas. There was seldom anything more specific than that. Nevertheless, a viewer could easily understand that Bush planned to work toward improving education.

Gore's education-referencing ads were even more overwhelmingly positive, with 90 percent categorized as promotional, and the remainder evenly split between contrast and attack ads. Gore's mention of education in advertising also used the language of accountability along with calls for smaller class sizes in elementary school and help with college tuition. This represents the most specific rhetoric on the issue in advertising.

Gore's attention to health care, like Bush's emphasis on education, begins by noting a problem—insurance companies and HMOs interfering with medical treatment—and posits his solution, a Patient's Bill of Rights. This is the focus of his two most heavily aired health-care ads, "Bean Counter" and "Patients" (see appendix A). The second most common theme in Gore's health-care ads highlights and defends his proposal to help seniors afford prescription drugs. The tone of his ads is relatively evenly split; among his aired ads mentioning health care, 37 percent are promotional, 31 percent are comparative, and 32 percent are attacking the opposition.

Bush generally didn't air ads that focused solely on health care but mentioned health care in conjunction with Social Security, proposing to make prescription drugs available and affordable to seniors (for example, "No Changes, No Reductions") and attacking Gore's plan for helping seniors with drug costs as the equivalent of a government HMO ("Notebook" and "Compare"). As such, Bush's attention to the issue is usually in direct contrast to Gore's more specific plan. In fact, 66 percent of his ads that reference health care were comparative, while 32 percent were primarily promotional and only 2 percent were attack ads. Further, while Gore treated health care as a distinct problem, Bush emphasized Medicare and talked about it in conjunction with Social Security. Although the candidates seem to implicitly agree on the problem underlying education, they clearly disagree on the underlying problem with health care. With regard to health care, the candidates are talking past one another.

Bush's early emphasis on Social Security in ads begins with the claim that now is the time to "strengthen and improve" Social Security. His most frequently aired ad focusing on Social Security ("This Generation," aired more than 8,000 times) proposes giving younger workers the ability to invest a portion of Social Security taxes in private accounts while assuring seniors that nothing will change for them. More commonly, Bush merely asserts the need to improve the program in his advertising (such as "No Changes, No Reductions" and "Hard Things"). Of the Bush ads aired that mention Social Security, 58 percent were promotional, only 11 percent were explicitly comparative, and 31 percent were primarily negative.

Gore's attention to Social Security was generally negative, attacking Bush for promising to use the Social Security surplus for both younger workers and seniors simultaneously and assuring America that he would protect the surplus. This was the message of his two most frequent Social Security ads ("Why," "Doesn't Add"). Every time Social Security comes up in Gore's ads, the ad includes an explicit critique of Bush's proposal. Indeed, of Gore's aired ads mentioning Social Security, 66 percent were characterized as mostly attacks, while only 16 and 17 percent, respectively, were positive or comparative appeals. Social Security talk, then, comprises some of the most specific policy talk found in the ads, with Bush, especially, stating a clearer policy intention and Gore outlining the negative consequences of those intentions. The rhetoric on Social Security comes closer to resembling dialogue.

Attention to taxes by both candidates is less straightforward. The only widely aired ad that highlights taxes as an issue, "Big Relief vs. Big Spending," was a Bush ad comparing Bush's preferred economic plan—cut taxes for everyone—with Gore's supposed economic plan—massive new spending. More commonly, tax talk gets thrown in with a list of other issues. To the extent either candidate identifies a problem that his tax plan will address, the problem is generally the opponent's tax plan. Bush ties tax cuts to the budget surplus ("I trust you" with the surplus) and critiques Gore's proposal as leaving out millions of families. Bush's ads mentioning taxes are less likely to be positive; only 22 percent are promotional ads, while 64 percent are comparative, and 14 percent are negative ads. Gore talks about tax cuts for the working and middle-class families and critiques Bush's plan as benefiting primarily the wealthy. Given his emphasis on the middle-class tax cuts, Gore's aired ads mentioning taxes are more likely to be positive (46 percent), though 30 percent are explicit attacks on Bush and 24 percent contrast the candidates. Unlike the other three issues, in which a problem or opportunity is the purported stimulus for candidate attention, for taxes, the opponent's wrong-headed intentions are the apparent stimulus.

Thus, while some intentions are laid out in the advertising campaigns, the direction, timing, and magnitude are never fully addressed. A viewer could readily ascertain that Bush wants to improve education or that Gore wants to protect health decisions from the interference of insurance companies, but the specifics of how either candidate might achieve these goals is largely left to the imagination—Bush will raise standards and demand accountability; Gore will fight the HMOs. When policy proposals are made explicit—letting younger workers invest part of their Social Security, adding a prescription drug benefit to Medicare—little in the way of details is offered.

In short, for Bush's most mentioned issues—education and Social Security—he generally began by identifying a problem and followed with a proposed solution, though he was more specific with regard to Social Security. Gore's narrative for health care, his most mentioned issue, was similar. Bush's health-care talk and Gore's Social Security talk generally began with an attack on his opponent's plan followed by a vague alternative. Both candidates' attention to taxes followed a similar script. Education and Social Security attention by Bush, and health-care attention by Gore, can be characterized as more promotional. Social Security and taxes for both Bush and Gore proved more positional than education and health care, though, and thus tended to contain a little more specificity. These differences will be considered in later chapters to unravel the nuances of hearing and connecting candidate issue priorities.

News Coverage and Issue Agendas

Presidential campaign advertising faithfully represents the message the candidates hope to communicate broadly, as campaigns exert direct control over this form of communication. Candidates' agendas, however, are also filtered and transmitted by the news before they reach much of the mass public. And candidate ads are often concentrated most highly in swing states, so campaign coverage by the mass media is the primary form of campaign communications those in the nonswing states receive. Do citizens receive similar messages about the candidates' respective issue priorities from these sources? Figure 3.2 depicts how frequently the television reports linked each candidate to the four dominant issues during the primary and the general campaign.

Television coverage of the campaign mentioned each of these issues roughly equally in stories about Bush and stories about Gore. The most noticeable difference occurs for education, where a higher percent of campaign stories about Bush bring up the issue. Slightly more of the campaign stories focusing on Gore raise the issue of health care. This broadly mirrors the candidates' own emphases, but the similarities, particularly in the general election season, stand out more than the differences. Especially for the issues of Social Security and taxes, the *NBC Nightly News* campaign coverage mentions the issues in connection to each candidate in similar proportions. Overall, television coverage of Gore mentions health care in 23 percent of the stories, Social Security and taxes in 14 percent of the segments, and education 12 percent of the

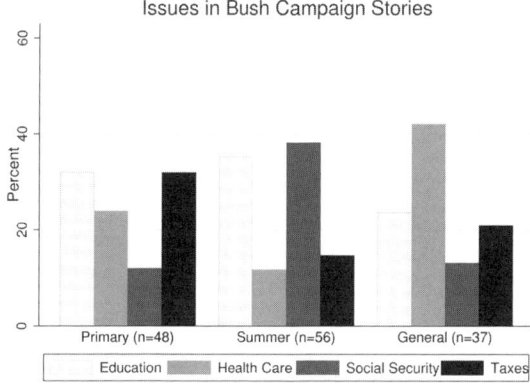

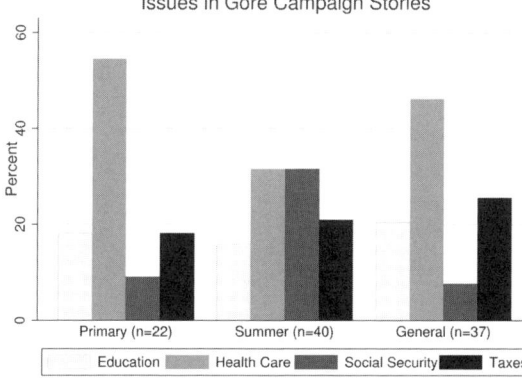

Figure 3.2 NBC Nightly News Campaign Coverage

time. Television coverage of Bush links him to education in 20 percent of the stories, Social Security in 18 percent of the stories, health care 17 percent of the time, and taxes in 15 percent of the news segments.

This similarity is not terribly surprising given the nature of campaign news coverage—the need to maintain some semblance of balance while highlighting the underlying competition of the campaign. But it does underscore a different way in which the needs of the newsroom may not serve the needs of the public. The emphasis on balance and on clarifying policy difference may obscure, to a degree, priority differences.

Conclusion

While brief, these data nonetheless provide a fairly concrete sketch of the campaigns' agendas and the coverage of those agendas in the mainstream press. Both candidates ran their campaigns on issues already of concern to the public at large. Bush tried to take the lead on education, an issue commonly perceived as belonging to Democrats. Gore took the lead on health care and Bush followed closely, though this issue, too, is generally part of the Democratic portfolio. Bush stayed ahead of Gore on Social Security reform. And while Gore started talking about taxes first in the general campaign, Bush matched his attention to the issue. The candidates spent much of the campaign reacting to one another's proposals with both criticism and counterproposals. Rather than trying to alter the issue agenda to include more "Republican-owned" issues, Bush chose to promote (and claim) issues that had previously benefited Democrats.

Candidates do not simply focus on their own agenda or on only the issues they believe will advantage them. Rather, the candidates engage one another in the development of the campaign agenda. This interaction constrains candidates. It forces them to attend to issues they might prefer to avoid and inhibits their ability to establish accountability standards based on personally beneficial but insignificant criteria. The competition prevents the candidates from focusing on peripheral issues, and thus helps ensure that whatever issues the campaign is ultimately about, they are not trivial.

Campaigns that ignore issues or talk only of the most trivial issues can hardly be expected to promote issue-based voting or expectations for problem solving for which a future president could be held accountable. It is a good thing, then, that most presidential campaigns do neither. Candidates talk about issues, though more often valence issues than issue positions, and they do so extensively and repeatedly. Given the campaign talk about issues, citizens can learn about candidate priorities based not just on what the candidates say but on how frequently they say it. The amount of valuable air time taken up by an issue is a signal about the candidates' priorities once in office.

The agenda priorities of Bush and Gore in 2000 provide a reasonable example of the issue talk to be found in contemporary presidential campaigns. And the dynamics of the issue talk in 2000 highlight some conclusions worth repeating. First, there is a clear correspondence between the messages of Bush and Gore in 2000. Presidential candidates do not autonomously choose the issues they address, and the candidate agendas are not independent of one another. What is most striking about the 2000 presidential campaign agendas is the degree to which the two dominant candidates followed one another's issue leads. In this case, the competition ensured the candidates focused on important issues that the public cared about. Competition may induce reassuring constraints on the candidates' attempts to shape what the election is about and to establish criteria of candidate evaluation and future accountability.

Second, the media coverage of the campaign pushes this convergence even further. Though the media portrayal of the campaign mirrors the candidates' issue priority messages—Bush mentions education in a higher proportion of his ads than does Gore and campaign stories are similarly more likely to link education to Bush, Gore mentions health care in a higher proportion of his ads than does Bush and campaign stories are similarly more likely to link health care to Gore—the pattern of media coverage serves to dampen these priority differences.

And finally, the candidates clearly conveyed a set of agenda priorities through the campaign talk; each emphasized only a handful of issues and had a single issue that dominated his agenda. Based on the candidates' campaign emphases, then, all four of these campaign issues have the potential to influence the public's expectations of the candidates. Gore's messages about health care and Bush's messages about education are sent at the greatest "volume," but Social Security and tax messages were repeated frequently enough to be influential as well. The issues were not all approached in the same way, though—Bush's attention to education and Social Security and Gore's attention to education and health care are most clearly framed as a problem the candidate wishes to solve, while Bush's attention to health care and taxes and Gore's attention to Social Security and taxes appear much more reactive. These different ways of talking about an issue may impact what citizens hear and what issues they connect to the candidates.

Of course, the presidential campaign is not a unitary entity. Campaign emphasis varies over time, as the seasons of the campaign ebb and flow. Some places receive advertising saturation while others are virtually ignored. Given the opportunity, do citizens accurately hear the agenda priorities of candidates? Several characteristics of modern campaigning we've seen here should aid citizen reception: the rise in volume of political information as the election approaches, the repetition of the candidates' key campaign themes, and an emphasis on issue priorities over issue positions. Characteristics of the public, too, encourage hearing the campaign: the growing attention to politics during the campaign, the public's greater concern with fixing problems versus pursuing particular policies, and the cognitive simplicity of candidate priorities compared to positions. It is to these questions and characteristics that we turn in the next chapter.

4 Hearing the Campaign

If a campaign talks about issues, and in doing so conveys the candidates' agenda priorities, do citizens hear these agenda priorities? This is the next necessary step for campaign-induced agenda accountability. If this key message of the presidential campaign is not accurately received by citizens, then citizens can hardly use these priorities as a standard of judgment for the new president.

Scholars of elections long doubted the effectiveness of campaigns in influencing the vote. The strong correlation between the vote and preexisting attitudes—partisan identification, incumbent approval and perceptions of the national economy, and so forth—at the individual level (Campbell et al. 1960; Fiorina 1981; Lazarsfeld, Berelson, and Gaudet 1944) coupled with the predictability of aggregate election outcomes based on presidential approval, economic conditions, and domestic and foreign tranquility (Gelman and King 1993; Lewis-Beck and Rice 1992) lent credence to the counterintuitive judgment that campaigns matter little to the outcome.

Candidates and political consultants stake their careers on the claim that what they do and say while running for office can influence the public. Certainly they spend considerable wealth in the doing of it. Scholarship, in a reversal, has begun to support this intuition, crediting campaigns with a number of short-term effects: increasing voter knowledge (Franz et al. 2007), reducing voter uncertainty (Alvarez 1997), and altering the weight voters give to issues in their electoral judgments (Johnston et al. 1992). This chapter adds to this list by empirically verifying that citizens learn agenda priorities. At the same time, it reinforces the empirical support for these other effects because hearing the campaign is a necessary, but largely ignored, condition for campaign influence.

The Message Citizens Hear

The presidential candidates disseminated a lot of messages in 2000 and these messages were highly concentrated on a handful of issues. Candidates repeat their dominant messages frequently, increasing the chances that voters have received them. Although candidates may try out new issues during the primary season, once the campaign has settled into the general election period candidate themes are more firmly established and campaigners heroically attempt to "stay on message." Consequently, the messages will be transmitted to the public over and over again, particularly via campaign advertisements.

Does this barrage of messages reach the voters? Hearing the campaign agenda is encouraged by the pervasiveness of the messages, by the repetition of the key themes, and by the candidates' emphases on priorities over positions—but these characteristics do not guarantee hearing. Most of the prior evidence at our disposal examines whether citizens learn candidate issue *positions* during the campaign. And on this score, the evidence is reasonably optimistic. For instance, the more attention folks pay to television news during the campaign, the greater their knowledge of the candidates' issues stances (Zhao and Chaffee 1995), and as the amount of policy information in the news coverage of presidential candidates has declined, more policy information in candidate advertising appears to have compensated so that citizens continue to learn about candidate positions via the campaign (Gilens, Vavreck, and Cohen 2007). Recently the content of candidate advertising, in particular, has been tied to greater knowledge about candidates: As exposure to more candidate advertising increases, so do the number of things citizens like and dislike about the candidates (Franz et al. 2007).[1] Knowing issue positions and possessing more thoughts about the candidates, though, are not quite the same thing as recognizing their issue priorities.[2]

Only a handful of studies have paid specific attention to candidate policy priorities rather than policy positions; these have focused on Senate campaigns and have come to contradictory conclusions.[3] Using the 1988 Senate Election Study, Dalager (1996) initially concluded that the campaign—measured by campaign spending—did not increase the odds that citizens could correctly identify the issues most talked about in the campaign as measured by the reports in political journals. In fact, he found a negative relationship. Kahn and Kenney (2001), studying the

1988 and 1992 Senate campaigns, measured the campaign emphasis of each campaign based on interviews with campaign managers and news coverage. They find that a greater emphasis on the economy, health care, the environment, or education in a Senate campaign did increase the likelihood that the audience for that campaign mentioned these issues.

Consequently, it remains an empirical question whether people accurately receive the policy priority messages of presidential candidates, and under what conditions. Certainly presidential campaigns seem likely, relative to lower-volume congressional campaigns, to be getting through to the public. And citizens in a presidential campaign context seem ready to receive these messages. As information becomes more available during the campaign, public attentiveness also increases. While much of the public pays comparatively little attention to politics between elections, presidential campaigns produce heightened awareness of and attention to politics, particularly in the few months preceding the election. Politics is "in the air" and citizens are encouraged to become more engaged in the political realm, if only momentarily.

Figure 4.1 presents three measures of citizen attention to politics from an original survey conducted during the 2000 presidential campaign.[4] Respondents were asked how closely they followed news about national politics and national affairs (news attention), how interested they are in national politics and national affairs (political interest), and how often they talk with others about politics and public affairs (political talk).[5] The trends are unmistakable. Political engagement increases during the primary period, falls off during the summer, begins a clear upward trend in the period just preceding the parties' national conventions, and peaks around Election Day.

Attention is a scarce resource, and citizens are unlikely to see a real gain from political attentiveness most of the time. Presidential elections, however, provide a motivation for attention as voters are being asked to make a politically meaningful and binding decision about who will lead the nation. Thus, the expected benefit of attention increases during campaigns while the expected cost of attention decreases due to the greater volume of political messages (Lupia and McCubbins 1998). Greater learning of agendas should take place when people are more actively paying attention to national affairs than when they passively absorb issue information via the nightly news. It follows that agenda learning is fostered during campaigns.

The candidates' tendency to emphasize issue priorities in their campaign rhetoric further increases the odds that citizens will accurately receive campaign messages. As work on issue ownership suggests, citizens

Hearing the Campaign 59

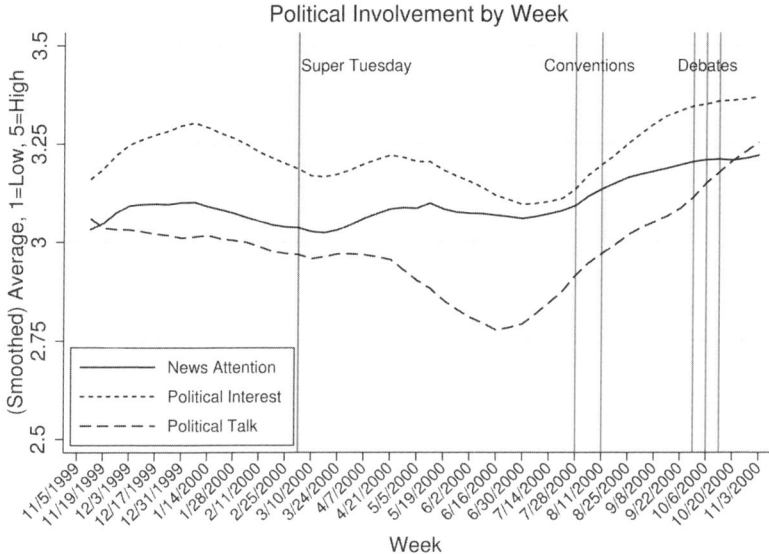

Figure 4.1 *Involvement with the Campaign*

frequently care more that a problem is solved than with how (Petrocik 1996), so these priority messages resonate with citizen concerns. Indeed, candidates often emphasize consensual valence issues precisely because these are frequently the issues most citizens care about. In poll after poll gauging "the most important problems," issues like the economy, health care, and education come out on top.[6] Problems are often consensual, though solutions are not; and problems are what citizens want addressed.

Candidate priorities have the additional benefit for citizens of being easier to understand than more complex policy proposals, which can involve technical details that make the lids of even the most wonkish eyes grow heavy. An individual need not understand a candidate's detailed proposal for a health insurance exchange, only that the candidate believes the current state of health care represents a problem that requires fixing with the help of government. Further, candidates are less ambiguous in the presentation of their issue priorities, and issue priorities are more easily communicated in the relatively superficial communication forms that dominate the campaign.

Greater public attention to politics during the campaign, combined with the repetition of a message that both resonates with citizens and is relatively easy for them to understand, increases the likelihood that citizens accurately hear the candidate talk about issues. Many candidate issue positions are vague and hard to come by in any given campaign, and therefore hard for citizens to learn, but issue priorities are prominently highlighted and ridiculously straightforward. Scholars have criticized the widespread reliance on valence issues in campaigns—they don't fit easily into the spatial models that dominate so much of the work on campaigns and elections, and don't present an easy contrast for voters. But they do supply an underappreciated contrast, a contrast of priorities and competing visions of what needs to be fixed most urgently to make the country better.

Distortions in Hearing

Some citizens are bombarded with campaign ads, a torrent of short campaign messages; others hear very little from the candidates themselves. Citizens who inhabit environments saturated by campaign communications should necessarily be more likely to receive the issue priority messages sent by the candidates. Nevertheless, what citizens "hear" a candidate talking about may also be a function of cognitive shortcuts like projection or a heuristic inference, or of cognitive biases like selective exposure.

Projection is a reasonable response to an ambiguous information environment. Projection leads citizens who are concerned about an issue to believe that a candidate they support is also concerned about an issue. This process could also work negatively—citizens who are concerned about an issue believe that a candidate they don't support is not concerned about the issue. Under projection processes, for instance, we would expect Democrats who prioritize an issue highly to report hearing Gore talk about it in 2000, *regardless of Gore's actual emphasis*. Such self-based inference, though, may not be that common. Krosnick (1990) fails to find notable projection on candidate issue positions when projection effects are appropriately distinguished from persuasion and changes in sentiment toward the candidate. Conover and Feldman (1989) find modest projection effects with regard to perceived issue positions in a panel study during the 1976 presidential election, but these effects decline as the campaign wears on and pale in comparison to the impact of other inferential processes. Projection of candidate issue positions, they conclude, is most likely when information on candidate issue positions is most scarce, but essentially disappears given some information. As candidate priorities are more readily available than many candidate positions, projection should be less common for these considerations.

Conover and Feldman (1989), instead, emphasize inferences on the basis of candidate categorization. Citizens use cues provided by a candidate's party, geographic origin, and demographics to produce perceptions of candidate positions (see also Popkin 1991). Given such a "heuristic hearing" process, we would expect individuals to hear Gore talking more about education or Bush talking more about taxes, *independent of the actual candidate emphasis or citizen concerns*, simply because the public is more accustomed to Democrats talking about education and Republicans talking about taxes. These party-based inferences often serve people well, but if they persist in the face of a campaign that does not conform to the expectations, they operate as a roadblock to real accountability. The need to make inferences on the basis of heuristic information, like projection, is greater when the information that is being inferred is ambiguous or difficult to obtain. Given the much stronger party inferences found in past research, we should expect some heuristic hearing as well, but not to the degree found for perceptions of issue positions. Heuristic inferences are still possible with regard to "hearing" what a candidate is talking about, but they should play a lesser role than they do in "knowing" a candidate's position.

Additionally, citizens may hear only part of the campaign as a result of selective exposure—the tendency to see and hear media communications congruent with one's predispositions, or to avoid communications that run counter to those predispositions (Klapper 1960). Such a process would predict that citizens would be more likely to hear the more agreeable campaign agenda of their own party candidate. Thus, Democrats would be more likely to hear Gore, particularly on "Democratic" issues like education and health care, while Republicans would be more likely to hear Bush, especially on issues traditionally favored by Republicans, like tax cuts. Note under such a process that hearing the candidate on an issue is conditioned on the frequency with which a candidate talks about the issue, unlike the prior processes in which perceptions are divorced from actual candidate talk. Still, experimental research into selective exposure has been, at best, mixed (Frey 1986), and survey work connected to actual media content has failed to find support for the theory (Milburn 1979; Mutz and Martin 2001). Despite the proliferation of news channels and other avenues of communication that could promote selective partisan attention, in the context of a presidential advertising campaign, designed to reach as many viewers as possible, selective exposure on the part of citizens is still relatively difficult to implement effectively.

Hearing the Campaign in 2000

In survey data collected throughout the 2000 campaign, from November 12, 1999, through Election Day, respondents were asked about their attentiveness to the campaign (described near the beginning of this chapter), as well as about their perception of whether the candidates were talking about four of the key 2000 campaign issues—improving education, reducing federal taxes, saving Social Security, and reforming health care.[7] Specifically, individuals were asked:

> The presidential candidates have been talking about a variety of issues during this campaign. Thinking about [George W. Bush], how much did you hear him talking about [improving education] during the campaign? A great deal, quite a bit, some, very little, or not at all.

How do perceptions of candidate attention compare across candidates? Across time? We begin with an examination of these trends.

HEARING OVER TIME

The daily structure of the survey data allows us to capture changes in perceptions of hearing over time. Figure 4.2 illustrates the trends in hearing for the sample as a whole. The "hearing" measures were aggregated by week, and, since each week only consists of a sample of about thirty, the weekly means are smoothed via lowess regression. This provides an initial look at how hearing changed over the course of the campaign and whether those themes emphasized by the candidates appear more likely to have been heard.

A general over-time pattern is common to each of the issues: Citizens are more likely to report hearing candidates talk about each issue during the height of the primary season; hearing falls off during the summer "silly" season and peaks as Election Day approaches. In that sense, "hearing" reflects the progression of the campaign.

Comparing across candidates, the first panel of figure 4.2 depicts changes in perceptions that each candidate was talking about education. At the onset of the campaign, individuals were more likely to perceive Gore (the solid line) to be talking about education, but as the campaign progressed, Bush (the dashed line) and Gore were perceived to be highlighting the issue roughly equally. Party reputations and expectations are clearly playing a role in the beginning of the 2000 campaign; as the volume of the campaign increased, however, citizen hearing begins to catch up with the actual emphasis of the respective candidates.

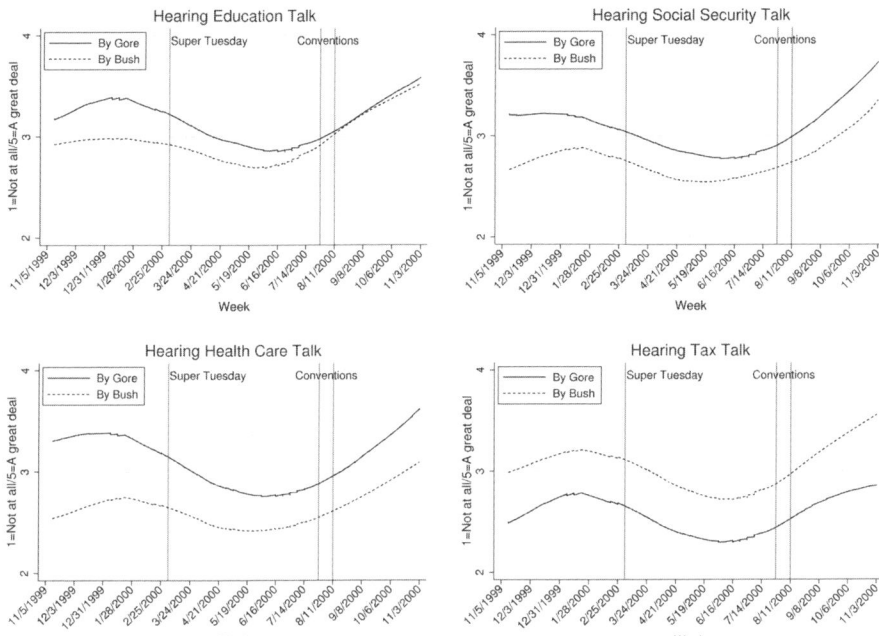

Figure 4.2 Hearing Candidate Issue Talk

Moving to the next panel of figure 4.2, for Social Security individuals were more likely to perceive Gore to be emphasizing the issue throughout the campaign despite Bush's heavy attention to this issue. And unlike the case of education, "hearing" Bush never quite catches up to "hearing" Gore, though the gap narrows some from the very beginning of the election cycle.

Looking at the last two panels, for health care and taxes, throughout the campaign, citizens perceived Gore to be talking more about health care than Bush, and perceived Bush to be talking more about taxes than Gore. The initial difference between the candidates is bigger for these issues than for education or Social Security and remains so.

At first blush, hearing candidate talk looks to be influenced by the volume of the campaign, by what the candidates are actually emphasizing, and by prior party expectations. Given roughly equal attention to the issue—as was the case for taxes and health care, party reputations exert some continuing influence. Only when Bush's attention to the issue far surpassed Gore's—as was the case for education—do we see the party-reputation-driven gap close. Talking more about the issue than your opponent hardly seems to guarantee the gap will close, however, as Bush also surpassed Gore in attention to Social Security. While the difference between Bush and Gore in perceptions of candidate talk grew smaller for Social Security, presumably in response to Bush's heavy emphasis, candidate trespassing into the opposition's issue space clearly was an uphill battle. Of course, heavy attention to an issue in the advertising campaign does not reach all, or even most, citizens so perhaps we should not expect the gap to narrow universally. Next we'll move to an exploration of the impact of the volume of advertising attention, along with these other influences.[8]

EXPLAINING HEARING

To get a better handle on what influences hearing, and in particular the degree to which hearing responds to candidate issue talk, I model the probability that an individual heard Gore or Bush talking about an issue as a function of the actual emphasis each candidate placed on that issue in the advertising aired within a respondents' media environment and up to the date the respondent was surveyed. Using the daily advertising data from chapter 3, I can construct a measure of the presidential campaign advertising environment for each day in each media market.[9] The measure counts the number of times a candidate aired an ad in a respondent's media market that mentioned one of the central issues, but only up to the date of the respondent's interview. Thus, two respondents from the same city will have different measures of candidate issue emphasis if one is interviewed early in the campaign and one is interviewed late in the campaign, with much candidate advertising occurring in between.[10]

The models of citizen perception also control for a citizen's own prioritization of the issue, party identification, political awareness, the proximity of the election, age, education, race, and gender. To allow for projection effects, I include interactions between issue prioritization and partisanship. This addresses the question: Do citizens who care about an issue project those concerns onto their party's candidate? To allow selective exposure effects, I include interactions between party and candidate emphasis. This helps answer the question: Do partisans hear their own candidates' priority messages more clearly? Finally, if individuals are primarily making party-based inferences, this will impact baseline hearing—that is, Gore will always be perceived to be talking more about Democratically owned issues (education, health care) and Bush will always be perceived to be talking more about Republican-owned issues (taxes), regardless of each candidate's real agenda emphasis.

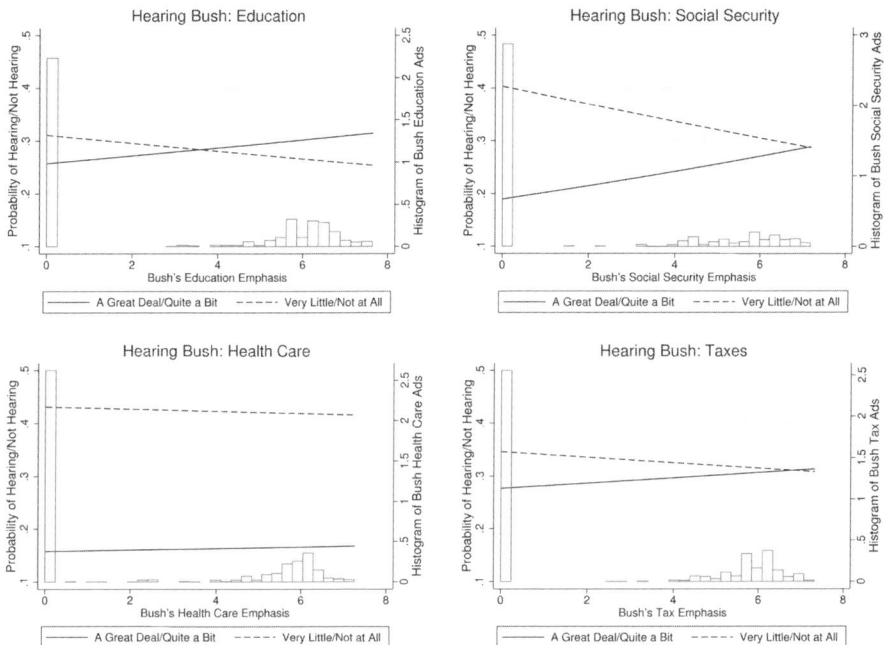

Figure 4.3 Impact of Campaign Advertising Emphasis on Hearing Bush

The influence of Bush's actual issue emphasis on whether citizens believe they've heard him emphasizing an issue is relayed in figure 4.3, and the influence of Gore's actual issue emphasis on whether citizens perceive him to be talking about an issue is shown in figure 4.4. Each issue is relayed in a separate panel; each panel in these graphs illustrates how likely a respondent was to say that Bush or Gore was talking about an issue a great deal or quite a bit (the solid line) or was talking about the issue very little or not at all (the dashed line) as actual candidate attention to the issue in the advertising available to respondents increases. In addition, to provide a sense of range, each panel includes a histogram of the relevant (logged) number of ads Gore or Bush had aired in the relevant respondent's market.[11] The full results are presented in appendix B.

In almost every case depicted in figures 4.3 and 4.4, the probability that citizens believe a candidate has emphasized an issue increases the more attention the candidate has paid to the issue in the citizens' media markets—the solid line rises. The probability of saying the candidate has talked very little about an issue or not at all declines the more candidate advertising has focused on the issue in the citizen's environment—the

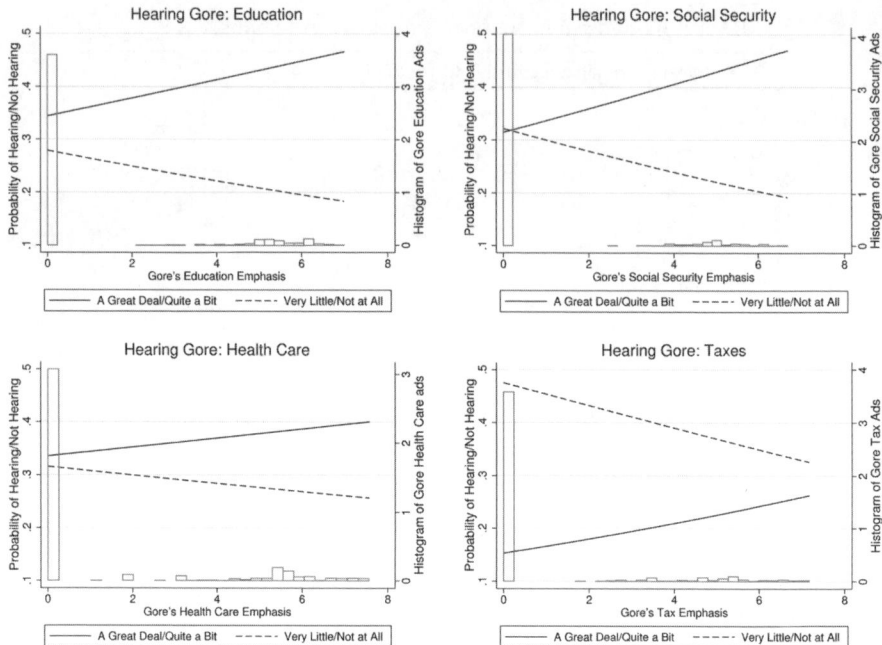

Figure 4.4 Impact of Campaign Advertising Emphasis on Hearing Gore

dashed line falls. And throughout, Gore's advertising emphasis has a bigger impact on accurate perceptions of candidate talk, based on the difference in the likelihood of hearing the issue when a citizen's environment has received no advertising by the candidate mentioning the issue and when a citizen's environment has received the highest degree of advertising on the issue.

Take the first panel in figure 4.3; this displays the impact of Bush's attention to education and the probability of hearing Bush emphasize education. In places where there have been no televised ads by Bush mentioning education, individuals have a 24 percent chance of saying Bush has been talking about education a great deal or quite a bit. Others, similar in party, issue ranking, attention to politics, age, education, gender, and ethnicity but who live in markets where there have been the most ads by Bush that mention education have a 31 percent chance of saying Bush has been talking a lot about education. This is a statistically significant increase in the odds of hearing Bush talk about education.

The first panel in figure 4.4 shows the analogous effect for Gore. Though Bush actually emphasized education more heavily than Gore, individuals, on average, perceived Gore to be talking more about the issue. Gore's attention to education increases perceptions that he's talking about education: A respondent from a place and time where Gore has run no ads on education has a 34 percent chance of saying Gore's been talking about education a lot, while a similar respondent from a place and time that has seen the maximum number of Gore ads mentioning education has a 47 percent chance of saying Gore has been talking about the issue a great deal or quite a lot. Again, this is a statistically significant increase.

The biggest impact of actual candidate talk on perceptions of candidate talk occurs for Social Security (the second panel of figures 4.3 and 4.4). Starting with Bush, given a media market where Bush has yet to air any ads mentioning Social Security, respondents have a 19 percent chance of perceiving Bush to be talking about Social Security. People living in areas that have seen the most advertising attention to the issue by Bush are more likely, with a 29 percent chance, to perceive Bush to have emphasized the issue. Moving to Gore, his attention to the issue similarly impacts perceptions of his emphasis—from a 31 percent chance of perceiving Gore to be talking about Social Security in contexts with little to no Gore ads that mention the issue to a 47 percent chance of perceiving Gore to be talking about Social Security in contexts with lots of Gore ads that mention the issue. Again, the effects of candidate talk on perceptions of candidate emphasis are significant for both Bush and Gore. For Bush, though, public perceptions of him talking about Social Security are never as high as public perceptions of Gore's emphasis on the issue.

Neither candidate's attention to health care affects public perceptions that the candidate is talking about the issue significantly. For Bush, the third panel of figure 4.3, the probability of perceiving Bush to be talking about health care barely moves at all as his campaign airs more ads mentioning the issue. But Bush's attention to health care was generally related to Medicare and mentioned in conjunction with Social Security. Attention to Medicare may simply not represent attention to health care for most citizens, those under age sixty-five. Greater emphasis does increase the probability of perceiving Gore to be talking about health care, the third panel of figure 4.4, but the increase is small—from a 33 percent chance in times and places with no advertising on health care to a 39 percent chance when and where Gore's ads have paid considerable attention to health care—and statistically insignificant.

Finally, for taxes, shown in the last row of figures 4.3 and 4.4, greater candidate attention increases perceptions that each candidate is talking about taxes, but the difference is only statistically significant for Gore. While the probability of hearing Gore talk about taxes increases when Gore airs more ads mentioning taxes (from a low of 15 percent to a high of 26 percent), even in places that have seen a heavier dose of Gore's tax ads, the probability of *not* hearing Gore talk about taxes is higher than the probability of hearing such talk.

Overall the impact of candidate advertising attention has a positive effect on citizen perceptions of candidate emphasis in seven of the eight cases analyzed here; the effect is statistically significant in five cases. These five—Gore and education, Bush and education, Gore and Social Security, Bush and Social Security, Gore and taxes—vary in terms of the dominant advertising tone, though they do tend toward the positive. Gore's education emphasis was overwhelmingly positive, with 90 percent of his aired ads mentioning education deemed promotional. Gore's aired ads referencing Social Security, on the other hand, were coded as promotional only 16 percent of the time. Across a range of tone, then, greater emphasis on an issue in the advertising campaign increases the public's perceptions that the candidate is focusing on the issue.

Candidate talk, though, is not the only thing that influences these perceptions. In the absence of candidate advertising attention, respondents were more likely to hear Gore talking about education, Social Security, and health care, and more likely to hear Bush talking about taxes. These results are consistent with a process of partisan heuristic "hearing."

Importantly, as Bush's attention to education and Social Security increases, the perceptions of Bush talking about these issues increases to become about equal to the default hearing for Gore. This, on its own, is pretty remarkable given how Bush deviated from the partisan script in 2000. One of Bush's campaign advisors notes the deviation: "George W. Bush is a different kind of Republican. This is not the kind of Republican that you're used to. He's reaching across old boundaries and borders, talking about issues you're not used to hearing Republicans talk about" (Mark McKinnon, quoted in Jamieson and Waldman 2001, 7). In places where Gore's campaign has mentioned taxes most frequently, perceptions of his attention to taxes catches up to the default perceptions for Bush. Unquestionably, party does matter in citizen perceptions of candidate emphasis—it would be surprising if it did not—but so, too, does candidate talk.

There is also some evidence of citizens projecting their own issue concerns onto their party's candidate. Though not conveyed in the figures, Democrats who place a high priority on health-care reform are more likely to perceive Gore to be talking about health care, independent of his advertising agenda. Similarly, Democrats who prioritize Social Security and taxes highly are more likely to perceive Gore to be emphasizing the issue. Republicans who prioritize taxes are more likely to perceive Bush to be talking about tax cuts. There are four cases of possible projection,[12] and it is more common in perceptions of Gore's agenda priorities. Two of the cases of potential projection—Gore and health care, Bush and taxes—occur for perceptions of candidate priorities that were not impacted significantly by candidate talk. When candidate talk does matter, projection appears to be less likely.

In no case was the influence of candidate talk conditioned by individual partisanship. The more each candidate emphasized education, Social Security, and for Gore, taxes, in a respondent's environment, the more likely respondents were to indicate hearing the candidates talking about these issues. In this sense, then, the candidate's messages, as conveyed in advertising, are getting through. And the effects are relatively general. Selective exposure—where Democrats are primarily picking up the messages of Democratic candidates and Republicans are more tuned in to the message of Republican candidates—is not a process in evidence here.

Individual-level characteristics also play a role. Partisan identification and the level of attention to politics are consistently related to "hearing" issue talk. Partisans were more likely to report hearing their own candidate emphasize every issue. Democrats are more likely than Republicans to perceive Gore talking about education, health care, Social Security, and even taxes; Republicans are more likely than Democrats to perceive Bush talking about taxes, Social Security, education, and health care—regardless of actual candidate talk. Partisans perceive their own party's candidate to be paying greater attention to every issue, whether the candidate actually does so or not. This is consistent with a general favorability effect. In addition, while controlling for the amount of candidate talk, the more politically aware are more likely to perceive both candidates talking about each issue. This general increase in hearing among the more politically aware and involved might well be in response to issue talk in other message media (newspapers, broadcast news) that vary less across media market.

We might expect, as a result of other message venues and the rise in campaign-related information available as Election Day nears, that citizens would report hearing candidates talk about the issues more when interviewed later in the cycle. Hearing could be a function of time. In fact, controlling for actual candidate emphasis, the proximity to the election does not alter the likelihood of hearing the candidates talk about the issues, with the sole exception of Gore and health care. Health care, recall, did crop up a bit more than the other issues in the newspaper and television campaign stories.

Conclusion

In the 2000 campaign, the advertising emphasis of both Bush and Gore influenced what citizens believed they heard the candidates talking about—with Gore's emphasis influencing perceptions of his talk on education, Social Security, and taxes, and Bush's emphasis influencing perceptions of his talk on education and Social Security. This is a reassuring result; citizens are often perceived to be quite ignorant of issue talk in campaigns, but individuals do, at least some of the time, accurately perceive what the candidates are talking about. Much work on candidate perceptions focuses on the cognitive biases citizens use that are likely to induce a distorted understanding of candidates—selective attention, projection, or informational shortcuts. Surely citizens employ these cognitive mechanisms—otherwise, the campaign environment should be one of the only things that matter—but so, too, do they respond to the actual information made most available by the campaign.

As for the cognitive biases, citizens are using candidate party as a basis for inference about candidate talk. Particularly when there is no advertising emphasis to counter them, citizen perceptions of who's talking more about the issues are entirely consistent with patterns of issue ownership. Projection, too, appears to influence perceptions of candidate issue emphasis, though not as often as candidate issue talk. In this analysis, projection was more common for Gore and less likely for issue emphasis perceptions that were influenced by candidate talk. There is no evidence, on the other hand, to suggest respondent perceptions were being distorted by selective exposure.

While it is comforting, for purposes of later accountability, that citizens' perceptions of candidate issue emphasis depend on actual candidate issue emphasis, candidate talk does not matter for every case examined here. Health care, in particular, stands out as an exception in search of an explanation. Recall that Bush's health-care talk centered on adding a prescription drug benefit to Medicare while Gore's emphasis was primarily on a Patient's Bill of Rights and only secondarily on a drug benefit for Medicare recipients. This divergence may muddle the health-care discussion. Alternatively, the focus on Medicare may simply not speak to broader citizen understanding of health-care reform.

For the most part, the candidate agenda priorities, as conveyed by candidate advertising attention, are getting through to the public. The repeated and accumulated messages of the campaign advertising serve to ensure that a wider audience hears the candidates' agenda priorities. This is a key step in establishing accountability standards. Does candidate talk, in turn, aid citizens in connecting their own concerns about the issues to their evaluations of the candidates? Does this repetition of priorities begin to build policy momentum for the winner? These are the questions to which the next chapters turn.

5 Candidate Messages and Citizen Expectations

Presidential candidates offer clear and competing agendas in the campaign. Citizens, for the most part, pick up these agendas. If citizens select a candidate in part on the basis of that agenda, this is a version of issue voting, one based on priorities, not positions. Thus, the public need only vote for the candidate whose priorities best align with their own for the campaign to produce informed choice. One way this might occur is through priming, where a citizen who considers a problem—for example, climate change—a high government priority comes to weight that priority more heavily in evaluating the respective candidates. A candidate who shares her sense of urgency about the issue becomes increasingly likely to be viewed favorably by our environmentally concerned citizen.

Priming, as a campaign effect, has received considerable attention. In fact, the idea of priming, or something very similar, dates back to classic voting studies from the 1940s. These early studies describe the campaign as "activating" particular issues, making them more salient in voter decision-making: "It is difficult to change people's preferences; it is easier to affect the priorities and weights they give to subpreferences bearing on the central decision" (Berelson, Lazarsfeld, and McPhee 1954, 206). Despite this early recognition of priming, the idea languished in scholarly work on campaigns, though it flourished in studies of media effects. By now, it is commonly accepted that when the news emphasizes a consideration—unemployment, scandal, military action—that consideration becomes a more important predictor of presidential approval (Iyengar and Kinder 1987; Krosnick and Kinder 1990).

Campaigns, too, can prime. But to understand how campaigns can create and reinforce enduring connections between candidates and issues, we must start by reconsidering the psychological underpinnings of priming. My argument relies on recognizing the critical distinction between two mechanisms of priming—that induced through recency and that induced through frequency—and noting that the effects of exposure to the campaign fit better with a frequency mechanism than a recency mechanism. Indeed, this distinction between recency- and frequency-induced priming is especially important because the *political* implications of the two are qualitatively different: Frequency priming helps build accountability whereas recency priming inhibits it.

Priming Reconsidered

Presidential candidates emphasize an agenda in hopes of encouraging citizens to make their vote choices on the basis of those issues and ideas that favor the candidate (Jacobs and Shapiro 1994; Johnston et al. 1992; Petrocik 1996). At least, that's the consensus in most of the campaign effects research (Iyengar and Simon 2000; Kinder 1998). Iyengar and Kinder define this "priming effect" as "influence[ing] the standards by which governments, presidents, policies, and candidates for public office are judged" (1987, 63). Rather than evaluate political objects exhaustively, individuals rely on the information that is most accessible. Information is more accessible if individuals have been recently exposed to it, or if individuals have been frequently exposed to it and the information has become connected in memory to the political object being evaluated. Much of the work on priming emphasizes the recency argument; I focus on the role of frequent exposure. This difference in focus, from recency to frequency, follows from concern with the impact of campaign effects after the campaign, with agenda accountability.

When political scientists talk about priming, or altering the dimensions of leader evaluation (Iyengar and Kinder 1987), they characterize the weight given to particular considerations in judgment as a function of accessibility, that is, how easily the consideration is retrieved from memory (Miller and Krosnick 2000). Accessibility of a consideration is increased through recent exposure (Iyengar et al. 1984; Mendelsohn 1996) or frequent exposure (Krosnick and Brannon 1993; Krosnick and Kinder 1990) to a message, or both (Iyengar and Kinder 1987; Price and Tewksbury 1997). Work on political priming seldom distinguishes between these processes, yet these are different mechanisms produced by different environments and for which psychologists posit different outcomes.

The social psychology literature concurs that priming is a function of accessibility. Yet social psychologists distinguish further between two types of accessibility—temporary and chronic—and add another inducer of priming to this list: applicability (Bargh et al. 1986; Higgins and Brendl 1995; Higgins 1996). These sources of priming have different antecedents—recency, frequency, and strength of associations, respectively. Acknowledging these different mechanisms of priming is key to reconciling contradictory conclusions about the duration, short or long, of priming effects (Althaus and Kim 2006) and about who is most susceptible, the well or poorly informed, to priming effects.[1] This distinction, too, is central to drawing the appropriate political implications of campaign priming.

Recent exposure to an issue increases temporary accessibility by momentarily bringing the issue into working memory. When asked to evaluate a president, considerations already in working memory are more likely to be used. In the context of campaigns, recency priming suggests that a consideration is used in evaluation because a candidate like Barack Obama, when brought to the top of the voter's head, meets up with other considerations already sitting there due to recent exposure. Having just seen a television news story about the rising cost of health care, a citizen uses health care as a more important basis for judgment when constructing an evaluation of Obama.

Frequent exposure makes an issue more chronically accessible or more generally available in working memory. Such chronically accessible issues are more likely to be used in evaluation regardless of the recency of a stimulus. In a campaign, repetition of an issue makes the issue chronically accessible, so even if the consideration has not been encountered recently, it is more likely to be found at the top of the head at the moment of evaluation. Considerations like the economy, by virtue of their prominence in political discourse, are chronically accessible for political evaluation.

Stronger associations between an issue and a target of evaluation increase the perceived applicability of the issue to the evaluation. An issue that is strongly connected to a politician in the mind of a citizen is more likely to be used in evaluation because when the politician is pulled into working memory, so too are the issues connected to him (Anderson 1983). Peace and prosperity, for instance, are thought to be strongly attached to a president's evaluations automatically. But how do associations become stronger? Usually through repetition.

Conceptualizing an individual's knowledge as an associative network comprised of linked nodes (Anderson 1983; Hastie 1986; McGraw and Steenbergen 1995) helps to clarify associational strength. In evaluating persons, people prefer to organize information around a "person node," even for unfamiliar types of individuals (Sedikides and Ostrom 1988). McGraw, Pinney, and Neumann (1991) offer evidence of such informational organization for political candidates. So a candidate node—for example, Bush—is linked to multiple subordinate ideas, or nodes representing information about Bush—for example, that he was the governor of Texas or that he favors accountability in education. The links vary in strength, and stronger links, formed by more frequently activating the two ideas *simultaneously*, imply that when one of the nodes (such as Bush) is activated, activation spreads to the strongly linked nodes (such as education) as well.

All presidents begin as candidates, and there is little reason to believe that individuals process and store information differently for candidates and for presidents. The "Bush node" developed while Bush was a candidate will not be replaced by an entirely new "Bush node" as president. Instead, the same information will be linked to candidate Bush and to president Bush in a similar structure. New information will be added, of course, and old information will decay if it is never reinforced. But the associations between the issue agenda of a candidate and the candidate will be some of the strongest during the campaign, and persistence of candidate–issue connections implies they will remain some of the strongest links after the election is over.

Because campaign communications necessarily invoke a consideration, often an issue consideration, and a candidate at the same time, repetition strengthens the association between the candidate and the consideration, and the consideration seems more applicable. Greater applicability suggests that a consideration is used in evaluation because when a candidate like George W. Bush is brought to the top of the head, it brings along with it those considerations to which it is strongly attached. Although such connections already exist for individuals prior to the campaign—issue ownership (Petrocik 1996) is another way of thinking about these preexisting associations—candidates work to reinforce or challenge these associations through their repeated emphasis in their campaigns. Frequent attention to an issue, then, both promotes chronic accessibility as well as stronger associations due to greater perceived applicability of the issue for candidate evaluation.

While priming is understood to be of consequence because it can change political judgments, it may do even more.[2] Priming can shape expectations of a leader by strengthening the association between a consideration and the evaluative target in long-term memory. Why, then, does so much work on priming ignore this possibility? Primarily because priming was introduced to public opinion scholars as a mass media effect.

Media Priming, Campaign Priming

That news media shape public opinion through priming is one of the most widely accepted results in political behavior. The most persuasive evidence of media priming comes from experimental research. Experimental studies, by definition, are primarily capturing recency effects because evaluations are normally requested soon after exposure to a treatment; the recency mechanism, as a result, has received greater empirical support. The pioneering work on media priming by Iyengar and Kinder (1987) is one of the few studies to incorporate an explicit comparison between repeated and one-shot message exposure. They find more powerful priming effects in their five-day sequential experiments than in their one-day studies, hinting at the potential differences between recency and frequency mechanisms.[3] Iyengar and Kinder further demonstrate experimentally that stories directly connecting a problem to the president produce even more powerful priming effects, supporting the role of applicability. These nuances, though, have been lost in much of the research that followed.

The psychological theory of priming entered the political science lexicon through studies of the news media and brought with it a particular perspective: that priming is a worrisome power of the press, that citizens are "victims of priming" (Iyengar and Kinder 1987, 90). Even media priming studies that are logically concerned with the impact of frequency—for instance, studies focusing on major political events as they occurred at the time, such as the Iran–Contra scandal (Krosnick and Kinder 1990) or the Gulf War (Krosnick and Brannon 1993; Pan and Kosicki 1997)—still presume this frequent coverage serves to activate primed considerations temporarily, making citizens "victims of the architecture of their minds" (Miller and Krosnick 1996).

That media priming research has emphasized the consequences, and usually the mechanism, of recency priming makes sense. This fits well with the structure of the news media, which itself emphasizes the rapid refocusing of attention to a news stream. News coverage of issues tends to be relatively transitory as the press responds to an ever-changing set of events. Combined with a preference for stories that are timely and novel (Shoemaker and Reese 1996), these incentives reduce the likelihood of sustained coverage of an issue outside of unusual crises and scandals. Further, in news coverage of issues, stories do not consistently tie issues directly to political leaders in ways that strengthen the applicability of the message to leader evaluation (Iyengar 1991). Even in the context of campaigns, in which news media cover the same candidates over extended periods of time, journalistic standards are ill suited to providing the stimulus for longer-term associations between issues and candidates in the minds of citizens, that is, repeated coverage of candidate issues and themes (Patterson 1993).

Campaign scholars have recently rediscovered priming as a potentially powerful campaign effect (Carsey 2000; Druckman 2004; Johnston et al. 1992; Just et al. 1996). The puzzle of Gore's loss in 2000, in the face of his more popular positions, is usually answered by his failure to make the economy salient for voters.[4] To date, most studies of campaign priming do not directly link the campaign *content* with public opinion, instead looking for outcomes like differences in the size of issue or trait coefficients as time passes within a given campaign (see, for example, Mendelsohn 1996) or across different campaigns that did or did not emphasize particular issues (such as Carsey 2000; Druckman 2004).[5] The latter are more persuasive, as they involve some measure of the campaign content, but these measures do not distinguish between levels of campaign emphasis. Nor do they distinguish between candidate emphasis and the emphasis in media coverage of the campaign.

Studies of campaign priming generally reference media priming, assuming the process is similar in the campaign context, while ignoring the distinction between mechanisms of priming—recent exposure, frequent exposure, and associational strength. One-shot election surveys that investigate whether themes prominent in the campaign are granted more weight in vote choice seem to assume priming is induced through frequent exposure to a message (Carsey 2000; Druckman 2004). Research into campaign effects that directly incorporate campaign dynamics, on the other hand, often rely on truncated measures of campaign communications—for example, a seven-day moving average—that necessarily assume priming effects are transitory (see, for example, Johnston et al. 1992; Johnston, Hagen, and Jamieson 2004). Thus, the incorporation of priming research into campaigns hasn't allowed for priming to be a useful or enduring effect.

The conclusions drawn from these studies—that priming does occur—ultimately theorize priming as a transitory effect. For instance, Aldrich, Sullivan, and Borgida conclude that "campaigns may *temporarily* activate foreign policy attitudes, although they may not change many minds" (1989, 135, italics mine), while Carsey posits that "candidates can create a *short-term* influence on voting behavior if they can alter the salience of particular dimensions at the time of the election by shifting voters' attention to different issues" (2000, 15, italics mine).

The general media context and the campaign context are sufficiently different to expect the mechanisms influencing priming to differ across these domains. Campaigns, and modern presidential campaigns in particular, are structured to promote repetition. Campaign texts preach to candidates to choose themes likely to advantage them and to repeat these themes endlessly, a sermon candidates enact pretty well. And, as chapter 3 details, what the candidates tend to repeat are issue priorities rather than issue positions. Consequently, the candidate messages about goals and priorities will be transmitted to the public over and over again, via campaign ads, reports of speeches and events, and debates, increasing the chances that dominant themes will be more chronically accessible and, importantly, more strongly connected to the candidate. We've already seen that citizens are likely to perceive these emphases if the information environment gives them the chance. Hearing Bush talk about tax cuts further bolsters the inference that Bush prioritizes tax cuts.

Since citizens pay more attention to national news as the campaign heats up, they are more likely to process this relevant information. The more actively individuals attend to the information they process, the more likely it will be stored in memory rather than serving as simply a transitory consideration. The clarity of issue priority messages further eases the necessary information processing for the development of connections. It is difficult to properly process and store information about which one is not quite confident. Ambiguity on the part of the candidate, and uncertainty on the part of individuals, will inhibit effective links. For instance, in 2000 Bush strategically avoided use of the phrase "school vouchers" when talking about his education reform proposals. An individual listening to him speak about his plans for improving education or exposed to his ads might have a hard time connecting Bush to a pro-voucher position and encoding that connection in memory. However, she will have little trouble understanding that he places a priority on improving education. The Bush–education connection is an easy one to make; the Bush–voucher connection is not. Because issue priorities are more readily apparent than issue positions, they will be more effectively linked to the candidate.

Repetition also ties the themes directly to a candidate by bringing the issue and the candidate to mind together. Candidates actively endeavor to convince citizens that particular problems, often those they are perceived to be better able to handle, are relevant and within the realm of the federal government. Presidential candidates implicitly frame their campaign issues as presidential responsibilities. In-party candidates talk about problems they have solved or intend to; out-party candidates, in addition, bring up problems the incumbent administration has presumably failed to address. Either way, presidential responsibility is implied. Thus, repetition, in strengthening the link between an issue consideration and a candidate, serves to increase the odds that the theme will be judged applicable when citizens evaluate the candidates.

Campaigns, more than standard media coverage, are fortuitously designed to promote long-term accessibility of campaign issues and to consistently connect these issues to candidates in ways that increase the perceived applicability of the issues to judgments about candidates. The multiple pathways of influence, through chronic accessibility and strong associations, means citizens are more likely to learn to connect campaign information to the candidates in ways that increase the potential for future accountability.

These two mechanisms—temporary accessibility as a result of recent exposure versus associational strength and long-term accessibility as a result of frequent exposure—are tricky to disentangle observationally, to be sure. Both of these processes imply that primed considerations play a stronger role in evaluation; that is, they'll be weighted more heavily than nonprimed considerations. Still, the distinction is important because the broader implications of these two processes are quite different. Recency priming is a transitory influence. If this is the dominant effect of campaigns, then there is considerably less cost to a bait and switch on the part of a winning candidate—professing one set of priorities in the campaign and focusing on another once in office. The frequency and associational strength mechanisms, on the other hand, encourage a more enduring accessibility and the development of stronger connections with clearer implications in the minds of voters. This more enduring phenomenon suggests that citizens can incorporate issue considerations into their evaluations in useful ways. While candidates may shape how citizens evaluate them, in the process they establish expectations of their future behavior, and thus standards for future accountability.

Candidate–Issue Priority Connections in 2000

Citizens may not evaluate candidates along precisely the same dimensions, so candidate evaluation and vote choice are not identical decisions (Lau and Redlawsk 2006). Indeed, candidates are generally trying to play down some considerations and to play up others in hopes of becoming identified with the issues they wish to make salient. To the extent that candidates define the standards for their evaluation as president during the campaign, it is important to examine how candidates are evaluated individually. The 2000 survey described in chapter 4 also captured candidate evaluations with the following question:

> I'd like to get your feelings toward the candidates for president by asking you to rate each one on a scale that runs from 0 to 100. 0 means you feel very unfavorable toward the candidate, 100 means you feel very favorable, and 50 means you feel neutral toward the candidate. Using any number from 0 to 100, overall how do you feel toward [Al Gore]?

The primary issue consideration is the priority citizens give to the key campaign issues. This is measured in the 2000 survey by asking the respondents, for each of the four key issues:

> As you know there are many important issues facing our country, but we have only limited resources for addressing these issues. Keeping this in mind, how much of a priority should the federal government give to [saving Social Security]: a very high priority, a high priority but not the highest, a medium priority, a low priority, or no priority?

Responses were coded from no priority (−2) to a very high priority (+2). The more highly citizens prioritize an issue, the more positively they should evaluate a candidate whom they believe also prioritizes the issue. Priming suggests the information environment created by the presidential advertising campaign should impact the strength of the connection between individual issue priorities and evaluations of the candidates. The main empirical question, then, is whether greater attention to an issue by a candidate in an individual's information environment increases the weight of that issue priority in the individual's assessment of the candidate.

In addition, an examination of campaign priming must allow for the fact that citizens need not respond en masse to candidate communications, but may be differentially influenced by the candidates on the basis of partisan predispositions (Zaller 1992). In particular, candidates may exert more influence on the evaluative criteria of their supporters. In the analyses that follow, I allow for the impact of issue priorities and of the information environment's effect on the weight of issue priorities to vary by partisan identification—Democrat, Republican, or Independent. In addition, in the full model of candidate evaluations, I control for political ideology, retrospective economic perceptions, political awareness, education, age, gender, and racial minority status.

Finally, all candidate attempts at priming need not be equally effective. Connections between candidates and issues are not developed anew in each campaign. As associational strength suggests, previously encountered associations will be more easily processed upon later exposure; thus, connections that exist before the campaign—built on party or candidate reputations—ought to be more readily activated and renewed than weak or previously nonexistent associations. This implies that issues owned by a candidate or his party (Petrocik 1996) will be more readily connected to that candidate during the campaign in response to the candidate's emphasis on the issue.

REPETITION VERSUS RECENCY PRIMING

I model the relationship between candidate evaluations and issue priorities, and seek to examine how the information environment of the advertising campaign impacts this relationship. But the "information environment of the advertising campaign" requires more clarification. I have argued that we need to better distinguish between repetition priming and recency priming. As a first step, then, I compare two models of campaign priming using two different measures of campaign advertising emphasis.

Priming as a function of associational strength and repetition relies on the intuition that individuals' information environments are not only a function of the ads aired on the day they are interviewed but on all the ads aired to which they could have been exposed over time. In other words, the campaign information environment is a cumulative one. Accordingly, the measure of cumulative candidate–issue ads on any given day in a given media market is the sum of the ads on all days leading up to that one. It captures the number of times a candidate–issue connection has been made explicit within the campaign ads aired in a citizen's viewing area at the time of his interview.

Recency priming, on the other hand, is predominantly concerned with whether the issue has been recently encountered. To compare more clearly the cumulative effect of exposure to the repeated ad message and the effect of recent exposure to an ad message, the second measure of candidate–issue ad emphasis incorporates only the three days leading up to a respondent's date of interview.[6]

First I want to test if the accumulated, repetitious advertising environment has a bigger impact on candidate evaluations than does the most recent advertising environment. Below I report the results of a non-nested model comparison test (see Clarke 2003 for details). This nonparametric test compares how likely each individual observation is with respect to each model—the one with accumulated advertising attention or with recent advertising attention. Table 5.1 reports three things: (1) which model is supported by the test; (2) the percent of observations for which the model with the cumulative ad measure produces a greater likelihood than the observations with the recent ad measure; and (3) the associated significance with which we can reject the null hypothesis—that neither model is better—in favor of the alternative hypothesis that the model with the cumulative ads is better. I compare the cumulative and recent ad emphasis for each issue separately.

In six out of eight comparisons, the model relying on the cumulative measure of issue emphasis in the advertising campaign is better supported by the data than the model that uses the recent measure of advertising attention. That is, modeling candidate evaluations, and in particular the weight given to issue priorities, as a function of accumulated advertising emphasis fits the data better than modeling these same evaluations and weights as a function of only the most recently aired ads. The two exceptions, where recent advertising emphasis seems to fit better, occur for Gore's evaluations: one with respect to education priority and one with respect to health-care priority. In other words, for Gore, on the issues most clearly owned by his party, recent attention and exposure appears more effective than repeated attention and exposure.

For Bush, the lesser known of the two candidates, the accumulation of repeated attention to each of these four issues had more impact on citizen evaluations and on the weight of their issue considerations than

Table 5.1 Cumulative versus Recent Ads

	Bush			
	Taxes	Education	Health Care	Social Security
Supported Model	Cumulative	Cumulative	Cumulative	Cumulative
% obs. where Cumulative > Recent	100.0	99.9	84.7	100.0
p-value of test*	0.000	0.000	0.000	0.000
N	1019	1021	1015	1015
	Gore			
	Taxes	Education	Health Care	Social Security
Supported Model	Cumulative	Recent	Recent	Cumulative
% obs. where Cumulative > Recent	100.0	0.9	1.0	99.9
p-value of test*	0.000	1.000	1.000	0.000
N	1023	1025	1019	1019

*$p < .05$ denotes evidence favoring the cumulative model over the recency model.

the issues most recently emphasized in his advertising campaign. This pattern of results suggests some additional caveats and possibilities. Repetition may be most effective at connecting issues to candidates who are not already well ensconced in the public mind. Repetition, too, may be more beneficial in developing new connections—Gore and taxes, Gore and Social Security—than priming links already well established. I consider these conditions more thoroughly in the next section.

REPETITION PRIMING IN 2000

What impact, if any, does a candidate's cumulative attention to an issue have on the dimensions of candidate evaluation? The full models are available in the appendix for those interested, but the key results are depicted visually in figure 5.1 for Bush and in figure 5.2 for Gore.[7]

Each panel in the figures graphs the marginal effect of an issue priority on candidate evaluation—that is, how strongly (and in what direction) do issue priorities influence evaluations?—as a function of (1) the candidate's accumulated advertising campaign in a respondent's media market at the time of her interview, and (2) the respondent's party identification. Stars denote at what levels of candidate-issue emphasis these

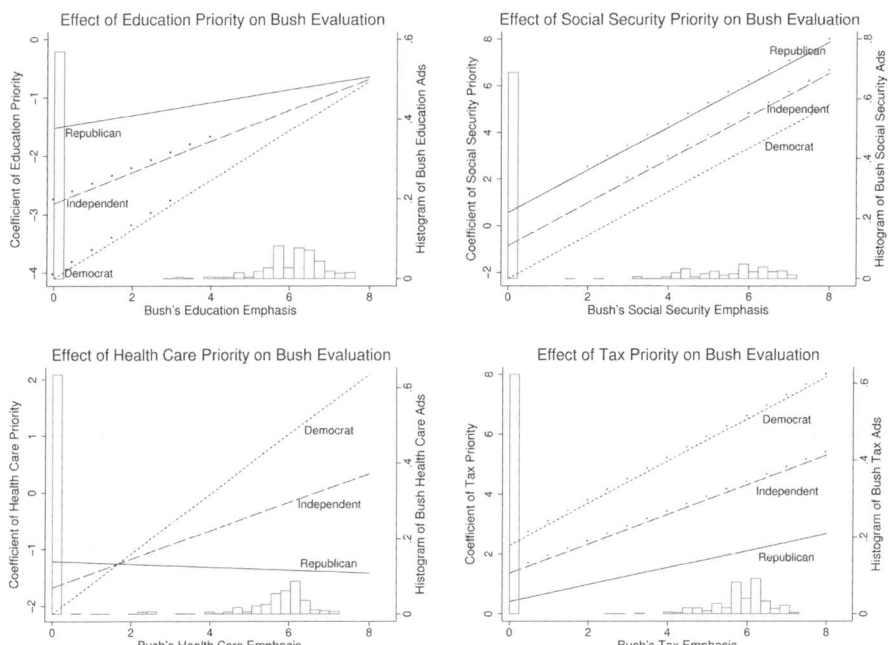

Figure 5.1 *Bush Issue Talk and Issue Priming*

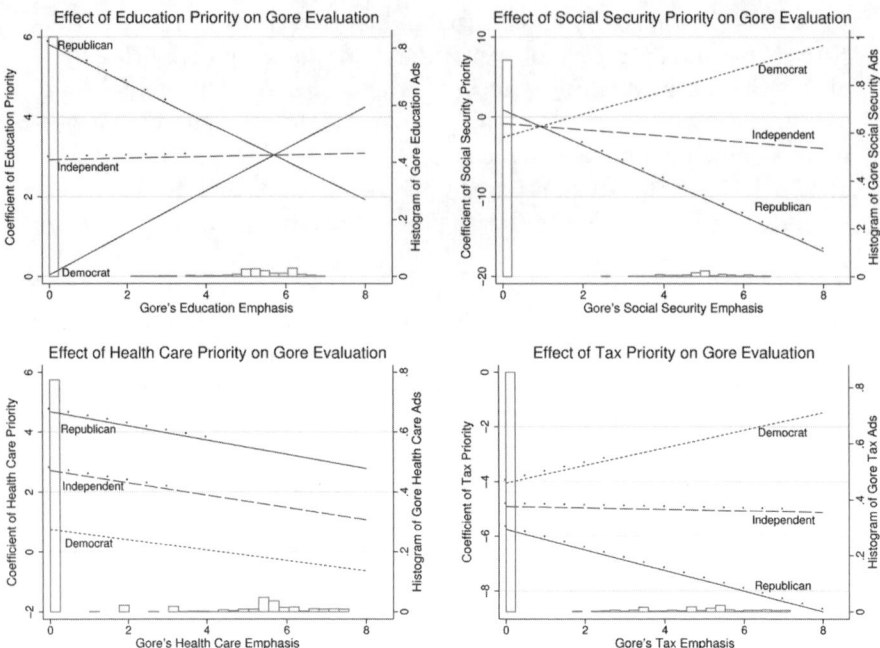

Figure 5.2 Gore Issue Talk and Issue Priming

marginal effects are significantly different from zero.[8] Finally, a histogram of the number of times a candidate's ads have mentioned the issue in a particular respondent's media market (logged) is overlaid on the graphs to convey a sense of how typical an effect is.[9]

The first panel of figure 5.1 provides the results for evaluations of Bush as a function of an individual's prioritization of education and references to education in Bush's advertising. A high priority attached to education initially disadvantages Bush, decreasing his evaluations, as is evident from the negative marginal effect. An Independent who thought education was a very high priority and who lived in a market that had witnessed no advertising by Bush that mentioned the issue would rate Bush about three points lower on the 100-point scale than a similar respondent who rated education a high priority but not the highest. Compared to an Independent who says education is not a priority at all, the citizen who cares the most about education would rate Bush about 12 points less positively.[10]

But what we really care about is how this connection changes as Bush emphasizes the issue more heavily. Does the line representing the marginal effect get closer to, or even greater than, zero? Based on figure

5.1, Bush's attention to education in his advertising campaign moves the initially negative influence of education priority on his evaluations in a positive direction for everybody, though not equally. Absent any attention, Democrats and Independents evaluate Bush less positively the more highly they prioritize education. For Democrats, the marginal effect of education priority absent any attention to the issue is about –4; for Independents, it is about –3. But in places and times where Bush's campaign has given even moderate attention to the issue, the weight of education priority reduces to something statistically indistinguishable from zero for both groups. Again, the initial negative connection means that someone who prioritizes education highly will evaluate Bush more negatively than a similar individual who doesn't prioritize education. While education initially disadvantages Bush, the prominent place education held in his campaign advertising serves to turn a negative effect into a neutral one. The weight of education priority in shaping evaluations of Bush among Republicans is never significant, and Bush's attention to the issue does little to alter that.

Figure 5.1 also presents the effect of Bush's ad emphasis on the marginal effect of prioritizing Social Security, highlighting the overall positive effect of Bush's Social Security advertising campaign on the weight citizens give to Social Security priority in their evaluations. As Bush's attention to the issue increases in respondents' environments, the weight Republicans give to the issue increases to significant levels, from about 1 to 8. The coefficient on the issue becomes significant for Independents as well, moving from about –1 to just over 6. Among Democrats, the effect of the issue changes from a slightly negative one, –2, to a moderately positive one, 5, but it is never statistically discernible from zero.

The next panel of figure 5.1 provides the marginal effect of health-care priority on evaluations of Bush conditional on the frequency of health-care ads. Greater attention to health care by Bush moves the weight of individual priority ratings from a slightly negative effect to a slightly positive effect for Democrats and Independents. Nonetheless, for no amount of observed attention does health-care priority significantly impact evaluations of Bush. Attention to the issue in his advertising campaign fails to significantly prime this consideration. Given the public did not accurately hear Bush's health-care talk when it occurred, the absence of any connection between the issue and his evaluation should not surprise us.

The overall positive effect of Bush's accumulated ads on the weight given to tax priority in his evaluations is evident in the last panel of figure 5.1. In the absence of any attention to the issue in his ads, the influence of tax-cut priorities doesn't achieve statistical levels of significance among Independents. As more ads are aired, however, the weight becomes significantly positive, moving from an effect size of about 1, representing only a 4-point difference between high tax-prioritizers and low tax-prioritizers on the 100 point scale, to just over 5, representing a 20-point improvement in evaluations of Bush for those who prioritize the issue very highly compared to those who prioritize the issue not at all. The influence of tax priority among Democrats is always positive and significant, but becomes noticeably more so as Bush's attention to the issue increases, from a low of about 2 to a high of nearly 8. Although the marginal effect becomes more positive among Republicans as Bush's ad campaign mentions taxes more frequently, the influence of tax priorities never achieves a conventional level of statistical significance.

What about Gore? Figure 5.2 presents the analogous effects of Gore's ads on the marginal effect of each issue priority on evaluations of candidate Gore. The first panel makes clear that the more accumulated ads Gore airs on education in a respondent's environment, the more weight Democrats place on the issue, the less weight Republicans place on the issue, and the weight Independents give to the issue remains relatively unchanged. Among Democrats, the average influence of education priority on Gore's evaluations increases from 0 to about 4, but it never attains any conventional level of statistical significance. Among Republicans, however, the weight given to education priority is significant absent any attention by Gore to the issue, with an effect size of about 6; greater advertising emphasis on education by Gore reduces the influence of the issue, ultimately making it statistically indiscernible from zero. Thus, while absent any attention by Gore, Republicans give greater weight to the issue in their evaluations, on average, than do Democrats, as issue attention increases to even relatively minimal levels, this difference disappears. In short, Gore's advertising campaign primarily serves to *deemphasize* the influence of education priority for Republicans.

Moving to the issue of Social Security, the next panel of figure 5.2, in the absence of advertising attention to the issue, the marginal effect for Gore hovers around zero, as it did for Bush. Neither candidate began with a clear advantage on the issue, in that the priority citizens give to Social Security is not consistently related to their evaluations of either candidate. The issue, at the start of the campaign, appears to be something of a wild card. And, like Bush, Gore alters the weight given to the issue as a function of how frequently he airs ads that mention the issue. But for Gore, his attention to Social Security has a disparate impact among partisans. The more Gore emphasizes the issue, the more negative the influence of Social Security priority becomes among Republicans, moving from neutral to –17. Republicans who place a high priority on the issue rate Gore 34 points worse than those who call Social Security a medium priority and 68 points worse than those who say Social Security is not a priority at all. Among independents, Gore's attention to the issue makes the influence of the priority on evaluations more negative, but the effect is never statistically distinguishable from zero. For Democrats, the weight of the issue priority increases quite a bit, from –3 given no Social Security ads to 9 given the maximum number of ads, though even this large coefficient never achieves a conventional level of statistical significance.

The effect of Gore's attention to health care in his advertising campaign on the relationship between health-care priority and evaluations of Gore is shown in the third panel of figure 5.2. Republicans and Independents who prioritize health care highly evaluate Gore significantly more favorably than those who do not, absent any attention to the issue on Gore's part. The marginal effect is about 5 for Republicans and 3 for Independents. As Gore's advertising campaign makes more frequent mention of the issue in a respondent's environment, however, the advantageous effect of health-care priority is neutralized. Democrats, for their part, never weight the issue significantly in their evaluations of the candidate, and Gore's advertising campaign does not change this. Although Republicans consistently weight this priority more highly than do Democrats, beyond a certain level of attention by Gore, the coefficients do not differ significantly from zero regardless of partisanship.

Finally, the last panel of figure 5.2 provides the results for Gore evaluations as a function of tax-cutting priority and mention of taxes in Gore's advertising. A high priority attached to taxes clearly disadvantaged Gore, decreasing his evaluations considerably, as is evident from the negative marginal effects for Gore, ranging from –4 to –6 absent any advertising emphasis. Even without any attention to the issue, then, tax priorities have a pretty big impact on evaluations of Gore. And Gore was generally unable to overcome his disadvantage on taxes by emphasizing the issue in his ad campaign. Indeed, among Republicans Gore's attention to taxes in his advertising campaign serves to strengthen the negative effect of prioritizing tax cuts, from a marginal effect of –6 to –9. The figure also reveals the differentiating effect of Gore's tax ads, leading to a more negative weight on tax priorities among Republicans and a less negative weight on tax priorities among Democrats. In environments with a moderate level of attention to taxes in Gore's advertising campaign, the initially negative influence of tax priority on Gore's evaluations is neutralized among Democrats.

Conclusion

What can we conclude? Overall, the accumulated, repetition measures of issue emphasis fare better than the more transitory, recency measures. The campaign appears to have done more to promote *longer-term associations* rather than *short-term accessibility*, particularly for Social Security and taxes. For Bush, too, the repeated attention to education had more beneficial effects than did recent attention, but here the campaign served primarily to neutralize a previous disadvantage.

The pattern of effects—across issues and across candidates—is instructive. For Gore, the most common effect of his issue emphasis, among the issues studied, is largely neutral for Democrats and negative for Republicans. Overall, his ability to influence the dimensions of his evaluations was more likely to be selective, conditional on partisan predispositions. For Bush, the more common pattern in response to his advertising emphasis is to move the weight of issue priorities in a positive direction for the electorate as a whole, though the degree of responsiveness also varies by partisanship.

This pattern is consistent with the conventional wisdom that Bush won the air war and Gore ran a relatively ineffective campaign. That Gore's ad campaign was less successful than Bush's could be due to less compelling ads on the part of Gore, more effective opposition ads by Bush's campaign, or by asymmetries in how congruent the mass-mediated campaign was with each candidates' ad campaign. Unfortunately, these data cannot pinpoint a single explanation. It is worth noting that the strongest cases of candidate–issue connections include an issue for which ad references were primarily positive (Bush and Social Security), an issue for which ad references were primarily comparative (Bush and taxes), and an issue for which ad references were primarily negative (Gore and Social Security). It is possible that the negative nature of Gore's Social Security attention in his ads worked to polarize responses on the basis of party, though Gore's issue attention appears to produce disparate responses among opposing partisans and co-partisans even for issues on which his ads were mostly positive, like education and tax cuts.

Still, the pattern of results across these issues and candidates suggest further qualifications. First, the existence of a prior connection—as a function of issue ownership—can facilitate the development of a connection between the candidate and the issue in the campaign, as with Bush and taxes. Prior connections can also inhibit the development of an association between the issue and the trespassing candidate, as with Gore and taxes or Bush and education. With respect to education, Bush needed first to overcome a preexisting negative connection. Indeed, that is all his emphasis on the issue seems to have accomplished; but that, itself, may be the goal. It is precisely such cases, when candidates work to counter prior connections, that highlight the role priming plays in de-emphasizing issues. Priming as accessibility cannot fully accommodate a negative relation between recent or frequent exposure to a consideration and a down-weighting of the consideration in evaluation; priming as building associational strength can. Gore, however, was not similarly successful when emphasizing taxes. Indeed, the evidence here suggests that Democratic candidates may only hurt themselves by engaging the issue (see Bartels 2005).

Second, the more information citizens are likely to have about a candidate, the more selectively responsive to candidate messages they are likely to be. Democrats, it would seem, were more open to the opposition party's candidate's suggestions for evaluative criteria than were Republicans. Given Gore's tenure in office and his inevitable connection to the policies and reputation of Bill Clinton's administration, it seems intuitively correct that Republicans, many of whom loathed the Clinton administration more than Democrats loved it, would be less responsive to Gore's redefinition of himself. Bush, on the other hand, was relatively unknown. Consequently, his attempts to define the appropriate dimensions of his evaluations may have simply fallen upon a more responsive audience. In the face of strong preexisting associations with a candidate like Gore, the campaign faces an uphill battle in influencing these connections, and success may be limited to favorably disposed partisans.

All priming effects are not created equal. It matters, when priming occurs in campaigns, if it is a transitory recency effect or a more enduring frequency and associational effect. We need to take this distinction more seriously. Candidates may hope to merely induce a short-term priming effect advantageous to their cause, one that carries through Election Day but no farther; but the repetitive strategy of contemporary campaigns favors the development of enduring connections that, once established, can harden into public expectations. Agenda accountability requires, first, that candidate priorities are clearly discernible; they are (chapter 3). Second, it requires that citizens accurately hear the candidates issue priorities; they do (chapter 4). Third, it requires that citizens develop connections, beyond a transitory recency priming effect, between candidates and the issues they discuss; this chapter demonstrates that, more often than not, they do. What this means for presidents is the topic of the next chapter.

6 Campaign Connections and Presidential Evaluations

Campaigns convey to citizens information about the priorities of presidential candidates. Citizens use this information in evaluating the prospective leaders, and for key issues they do so in a way that suggests the development of longer-term expectations. What effect do these citizen understandings have on leader behavior? And what effect does subsequent leader behavior have on the public's evaluations of a president?

The President: Priorities, Action, and Effort

Much has been written on the role of the president in policy making, particularly on his role in the legislative arena (Bond and Fleisher 1992; Jones 2005; Light 1999; Neustadt 1990; Peterson 1993). One thing past research has taught us is that a president cannot command, not in a system defined by separation of powers.[1] The diffuse responsibility inherent in a separated system means, as well, that we "cannot fairly hold the President accountable for the success or failure of his overall program, because he lacks the constitutional power to put that program into effect" (Jones 1999, quoting Cutler 1980, 127).

What, then, can a president do? What may we fairly hold the president accountable for? Presidents set and sequence government priorities. Indeed, there is nearly unanimous agreement among presidential scholars that a president must do so if he wishes to be successful. As Jones (2005) notes, upon entering office a president will encounter a governing agenda that is already full. Government cannot address the entire agenda at once, and so the collective congress awaits a designation of priorities by the individual president. "As in any organization with too much to do, there is a need for someone in authority to say 'Let's start here, with this.' A president who says 'Let's start here and here and here and here' fails as a designator" (Jones 2005, 219). Light calls this the "must list"— Congress needs to know what the president wants to act on immediately and what can wait (Light 1999, 157). Should a president fail to provide a list of priorities or provide one with too many items on the list, he will lose in the competition for space on the congressional agenda. In short, "Nothing an individual president can do breeds success like clear priorities" (Peterson 1993, 267). And yet, candidate priorities in the campaign and in the decision calculus of voters have been routinely dismissed as so much fluff.

Priority setting occurs early in a new administration. Getting the attention of Congress is crucial. The power of an electoral connection for members of Congress may be greater at the earlier stages of decision making, when deciding which problems to pursue, rather than at the final stages, when voting on particular amendments or bills (Arnold 1990). This provides a president's best opening, particularly for issues and problems highlighted in the campaign. If Congress avoids tackling some problems because they do not think citizens will tolerate the visible and traceable costs, then the presidential campaign can push members over this hurdle by signaling citizen interest in the issue and demonstrating that addressing the issue is electorally safe.[2]

It is not enough to convey clear priorities to Congress, though. To increase the odds of success in the policy arena, a president must act early. Light (1999) identifies a president's first term in office as critical, and the first year of that first term as especially so. The choices presidents make early about dominant themes and directions follow, or haunt, the administration throughout its tenure. As one of Light's informant's notes, "The president gets a second chance to set the program in the second term. But most of those choices are predetermined by the first. The failures of the first term are often the failures of the second" (1999, 41). Because, as Light notes, presidents face a cycle of declining influence, new presidents have the greatest opportunity for achieving domestic goals early. In his study, 72 percent of legislative items introduced by the president in the first three months of the new term (January through March) are eventually enacted. Only 39 percent of those introduced in April through June are enacted; and 25 percent of those introduced in the latter half of the year make it through.[3] These early actions, the top priorities, are foreshadowed in the campaign, or should be forecast in a campaign reasonably characterized as "informative."[4]

In addition to clarifying what parts of a president's program are key and pursuing these policies early, a president must expend effort in seeing those programs enacted. Presidential effort—how the president uses his scarce resources of time, lobbying, and speech making—matters for successful legislative action. Presidential effort is directly related to whether Congress acts on a president's proposal (Peterson 1993).[5] Gaining congressional attention and overcoming congressional inaction are key in forming any solution—the president's, his opponents', or some compromise between the two—to a problem.

In short, what a president can do in the legislative arena depends on the clarity of his legislative priorities, his ability to act early, and his willingness to spend his political capital. The campaign priorities ought to be reflected in the behavior of the president in this regard. The president's follow-through on the campaign priorities provides a sound basis on which to hold him accountable. It remains to be seen whether the winner's campaign priorities are reflected in his presidential activities early on and whether the public responds accordingly.

From Campaigning to Governing, from Voting to Approval

The presidential campaign is, among other things, an elaborate effort to establish expectations among the electorate. Though the campaign is hardly the only opportunity for such development, it is a defining moment.

As argued in prior chapters, the development of priority expectations during the campaign is more likely given clear and repeated issue emphasis by the nominee. The public is more likely to accurately hear such a message and to connect the expressed priorities to the would-be president. The ability of citizens to learn to connect the issues a candidate emphasizes to that candidate during the course of the campaign improves the likelihood of holding leaders accountable for the future policy agenda. If candidates are heavily and reliably evaluated on the basis of issue priorities promoted during the campaign, and these issues continue to serve as a criterion of presidential evaluation after the election, then presidents attuned to their public standing may feel constrained to act in accordance with their campaign rhetoric.[6]

Recall from chapter 3 that Bush's campaign ads most frequently mentioned education (51.4 percent of ad airings), followed by Social Security (36.4 percent), health care (26.5 percent), and taxes (22.3 percent). No other issue was mentioned in more than 20 percent of the ads aired. Citizens heard Bush talking most about taxes and education overall. The degree to which citizens understood Bush to be emphasizing education, taxes, and Social Security depended on how much emphasis these issues received in Bush's campaign ads aired in the citizens' media market (chapter 4). Finally, voter evaluations of Bush as a candidate were clearly and positively tied to the priority they gave to taxes, and the connection was stronger in areas where Bush's advertising campaign cited taxes more frequently. Voter evaluations of Bush were initially negatively tied to the priority they gave education, though this detrimental connection was weakened for citizens exposed to more of Bush's campaign ads emphasizing the issue. Education wasn't strongly and positively tied to Bush as a result of his repeated emphasis on the issue; instead, the issue was neutralized. It seems plausible that, given more time, Bush could have built a positive connection, but in the course of the 2000 campaign he did not manage to do so. Further, voter evaluations of Bush were initially unrelated to the priority they gave to Social Security, but where the Bush campaign emphasized the issue more, the connection became strong and positive (chapter 5).

In short, Bush emphasized education, citizens heard this emphasis, and Bush's repetitive talk of education served to overcome an initially disadvantageous connection. Bush emphasized taxes, citizens heard this emphasis, and repetition served to strengthen the connection between Bush and taxes. Bush emphasized Social Security, citizens heard this emphasis to a lesser extent, and repetition created a positive connection between Bush and the program. Finally, though health care was also one of Bush's top four issues, it was largely a response to the Gore campaign and was conflated in Bush's rhetoric with Medicare and Social Security in a potentially confusing manner. Consequently, citizens failed to register Bush's emphasis on the issue or to connect it to him in either a transitory or enduring way.

What does this mean for presidential accountability? The theory of agenda accountability posits that those issues connected to the candidate will continue to be more strongly connected to the president, via the impact on approval, than those issues not connected to the candidate. For Bush, the issues that became clearly connected were taxes and Social Security; education, despite Bush's efforts, and health care were not strongly tied to Bush as a candidate.

Second, this pattern of connections should occur regardless of what the president does—whether he follows through, prioritizing the issue, taking early action, and expending effort; whether he neglects the issue; whether he becomes distracted by a new issue; or whether he neglects noncampaign issues. The possible outcomes and where key issues fall for Bush's first year are shown in table 6.1. Follow-through, though, should bolster approval while neglect should worsen it. Issues that interrupt his campaign agenda or are consistently neglected should have a weaker effect on approval. Bush followed through on a connected issue, taxes, and an issue that was not tied to him in the minds of voters, education. In addition, he neglected both Social Security and his Medicare prescription drug proposals during his first year; the first was strongly tied to him, the second was not. And there are a variety of issues that played no substantial role in either the campaign or in the early administration—for example, the environment or campaign finance reform. The outcome Bush's early presidency does not readily provide for is agenda interruption. This will have to wait until the next chapter.

Bush's Priorities, Actions, and Efforts

> Together we will reclaim America's schools before ignorance and apathy claim more young lives. We will reform Social Security and Medicare, sparing our children from struggles we have the power to prevent. And we will reduce taxes to recover the momentum of our economy and reward the effort and enterprise of working Americans.
> —President George W. Bush, inaugural address, January 20, 2001

President George W. Bush alluded only briefly to his policy agenda in his first inaugural address. His references to domestic policy, occurring halfway through the speech, mentioned only education, Social Security and Medicare, and tax cuts—the very issues his campaign promoted most heavily. The priorities, at the outset, seemed sincere.

In Bush's address before a joint session of the Congress on admin-

Table 6.1 Agenda Outcomes

		Campaign	
		Emphasis	Neglect
Administration	Emphasis	Agenda follow-through *Taxes* *Education*	Agenda interruption None
	Neglect	Agenda neglect *Social Security* *Medicare Rx*	Consistent neglect *Environment* *Campaign finance*

istration goals (his non–State of the Union) on February 27, Bush again addressed education first, and at length, devoting seven of seventy paragraphs (10 percent) to promoting his education initiatives. "The highest percentage increase in our budget should go to our children's education. . . . Education is my top priority, and by supporting this budget, you'll make it yours, as well" (Bush 2001a). The only issue to receive more attention in the speech was tax cuts—Bush devoted fourteen paragraphs (20 percent) to defending his tax-cut proposals.[7] He briefly mentioned a proposal to add to Medicare a new prescription drug benefit for low-income seniors, and pointed to the need to reform Medicare more broadly by adding a prescription drug benefit for all seniors (three paragraphs, in all). Social Security, meanwhile, merited four paragraphs of attention, ending with the announcement of a presidential commission to reform Social Security and signaling a sidelining of the issue until a later time.

A similar pattern emerges in Bush's public remarks around the country. Some speeches clearly emphasized a particular issue, but a standard traveling speech began the policy talk with education and ended it with a somewhat greater proportion of time devoted to taxes. In his public remarks during his first 100 days, about 17 percent of the paragraphs in his speeches addressed education and about 20 percent addressed his tax cuts.[8] No other issues received anything close to this level of rhetorical attention. Though Bush's attention became more dispersed as time wore on, up until the attacks of September 11, education and tax cuts dominated his public remarks, receiving 12 and 14 percent of paragraphic attention, respectively. Social Security and the Medicare drug benefit, meanwhile, were largely neglected in Bush's rhetoric. The proportion of attention devoted to education, taxes, Social Security, and Medicare in Bush's public remarks during his first eight months in office is shown in figure 6.1.

Education and taxes were also emphasized in the president's budget proposal. Bush's budget proposed a $4.6 billion increase in spending for the Department of Education (Parks 2001a), the biggest increase over 2001 by agency. His proposed tax cuts totaled $1.6 trillion over ten years. In the positioning and attention given to the issues in Bush's presidential rhetoric and in his budget, education and tax cuts were unquestionably his top legislative priorities. Although these campaign priorities continued to receive top billing in his presidential agenda and public remarks, education and tax cuts followed different paths to fruition. Tax cuts traveled a purely partisan script, and education followed a genuinely bipartisan one. What does this commitment to, or neglect of, his key campaign priorities mean for the president and for the public? To understand the

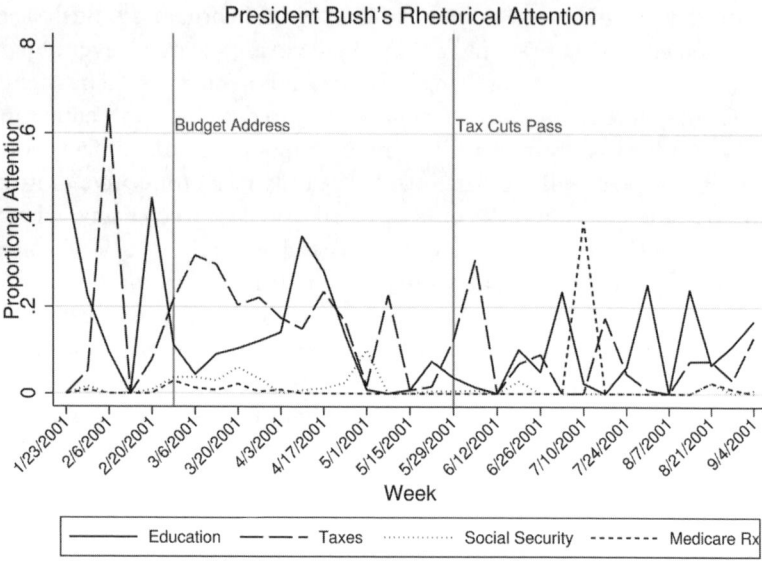

Figure 6.1 Attention to Campaign Priorities: President Bush

dynamics of the public response, we first need to review the relevant time line for each issue.

EDUCATION: AGENDA FOLLOW-THROUGH

Education reform was Bush's number one priority in his campaign rhetoric. He introduced his twenty-eight-page blueprint for education reform on January 23, 2001, his third day in office. The bill that ultimately passed, the No Child Left Behind Act (NCLB), is widely regarded as the biggest expansion of federal involvement in education policy since the Elementary and Secondary Education Act of 1965 (ESEA).

Prior to his inauguration, Bush held a meeting of education leaders in Austin, Texas, inviting leaders from both parties in a signal of his intent to pursue a bipartisan compromise. Notably, Senator Edward M. Kennedy (D-Mass.), a liberal champion of education and the ranking Democrat on the Senate Education Committee, was not included. But as the Bush team came to realize that the majority of Democrats would not follow the lead of the centrist Democrats, and as Kennedy recognized he might be excluded from a key role in the most important education bill since the ESEA, the two men came together. Bush reached out to Kennedy, calling him in late December "to express his interest in working together on education and other issues" (Kornblut 2001). Bush and Kennedy even appeared together at an inner-city school to highlight their areas of agreement in overhauling education (Enda 2001). And Bush embraced meaningful bipartisan centrism on education from the outset. As early as January 2, the *Washington Post*'s Dana Milbank reported that the Bush administration had decided to emphasize regular testing of students and increased education flexibility for states at the expense of the more divisive school voucher program, including vouchers as more of a symbolic gesture to satisfy conservatives (Milbank 2001).

The emphasis on education continued after the inauguration. The White House dubbed Bush's first week in office "Education Week" and expressed his intent to make the education initiative his first major domestic policy (Allen 2001). Bush used his first weekly radio address to promote education reform. In his second full week in office, Bush met with a bipartisan group of governors at the White House to discuss his education reform package.

Clearly, Bush intended his education efforts to be front and center in his policy agenda and in the minds of voters. The immediate peak in attention to education is clear in figure 6.1. He continued to speak on education, devoting about 45 percent of his public remarks to education the week before delivering his joint address to Congress in February. Bush's emphasis on education peaked again in mid-April, when he devoted one third of his public remarks to education after submitting his formal budget proposal and before the Senate began debating the legislation. A fourth set of peaks occurred in July and August as the House and Senate worked to reconcile their education bills.

NCLB was the first bill he sent to Congress, though Bush provided only a sketch outlining his general principles, leaving Congress to write the details and leaving himself the flexibility to negotiate (McGuinn 2006). The House and Senate had reserved bill numbers HR 1 and S 1 for education reform, signifying their consent to Bush's agenda (Nather 2001a). Bush's education proposal had a comparatively easy time in the Republican-controlled House. In the House, the bill made it out of committee on May 9, though only after the removal of the most contentious issues—school vouchers and block grants. The White House, nevertheless, claimed a victory for winning on most of their proposals: annual testing, consolidation of federal education programs, flexibility in spending at the local school district level, school report cards, and requiring poorly performing public schools to improve or face consequences (Nather 2001b). After defeating an amendment on the floor to strip the bill of required annual testing, a victory attributed to White House lobbying efforts (Nather 2001e), and narrowly accepting an amendment to allow 100 school districts to spend funds from four federal programs flexibly, the House passed HR 1 on May 23, by a vote of 384 to 45.

The legislation was actually introduced first in the evenly divided Senate and faced its biggest obstacles there. Though the Senate Health, Education, Labor and Pensions Committee voted the bill out of committee on March 8 with unanimous support, it, too, managed this only by moving consideration of school vouchers and block grants to the Senate floor. The Senate expected to take up the bill in late April, but disagreement with the White House over spending delayed the bill's introduction on the floor. Bush initially proposed increasing spending for ESEA by $1.6 billion, but Senate Democrats proposed an increase of $14.4 billion (Nather 2001f). After the administration offered a $2.6 billion increase and Senate Democrats lowered their request to $8.8 billion on April 23, the negotiations came to a standstill (Nather 2001c). Even so, in the now-standard 100-day media assessment of the president, President Bush told CNN's John King he was feeling "pretty darn good" about his presidency, citing progress on a tax cut and negotiations with Democrats on his education agenda (King 2001).

Negotiations between the White House and the Senate became more precarious as Senator James M. Jeffords (Vt.) announced on May 24 that he was leaving the Republican Party and would vote to turn control of the Senate over to the Democrats. Jeffords, who had been one of the key Republican negotiators on the bipartisan education bill, cited his disagreement with Bush on education spending—Jeffords was advocating for more funding, particularly for special education—as one of the primary reasons he was leaving the GOP (Nather 2001e).

After six weeks of Senate floor debate, the bill passed the Senate on June 14 with a vote of 91–8. The House and Senate versions both included a focus on testing and accountability but differed significantly on financing. The Senate's version outlined $41.8 billion, overall, for education for the following year; the House version allocated $24 billion, much closer to Bush's proposed $19 billion (Wilgoren 2001). The House–Senate conference would need to close the gap. Nevertheless, passage of the education reforms in both chambers was generally hailed as a triumph for President Bush. In a statement following the Senate vote, Bush praised the bill: "The reforms in this bill reflect the core principles of my education agenda: accountability, flexibility, local control, and more choices for parents" (Bush 2001b).

Though Bush began highlighting education again in June to encourage Congress to finalize a bill, the conference committee did not meet until July 19. By the August recess, the committee had not begun to tackle the major points of disagreement. During the recess, conference committee staffers worked out "potential compromises on approximately 2,750 issues in the bills" and key negotiators were expected to meet as many as three times the week of September 10 to push the bill along (Nather 2001d). Of course, those meetings were delayed by the terrorist attacks. Memorably, Bush was in a school promoting No Child Left Behind when he learned that airplanes had struck the World Trade Center towers.

Although most of the domestic legislation in the pipeline was temporarily shelved after 9/11—the patients' bill of rights, campaign finance reform—the education bill maintained some momentum. Unlike much of the other domestic legislation, the education bill was a priority for Bush from the start. And polling data consistently showed education ranking first among the public's concerns early in 2001. Even after 9/11, education ranked third, behind concerns about terrorism and the economy (Gorman 2001).

The conference committee began meeting again on September 25 to resolve the remaining conflicts. After months of negotiations, the House adopted the conference report on NCLB on December 13 by a vote of 381-41; the Senate followed suit, approving the final version on December 18 by a vote of 87-10. The president signed No Child Left Behind into law on January 8, 2002.

Bush's work on education during the transition, the number one position education reform enjoyed in his legislative queue, his rhetorical attention to education, and the survival of education even after the agenda-changing events of September 11 attest to the priority and effort Bush afforded the issue.

TAX CUTS: AGENDA FOLLOW-THROUGH

While Bush used the language of priority with reference to education and emphasized it more heavily than any other issue in his campaign, tax cuts were perceived by many as a close contender for the top spot. Journalists routinely referred to the tax-cut proposal as "the centerpiece of his campaign" (Nitschke 2001e). At an economic forum he convened in Austin, Texas, on January 4, he reaffirmed his commitment to the ten-year, $1.6 trillion tax-cut proposal he campaigned on. The key difference between the early presidential rhetoric on tax cuts and the rhetoric from the campaign was that now the tax plan was being billed as economic stimulus in response to signs of a slowing economy.[9]

In his second week in office, Bush met repeatedly with leaders of the congressional tax-writing panels. The week of February 5, Bush's third week as president, was dubbed "Tax Week" by the White House, as Bush began publicly lobbying for his proposal and sent his tax plan, "Agenda for Tax Relief," to Congress. The plan was, like the education outline, a blueprint, not a detailed proposal (Parks and Nitschke 2001). On June 7, he signed into law the deepest tax cut since the 1981 Reagan tax cuts.

House Republicans granted Bush early symbolic victories and momentum by passing four discrete pieces of the tax proposal—a reduction in income tax rates on March 8, tax cuts for married people and people with children on March 29, a phase-out of the estate tax on April 4, and tax incentives for retirement savings on May 2. The real struggles were, again, in the Senate, where the White House recognized early on that the tax cuts would not pass without the protection afforded by the special budget reconciliation process, a strategy to evade the possibility of a filibuster and thus to pass tax cuts by a simple majority. Consequently, the key legislative maneuvers began with the 2002 budget resolution where tax cuts could win, or not, reconciliation rules.[10]

Kent Conrad (D-N.D.), the Senate Budget Committee's ranking Democrat, said of the tax-cutting strategy: "Let's be realistic here. If it's in the budget resolution, it's going to happen" (Parks and Nitschke 2001). Conrad also made clear, though, that no Democrat would vote for a budget resolution calling for a tax cut as deep as Bush had proposed (Nitschke 2001a). Then-Republican James Jeffords became the first Republican senator to announce his opposition to Bush's tax proposal on February 13, asserting, like the Democrats, that he would not support such a large tax cut; Lincoln Chafee (R-R.I.) quickly followed suit (Nitschke 2001a). Even with the support of Democrat Zell Miller (Ga.), the opposition of Jeffords and Chafee would leave Republicans short of the needed votes in the 50–50 Senate.

Bush clearly still had some selling to do, and sell he did. Tax cuts were Bush's key rhetorical theme in March, following his February 27 budget address. His persuasive appeals appeared designed to persuade members of Congress as much as to elicit public support; Bush favored speaking in states that he had won in the campaign but that were represented by Democratic senators—Georgia, Louisiana, Arkansas, Missouri, North Dakota, South Dakota, Montana, and North Carolina (Edwards 2008).

Charles E. Grassley (R-Iowa), Senate Finance Committee chairman, delayed working on tax legislation until May, expecting the budget resolution for 2002 to be adopted by then (Nitschke 2001c). The House adopted an initial 2002 budget resolution, closely mirroring the president's plan, on March 28 (Parks 2001a). The Senate, unable to move a budget resolution through the evenly divided Finance Committee, put the measure directly before the full chamber. A budget resolution passed the Senate on April 6 (63–35), but the Senate's version limited the tax cut to $1.18 trillion, $448 billion less than Bush proposed, essentially splitting the difference between Bush's proposal and an alternative proposal offered by Senate Democrats. Three Republican moderates were central in cutting the tax ceiling—Jeffords, Chafee, and Arlen Specter (Penn.). In addition, the Senate's budget resolution called for retroactive tax cuts for 2001, as much as $85 billion worth, a measure embraced by the Democrats in an effort to promote a greater stimulative effect for the tax cuts. Republicans claimed a key success in gaining reconciliation protections for the tax-cut legislation (Parks 2001c).

Both chambers passed the reconciled budget resolution on predominantly party lines. The House voted 221–207, gaining the support of six Democrats, on May 9. The Senate voted 53–47, gaining the support of five Democrats, on May 10. The compromise resolution allowed for a ten-year tax-cut ceiling of $1.35 trillion, allowed for $100 billion to be used as tax rebates for 2001, and retained reconciliation instructions for tax-cutting legislation (Parks 2001b). This legislative vote was key, all but ensuring significant tax cuts and a policy success for Bush.

The actual tax legislation followed quickly, in congressional terms, on the heels of the budget resolution. The House repassed its income tax reduction piece as an official reconciliation bill on May 16. The Senate passed its own comprehensive tax legislation, including a reduction in income tax rates, alleviation of the marriage penalty, a phase-out of the estate tax, and an expansion of the child tax credit, on May 23. The Senate version contained several "gimmicks" meant to keep the cost within the parameters defined by the budget resolution in order to avoid a point of order that would require sixty votes to overrule. The most noted of these was the "sunset" provision, set to automatically repeal all of the cuts on December 31, 2010 (Nitschke 2001b).

These latest successes were quickly overshadowed by Senator Jeffords's announcement that he would leave the Republican Party and begin caucusing with the Democrats as an Independent as soon as the tax legislation reached Bush's desk. Given the end of Republican control of the Capitol, the White House "urged their Republican allies to quickly embrace any version of a tax cut deal that could become law" in the House–Senate conference negotiations (Nitschke 2001d). The final bill was only slightly altered from the Senate's version. Both chambers stayed in session into the Saturday of Memorial Day weekend to pass the bill on May 26, 240–154 in the House and 58–33 in the Senate. Bush signed the Economic Growth and Tax Relief Reconciliation Act into law on June 7, proudly claiming the outcome as a resounding policy success.

SOCIAL SECURITY: AGENDA NEGLECT

Bush's early efforts on behalf of Social Security were largely symbolic, despite the prominent role Social Security and privatization played in his campaign. He announced in his February 27 budget address that he would establish a presidential commission on Social Security reform. On May 2, he officially introduced his Presidential Commission to Strengthen Social Security, a bipartisan group whose sixteen members all supported some form of personal investment accounts. The inclusion of individually controlled, voluntary personal retirement accounts to augment Social Security was a key guiding principle of the committee, along with the prohibition of any decrease of benefits for those near retirement (or retired) and a prohibition on any increase in the payroll taxes that fund the program. Democratic critics dismissed it as a presidential advocacy commission (Dentzer 2001). The commission began meeting on June 11, issued an interim report on the state of the Social Security program on July 24, concluded its work on December 11, and issued a final report on December 21. None of this resulted in legislative action or effort on the part of President Bush.[11]

MEDICARE PRESCRIPTION COVERAGE: AGENDA NEGLECT

Adding a drug benefit to Medicare, and helping seniors with the cost of prescription drugs more generally, was not wholly absent from Bush's agenda in 2001. But based on his rhetorical attention and legislative efforts, it was unmistakably a low priority.

On January 29, Bush introduced his "Immediate Helping Hand" prescription drug plan for low-income seniors; knowing it would be poorly received on Capitol Hill, the White House introduced it without fanfare (Carey 2001b). The plan, proposing $48 billion over the next four years to be delivered via block grants to states, was quickly rejected by both Democrats and Republicans in Congress. In his February 27 address to Congress and in his budget proposal, Bush included an $156 billion increase over ten years for Medicare modernization (including the block grant proposal), which he argued would fund a new prescription drug benefit for low-income seniors, though Democrats countered that anything less than $300 billion would indicate a lack of seriousness (CQ Staff 2001). These critiques were reinforced in late March when the Congressional Budget Office released new estimates for adding a prescription drug benefit to Medicare of $1 trillion over the next decade. Representative Billy Tauzin (R-La.) noted, "Everybody knows [Bush's] figure is gone" (Goldreich 2001). Democrats, meanwhile, repeatedly tried to tie the prescription drug proposals to the ongoing tax-cut debate, arguing that Bush's ambitious tax-cut plan might leave little for such health-care reforms. While Democratic and Republican senators continued to identify prescription drugs for seniors as a high legislative priority, offering competing proposals, no bill made it out of committee (Bettelheim 2001).

Bush didn't enter the congressional fray at all again until July, when he announced a set of principles for Medicare reform. A key element of his July proposal was a privately administered drug discount card program to help seniors buy medications at a reduced price, a plan he could implement without congressional approval (Carey 2001a). Within days, the trade associations for independent and chain drugstores filed suit to block the proposal and by September a federal court had blocked the plan on the grounds that the administration might have lacked the authority to create the program without congressional approval or writing a specific regulation (Goldstein 2001).[12]

THE PUBLIC RESPONDS IN 2001

What was the public response to the Bush's early presidential efforts? In March, pollsters began asking about approval of Bush's handling of issues. These responses, broken down by party, are shown in table 6.2 from March through September, along with overall presidential approval.[13]

Bush's overall job approval is relatively high in this early period, as we would expect. Bush's education approval is generally higher than his overall approval, while Social Security approval and approval of prescription drug coverage are generally lower. Approval of Bush's handling of taxes is positive, though markedly below his approval for education and generally lower than his overall numbers, until June and July when the rebate checks from the tax-cut bill started reaching the public. For Social Security, approval quickly falls below 50 percent. Given the primary activity on Social Security during this period involved the president's Social Security Commission, this is hardly surprising. Similarly, for his handling of prescription drug coverage for seniors and the cost of prescription drugs, his approval is comparatively low. Until his July announcement of, and subsequent court battle over, his discount drug card proposal, the public almost certainly did not understand Bush to have acted on the issue.

Bush received strikingly high approval among Republicans. And his overall approval from his co-partisans is consistently higher than approval on these issues; among these, however, Bush is rated most strongly on taxes. The picture is starkly different for Democrats and Independents.

Table 6.2 Issue Approval, by Party Identification

	Percent Approving Bush's Handling of Issue, Overall				
Survey Sponsor	Survey Date (Midpoint)	Presidential Approval	Education Approval	Tax Approval	Soc Sec Approval	Rx Drug Approval
Gallup	3/10/01	60.5	65.9	56.2	50.6	
ABC/WP	4/20/01	64.3	60.5	55.6		
Gallup	4/21/01	62.5	64.0	56.0		
ABC/WP	6/1/01	56.2	56.2	58.8	47.7	
Gallup	7/10/01	58.1	62.5	60.6	48.8	51.4
ABC/WP	7/28/01	58.9	62.9		46.2	40.6
ABC/WP	9/7/01	55.3	60.0		44.3	33.4
	By Party: Republicans				
Survey Sponsor	Survey Date (Midpoint)	Presidential Approval	Education Approval	Tax Approval	Soc Sec Approval	Rx Drug Approval
Gallup	3/10/01	90.6	84.0	85.4	75.1	
ABC/WP	4/20/01	92.9	82.3	83.0		
Gallup	4/21/01	92.0	84.2	85.9		
ABC/WP	6/1/01	86.4	77.2	86.1	75.4	
Gallup	7/10/01	87.2	82.7	86.1	73.0	67.0
ABC/WP	7/28/01	90.9	86.4		75.4	61.5
ABC/WP	9/7/01	86.8	83.3		71.1	52.3
	By Party: Democrats				
Survey Sponsor	Survey Date (Midpoint)	Presidential Approval	Education Approval	Tax Approval	Soc Sec Approval	Rx Drug Approval
Gallup	3/10/01	35.3	49.3	31.4	29.5	
ABC/WP	4/20/01	38.0	39.8	30.5		
Gallup	4/21/01	33.0	43.2	24.2		
ABC/WP	6/1/01	29.2	37.9	35.5	25.9	
Gallup	7/10/01	29.7	42.5	35.8	26.1	36.3
ABC/WP	7/28/01	32.0	43.6		22.6	23.5
ABC/WP	9/7/01	26.9	39.6		20.5	16.3
	By Party: Independents				
Survey Sponsor	Survey Date (Midpoint)	Presidential Approval	Education Approval	Tax Approval	Soc Sec Approval	Rx Drug Approval
Gallup	3/10/01	46.1	65.2	43.8	42.7	
ABC/WP	4/20/01	59.4	61.3	50.9		
Gallup	4/21/01	56.8	59.4	56.3		
ABC/WP	6/1/01	57.8	63.0	46.0	33.3	
Gallup	7/10/01	49.4	58.2	51.9	35.4	45.6
ABC/WP	7/28/01	58.6	60.0		39.0	40.0
ABC/WP	9/7/01	46.3	52.0		31.0	31.7

While Democrats give Bush a generally low approval rating, they rate him higher, begrudgingly, on education and particularly harshly on Social Security. Independents give Bush generally favorable marks overall and especially high marks for education.

EDUCATION: UNCONNECTED AGENDA FOLLOW-THROUGH

Though Bush followed through on his education emphasis, citizens did not, on average, connect the issue to him strongly during the campaign. Agenda accountability would, thus, expect positive evaluations of the issue, but the issue should not be strongly related to his approval as president.

The top panel of figure 6.2 ties together presidential attention to education (represented by the line) with approval of Bush's handling of education by the public (represented by the dots). Key events in the progress of educational reform legislation are also indicated. Again, the heavy attention Bush paid to the issue is evident. And approval of Bush's handling of education is over 60 percent until May, when Bush's attention to education drops off and before any major legislative successes. It rises again after the legislation has passed both houses of Congress and appears headed for final passage. This is among Bush's highest issue evaluations. The public responded to both presidential effort and apparent political success.

The bottom panel of figure 6.2 shows the individual-level *relation* between approval of Bush on education and overall presidential approval (represented, again, by the dots); this shows how heavily education is weighted in forming evaluations of the president.[14] This panel is key to the story. Education approval is consistently and significantly related to overall presidential approval throughout this time period, largely unmoved in any systematic way by either Bush's efforts or his legislative results. But as we will see momentarily, education approval turns out to be one of the weaker predictors of overall approval among the issue approval measures (the effect size ranges between .33 and .40). Given the high approval Bush received for education, he clearly would have benefited from a stronger enduring connection.

TAX CUTS: CONNECTED AGENDA FOLLOW-THROUGH

Tax cuts represent a case of agenda follow-through on an issue that was strongly connected to Bush as a candidate. If the public uses these campaign connections as the basis for expectations of presidential effort, as agenda accountability anticipates, then Bush's performance on taxes should be relatively high and should continue to be strongly related to his overall approval in office.

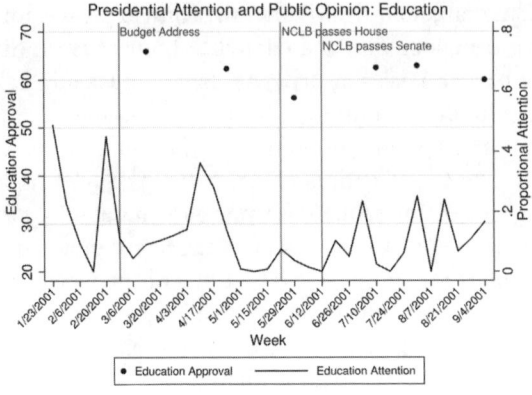

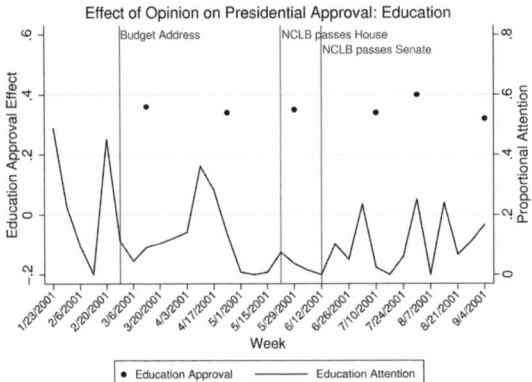

Figure 6.2 Bush and Education

Recall from table 6.2 that approval of how Bush was handling taxes was consistently above 55 percent, though markedly lower than his overall approval until the summer. Tax approval is, as in the figure for education, combined with presidential attention and key legislative events in figure 6.3. Tax cuts received a great deal of rhetorical attention by the president, particularly in the lead up to congressional passage of his signature issue. The top panel, showing the percent approving of Bush's handling of the issue, reiterates the favorable evaluations of Bush on the issue. And tax approval bounces up very modestly after Bush's political success in passing tax cuts in June and once the rebate checks start arriving in July.

The lower panel of figure 6.3 depicts the relationship between individual-level approval of how Bush has handled taxes and overall approval. The effect of tax approval on Bush's overall evaluations is significant, ranging between .38 and .52. The size of this relationship, between tax

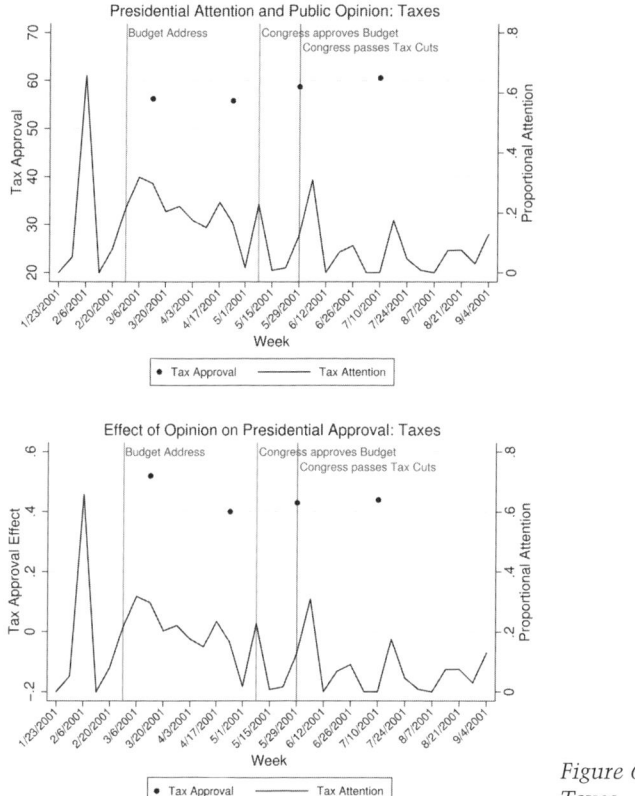

Figure 6.3 Bush and Taxes

approval and Bush approval, also appears modestly responsive to Bush's efforts and political success, declining somewhat as Bush's attention turns to other issues and rising again as the tax cuts become law. Importantly, the connection between taxes and Bush evaluations is consistently strong, and stronger than those between education and Bush evaluations.

SOCIAL SECURITY: CONNECTED AGENDA NEGLECT

Bush paid little attention to Social Security throughout this period and made little effort on behalf of Social Security reform until after his 2004 reelection. Consequently, Social Security provides an example of presidential neglect of a top campaign priority. Agenda accountability predicts that evaluations of Bush on Social Security should be comparatively low. And given the connection forged between Social Security and Bush during the campaign, Social Security should continue to play a notable role in presidential evaluations.

As was evidenced in table 6.2, Social Security provided some of Bush's lowest issue approval numbers, potentially dragging down his overall evaluations. The top panel of figure 6.4 reiterates these conclusions, presenting the slight decline in public approval of Bush's handling of Social Security over time. Further, the figure highlights the near omission of Social Security in his public remarks.

The bottom panel of figure 6.4 shows the connection between approval of Bush's handling of the issue and his overall approval. The impact is consistently strong and positive, with the effect size ranging between .36 and .50, strikingly similar to the effect of tax approval and noticeably stronger than the effect of education approval. The campaign succeeded in connecting Bush to Social Security reform and the connection appears to have endured, though not to Bush's advantage.

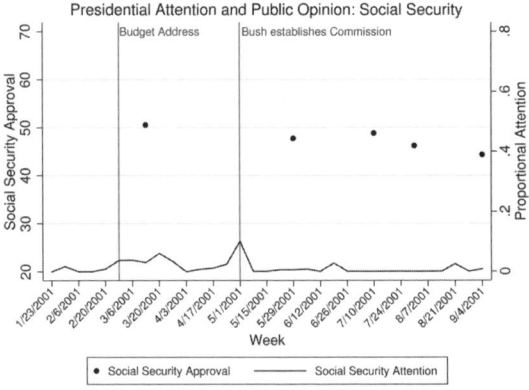

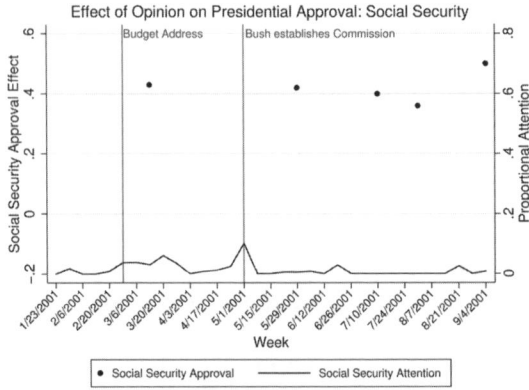

Figure 6.4 Bush and Social Security

MEDICARE PRESCRIPTION COVERAGE: UNCONNECTED AGENDA NEGLECT

Though Bush did not entirely neglect his campaign emphasis on "modernizing" Medicare by adding a prescription drug benefit, the efforts he made on behalf of the proposal were, at best, minimal and relatively quiet. And, of course, health care as an issue evidenced no connection to Bush during the campaign. This, then, is an issue that, though emphasized to a degree in the campaign, was neither connected to the candidate nor followed through in the administration. Evaluations of Bush on the issue are expected to be on the low end, but in the absence of a campaign connection, they should not be strongly tied to presidential popularity.

Though prescription drug coverage provides the fewest data points, as pollsters did not ask about the issue until July, itself a sign of the low position the issue enjoyed on the agenda, figure 6.5 still provides some suggestive evidence. Like Social Security, the almost complete absence of the issue from his rhetorical attention stands out. Aside from a set of remarks over three consecutive days in mid-July, Bush rarely mentions the problem of prescription drug costs and the absence of a prescription plan in Medicare. Though approval of Bush's handling of the issue is respectable when the question was first asked in July.[15] Nonetheless, overall, approval of his handling of prescription drug coverage is relatively low.

Further, the bottom panel of figure 6.5 reveals the weakest connections so far between an issue evaluation and Bush's performance ratings, with effects ranging between .25 and .33. Though Bush's comparative neglect of the issue produces relatively poor evaluations for the issue, these evaluations are not central in the formation of overall presidential performance ratings.

COMPARING ACROSS ISSUES

So far, the issue evaluations and, more importantly, the strength of the connection between these evaluations and presidential evaluations conform to expectations. Bush received relatively high approval for campaign issues on which he followed through—education and taxes—but the issue to which he successfully connected himself in the campaign—taxes—has a somewhat stronger effect on his overall evaluations. Bush received lower issue approval on campaign issues on which he exerted less effort—Social Security and Medicare drug coverage—but the issue that was more strongly connected to his evaluations in the campaign—Social Security—has a notably stronger effect on his performance ratings.

To help put the connection between education, taxes, Social Security,

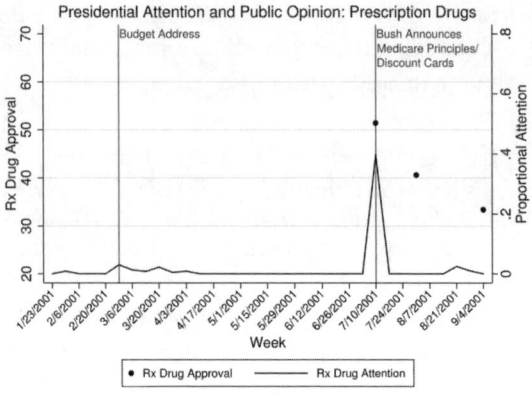

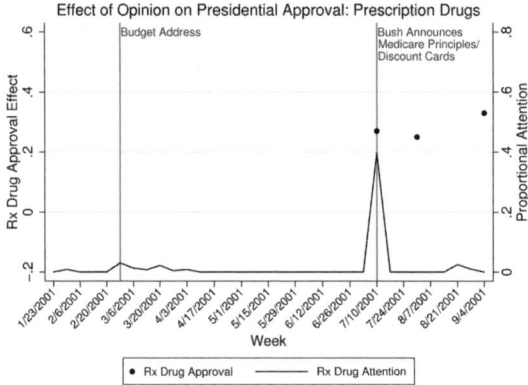

Figure 6.5 Bush and Prescription Drugs

and Medicare and President Bush in greater context, table 6.3 provides the average approval level for all of the issues asked about more than once in the Gallup and ABC/Washington Post surveys used above; the second column provides the average strength of the connection between each issue approval and Bush's overall job approval.

Again, table 6.3 reveals the stronger approval of Bush on education and taxes, the campaign issues for which he successfully followed through,[16] relative to approval on Social Security and prescription drugs. And the stronger effect on presidential approval of the issues that were connected to him in the campaign, taxes and Social Security, is also evident. But how do these compare to other issues?

Starting with issue approval, the issues on which Bush received strong evaluations, comparable to his evaluations for campaign issues he followed through on, are foreign affairs, his defense budget, and the economy. On foreign affairs, Bush enjoyed a successful resolution to his first foreign

Table 6.3 Comparison across Issues: President Bush

	Approval of Issue	Effect on Approval*
Education	61.7	0.35
Taxes	57.4	0.44
Social Security	47.5	0.43
Rx Drugs	41.8	0.28
Economy	54.5	0.50
Foreign Affairs	57.7	0.45
Campaign Finance	39.7	0.31
Environment	45.3	0.37
Energy	42.8	0.39
Federal Budget	51.0	0.50
Defense Budget	56.2	0.37

*Effect of issue approval on presidential approval controlling for partisanship, education, age, and gender.

policy crisis, the Hainan Island incident, in April. A U.S. spy plane had collided with a Chinese fighter jet and made an emergency landing on China's Hainan Island. The twenty-four-member crew was held for ten days before being released after Bush issued a letter of regret for the death of a Chinese fighter pilot. On the economy, when Bush entered office, economic reports showed the economy in its 112th month of expansion. The economy ultimately experienced a slowdown in 2001; indeed, Bush talked up the possibility as a justification for his tax cuts. But it wasn't until November of 2001 that the National Bureau of Economic Research announced a recession had occurred, classifying it as the mildest recession since WWII (Wood 2007). Though these issues did not play a prominent role in the campaign, these are precisely the issues a president is always expected to address. And neither presented a serious challenge in this period, before 9/11. High issue approval is, reasonably enough, largely a function of apparent presidential success.

Of the issues measured, three yield consistently low approval numbers, comparable to those Bush received on campaign issues his administration neglected: campaign finance, the environment, and energy. Of these, the White House granted only energy notable attention, and then under the auspices of Vice President Cheney's notoriously secretive task force. Campaign finance reform was not seriously on the president's agenda. And Bush came in for some early criticism for his actions regarding the environment in March when he reneged on a campaign promise to impose mandatory emissions reductions for carbon dioxide on the nation's power plants and withdrew U.S. support for the global Kyoto treaty to reduce greenhouse gas emissions. Put another way, his low approval on Social

Security and prescription drug coverage rivals that of an issue on which he openly broke a campaign pledge and defied popular consensus.

Turning to how strongly connected the issues are to approval of Bush, shown in the second column, the weight of tax approval and Social Security approval, the campaign-connected issues, rivals that of economic and foreign affairs approval, the two issues generally believed to be the strongest predictors of approval. Indeed, other than the economy and foreign affairs, the only issue to consistently relate more strongly to approval of Bush is the budget, an issue intimately connected to the tax cuts both legislatively and in Bush's presidential rhetoric. The effect of education and Medicare reform, meanwhile, are more akin to that of campaign finance reform and the environment, issues not widely connected to George W. Bush in the campaign or after. All of the issues are, of course, somewhat connected to overall approval. Given the similarity of the questions and their adjacent position in the series of questions asked of respondents in public opinion polls, it could hardly be otherwise. But job approval is not equally dependent on all of them. Conventional wisdom would find it surprising that in the face of his heavy rhetoric, effort, and eventual success, education never became as potent in shaping the ongoing referendum of Bush as taxes and Social Security. The agenda accountability process, though, accounts for this. While effort or neglect, and success or failure, have some impact on issue approval levels, they have little to do with whether the issue approval matters for presidential support.

Conclusion

Bush's campaign priorities were largely reflected in his early behavior as president. Education, Bush's top priority in the campaign, continued to be one of his top priorities in his administration, itself a reassuring result. And though his campaign managed to neutralize the previously negative connection between education and the Republican candidate, the failure to forge a positive connection during the campaign haunted the early administration. Bush behaved as if he would be rewarded for fulfilling a campaign priority—working to maintain bipartisan support by dropping the most divisive issue early on. That the bill survived the shakeup in the Senate and the more jarring terrorist attacks is testament, in part, to the priorities Bush set in motion. Yet the reward was relatively modest, at least compared to other big campaign issues or the standbys like the economy and foreign affairs. The lack of a positive connection between Bush and education in the public mind limited the benefit of positive accountability judgments.

Bush also followed through on tax cuts. Tax cuts, though, represented an issue that the public already connected to Republican candidates. And Bush was able to reinforce and strengthen that connection to himself in the campaign. As a result, approval of Bush's handling of tax cuts exerted a stronger positive pull on his overall job rating. His follow-through on this campaign priority benefited Bush with regard to public prestige.

Bush also highlighted Social Security in his campaign, and citizens made the connection between Bush and Social Security. But this was an issue for which Bush did not enjoy the clear political will of the Congress to pursue, and he did not seriously pursue it. The White House neglect of Social Security reform led to some of Bush's lowest issue approval numbers. Given the strong connection forged between Bush and Social Security during the campaign, these numbers pulled his overall approval down more than his positive education approval numbers pulled them up. This issue connection appears to have endured; the public did hold Bush negatively accountable for failing to promote or produce reform on the issue.

And while Bush also put off Medicare reform and prescription drug coverage, these health issues did not make much of an impression on the public during the campaign. His subsequent delay on the issue did not, as a consequence, produce a notable sanction with respect to his public support.

The pattern across these issues strongly supports the overall argument of agenda accountability. The issues ignored in the campaign, barring the economy and foreign affairs, are less strongly related to presidential approval afterwards. The issues emphasized in the campaign, heard by the public and connected in the minds of citizens to the future president, are more strongly related to presidential approval afterwards, even rivaling the long-standing connections, almost certainly chronically accessible, between the president and economic and international considerations. Still, President Bush's early administration represents only one case, and necessarily provides only a handful of agenda outcomes. The next chapter looks to the first years of President Clinton's and President Obama's administrations to generalize and expand the argument.

7 Beyond the Voting Booth

CLINTON 1993 AND OBAMA 2009

Bush's early presidency allowed us to examine the consequences for accountability of three of the four campaign agenda outcomes—agenda follow-through (education and tax cuts), agenda neglect (Social Security), and consistent neglect, or de-emphasis in both the campaign and administration. To further generalize the expectations of agenda accountability and to add some cases in the as-yet-unobserved outcome, agenda interruption, this chapter turns to a similar, though necessarily briefer, examination of President Clinton's and President Obama's first years in office.

Clinton and Obama offer the opportunity to consider the theory for Democratic presidents and in the context of negative economic conditions. Although Bush, prior to September 11, did not tackle issues that were not key in his campaign, both Clinton and Obama felt compelled by circumstance to work on issues beyond the problems prominently identified in their campaigns.

In addition, these cases provide variation in the congressional context—the party in power, the polarization of the parties, and the behavior of the out-party—which gives us some purchase on whether these impact public accountability of the president.

Clinton's Campaign and Accountability

Clinton's first year in office affords multiple interesting issues for comparison. Among his campaign issues, he attempted to follow through on jobs and the economy and on health care. On the first, he met with early failure; on the second, he began late in the year and as the year ended, success still looked possible. Clinton dropped his middle-class tax-cut proposal immediately, offering another example of agenda neglect, albeit on an issue not traditionally connected to Democrats. And importantly, Clinton's first year includes two cases of agenda interruption, with the budget deficit and NAFTA, coupled with notable policy success. This provides some leverage on disentangling agenda accountability from an alternative explanation that citizens simply reward success.

Recall from chapter 2 that Bill Clinton's most repeated advertising emphasis centered on the need to create jobs (mentioned in 71 percent of his ads) and his proposed middle-class tax cut (63 percent). In addition, candidate Clinton highlighted problems in the overall economy (33 percent) and the growing problems of the health-care system (29 percent). These issues comprise the bulk of his campaign themes, captured as well in the now-famous slogan in his campaign headquarters: "Change vs. more of the same; The economy, stupid; Don't forget health care."

The public opinion data needed to determine whether citizens actually heard these themes and connected them to Clinton do not exist, but based on the findings from the 2000 campaign, it is safe to say that jobs, a traditionally Democratically owned issue, was more readily connected to Clinton than were taxes. Indeed, reports at the time suggest that the White House believed voters had not taken the tax-cut promise seriously (see, for example, Kelly 1993). Health care, though not as evident in the advertising focus, was central to Clinton's campaign. When talking about his priorities, he routinely listed health care—reining in costs, increasing access—among his top three agenda items (see, for example, Ifill 1992).

Clinton's biggest achievements during his first year came on deficit reduction and the passage of NAFTA, neither a major part of his campaign. Clinton spent a great deal of effort on his economic stimulus plan to spur job growth in the early part of the year, though this was ultimately defeated by Republicans in the Senate. His efforts on health care began late in the year, beginning with his September address on health care, though the Health Care Task Force, chaired by Hillary Clinton, spent most of the year quietly putting together a detailed program. And the middle-class tax cut was dropped entirely from Clinton's legislative and rhetorical efforts.

The path of Clinton's attention on these themes—those on which he attempted to follow-through, jobs and health care; those he neglected, taxes; and those that arose after the campaign, the budget deficit and trade—are shown in figure 7.1 in order from the most frequently referenced to the least.[1]

After a brief rhetorical flirtation with health care, Clinton's top focus is on jobs. But after the economic stimulus package fails, the budget deficit receives more attention in Clinton's public remarks. Health care is, quite pronouncedly, the top theme after the deficit plan is signed into law; and NAFTA rises to the fore at the end of the year in the run-up to the bill's passage. Clinton's rhetoric, as we'll see in the next section, follows his legislative efforts quite well. What remains to be seen is how his attention or neglect on problems highlighted or not by his campaign impacts his evaluations

CLINTON AND THE ECONOMY:
FROM FOLLOW-THROUGH TO INTERRUPTION

As president, Clinton was criticized for taking on too much while understanding the ways of Washington too little. This is one explanation for his early "gays-in-the-military" distraction, though for the most part this issue was resolved during the presidential transition. For Clinton, the bigger distraction from the campaign agenda was the budget deficit. In his speeches early on he would repeatedly note that, after the election, the government revised the deficit figures up by as much as $50 billion

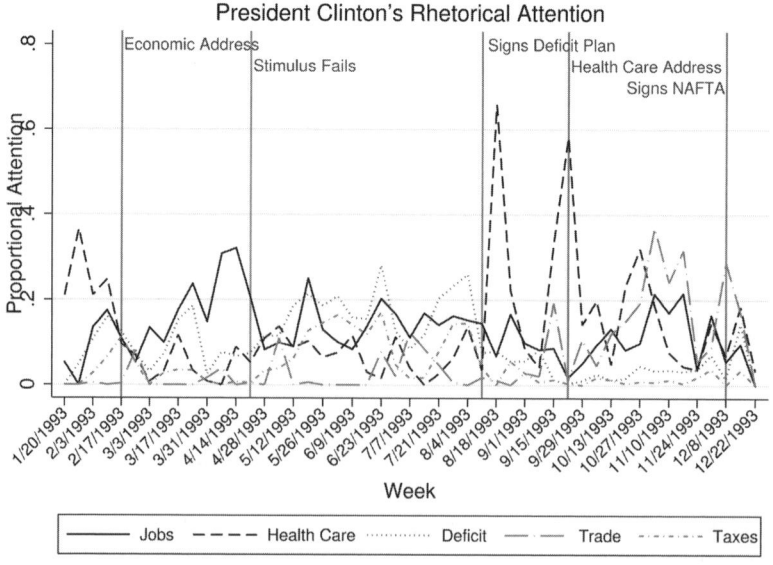

Figure 7.1 Attention to Campaign Priorities: President Clinton

per year from the estimates in August 1992. When Clinton entered office, the federal debt as a percentage of GDP and the federal deficit were at highs not seen since the government was paying down the debt for WWII (Wood 2007). The larger-than-anticipated deficit compelled the Clinton team to ax the promised middle-class tax cuts, though Clinton continued to push for an expansion of the Earned Income Tax Credit to aid lower-income families.

On February 17, Clinton delivered a major economic address to Congress outlining the three pieces of his economic plan: a short-term stimulus package of $30 billion over two years to bolster job creation; nearly $160 billion in investment spending over four years to correct the "investment deficit" in infrastructure, education, child care, job training, and health-care spending; and the plan to reduce the budget deficit by almost $500 billion over four years, half from spending cuts and half from tax increases (Hager 1993).

Clinton achieved an early victory on his economic program as the House and Senate passed budget resolutions in March that left Clinton's proposed budget largely intact. Both versions included deficit reduction targets of over $500 billion in five years, achieved through additional revenue from tax increases on top income earners and corporations and a new broad-based energy tax, and reduced spending on defense and entitlements (Pianin 1993b, 1993c).[2] This victory, though, was quickly overshadowed by the defeat of Clinton's economic stimulus package. Although the House had passed the package in March, alongside the budget resolution, the Senate Republicans successfully filibustered the bill, offering Clinton his first major legislative failure as president on April 21. Congress, instead, passed an extension of unemployment benefits, one small part of the overall stimulus proposal.

Clinton's battle with Congress over his budget and economic policies would continue as Congress began writing the legislative details of the Omnibus Budget Reconciliation Act. After the economic stimulus package failed, Clinton's focus shifted from the short-term recovery efforts of stimulus spending to long-term recovery efforts of deficit reduction. The House initially passed the budget reconciliation bill on May 26 by a narrow margin of 219–213. It contained a combination of tax increases and spending cuts to reduce the budget deficit. The Senate passed a version a month later, but only with the removal of the controversial energy tax and with Vice President Gore casting the tie-breaking vote. To pass the final version of the bill, Clinton had to forgo large chunks of his investment spending plans for economic growth, accept a gas tax he had argued against in the campaign, and accept deeper cuts in Medicare spending.

Even then, it was a close call: the bill passed the House on August 5 by a vote of 218–216; it passed the Senate on August 6 by a vote of 51–50, with the support of no Republicans and with Gore again breaking the tie. The bill, signed into law on August 10, raised the tax rate for wealthy Americans and corporations and provided significant tax credits for the working poor. Congress projected the bill would achieve $496 billion in deficit savings over five years. In short, Clinton won some, mostly on the deficit, and lost some, mostly on investments for economic growth.

The public response, along with the path of Clinton's attention to jobs and the economy, are shown in figure 7.2. Like the figures in chapter 6, the line represents the proportional attention Clinton paid to the issue in his public remarks. The percent approving of Clinton's handling of an issue is shown by the circles in the top panel[3] and the connection between issue approval and Clinton's overall ratings are shown by the circles in the bottom panel.[4]

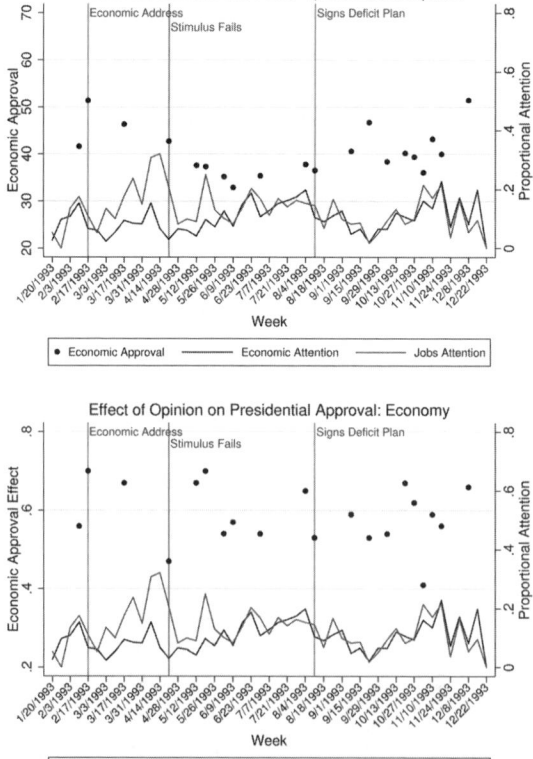

Figure 7.2 Clinton and Jobs/Economy

Approval of Clinton's handling of the economy trends quite clearly down after peaking upon Clinton's major economic address to Congress, reaching its nadir about six weeks after the Senate handed Clinton his first major legislative defeat with the filibuster of the economic stimulus bill. The passage of Clinton's budget bill marks a rise in Clinton's economic approval. Here the trend seems to move, reasonably enough, in response to Clinton's policy failures and successes. Clinton's consistent attention to jobs and the economy, on its own, does not bolster his economic approval.

In contrast to his economic approval rates, the impact of economic approval on Clinton's performance ratings demonstrate no obvious trend during his first year in office, hovering around a mean of .59 (see the lower panel of figure 7.2). Economic approval has the biggest effect on Clinton's ratings compared to any other issue asked about. The consistency of economic accountability is hardly surprising; nevertheless, an effect that declined quickly or as a function of presidential failure would have undermined the theory of agenda accountability. Interestingly, the effect of economic approval on President Bush's performance ratings during the first year, which were also reasonably stable, averaged .50. The noticeably stronger impact of economic approval on Clinton's ratings, compared to Bush's, also works in favor of agenda accountability and the flexibility of expectations established during the campaign.

After the failure of the economic stimulus plan, Clinton began to emphasize his deficit-cutting budget plan. The increasing attention to the deficit is visible in figure 7.3. References to the deficit averaged 13 percent before the stimulus bill was defeated, but received, on average, 26 percent of his paragraphic attention between this legislative defeat and the successful passage of the deficit plan. After this, attention to the deficit trails off, averaging only 6 percent of references through the end of the year.

The top panel of figure 7.3 reveals the relatively low ratings the public gives Clinton on his handling of the budget deficit. Deficit approval shows no obvious trend in response to events or Clinton's attention in public remarks. The public's failure to recognize his remarkable success on the issue is troubling. Perhaps an emphasis on the issue in the campaign would have improved his credit-taking credibility. Or perhaps the clear resistance by Republicans served to muddle the signal that passage of the deficit-reduction package sent to the public.

The effect of deficit approval on Clinton's overall support, though, does appear to follow Clinton's attention to the matter. The average effect of deficit approval on job approval is .48, but the size of the effect is a bit higher during the period in which Clinton was campaigning for his

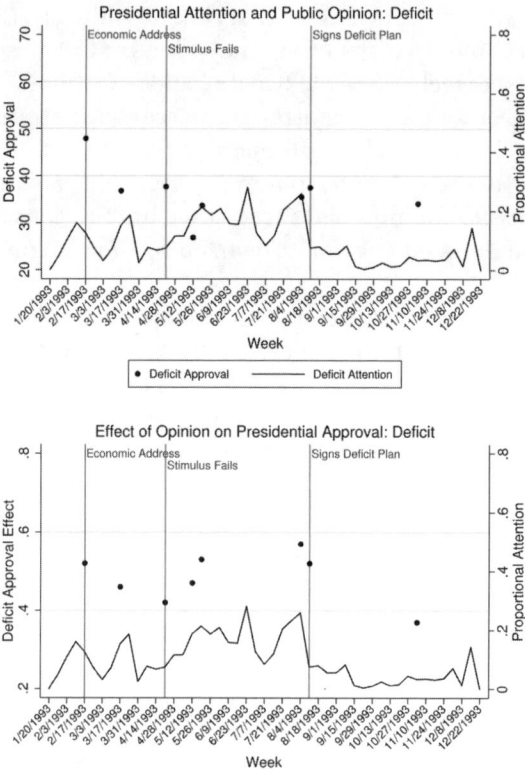

Figure 7.3 Clinton and the Budget Deficit

deficit plan. And the effect size drops to its lowest point after the budget battle was over and as the deficit receded in Clinton's public remarks.

The impact of deficit approval, while stronger than expected given Clinton's inattention to the issue during the campaign, is noticeably weaker than the impact of economic approval on overall evaluations. This case suggests that problems not connected to the candidate during the campaign can become a moderately important basis of evaluations, though the effect looks to be more transitory and dependent on ongoing presidential attention. The clarity afforded in the campaign may assist in promoting the longer-term connections that can benefit (or harm) a president.

CLINTON AND TAXES: AGENDA NEGLECT

Because jobs, the deficit, and taxes were not fully separable in Clinton's rhetoric during his first year—all strands of Clinton's key economic proposals—we'll turn next to Clinton's treatment of taxes and the consequences for his evaluations.

Despite his commitment during the campaign to a middle-class tax cut, after his postvictory economic summits and briefings he abandoned any hope of fulfilling this part of his agenda. The budget he signed in August raised income taxes for the top 1.2 percent of taxpayers, increased taxation of Social Security benefits for the top 12.8 percent of recipients, and expanded wage subsidies for the working poor. In that sense, then, the president fulfilled in part the spirit, if not the letter, of his commitment to shift more of the tax burden to the wealthy. But there was no tax relief for the middle-class.

His attention to taxes, limited as it was, generally emphasized his continued desire to expand the Earned Income Tax Credit for the working poor and his defense of raising taxes on wealthier Americans. Figure 7.4 shows the trend in Clinton's rhetorical attention to tax policy, most of which occurred while campaigning for his budget proposal.

In addition, the top panel of figure 7.4 provides the public's approval of Clinton's handling of the issue. Notably, pollsters rarely asked about approval of Clinton's handling of taxes, underscoring the degree to which the issue fell quickly from the agenda. Nonetheless, based on the points when this question was asked, approval of Clinton's handling of taxes is consistently low, averaging 32 percent. Further, the bottom half of the figure shows tax approval was only modestly related to his overall evaluations, averaging an effect size of .38. Relative to the economy and the deficit, taxes evidence a much weaker connection to President Clinton.

CLINTON AND HEALTH CARE: LATE FOLLOW-THROUGH

The economy in its various forms—stimulus spending, jobs, deficit reduction—had occupied the president for the majority of his first year in office. By all accounts, Clinton considered health care, too, primarily an economic issue, a needed step to promoting economic growth and reducing the budget deficit (Jacobs and Shapiro 2000).

As in the case of Clinton's economic plan, the president's approach was to present a detailed policy proposal to Congress. Towards that end, Clinton established the Health Care Task Force on January 25 and named Hillary Clinton to head it, signaling that health care would remain a high priority for his administration. Though the task force ballooned to include 630 experts, and the process took far longer than the 100 days Clinton had promised, the task force itself was primarily a political tool to help the president build credibility and consensus for his preferred plan (Jacobs

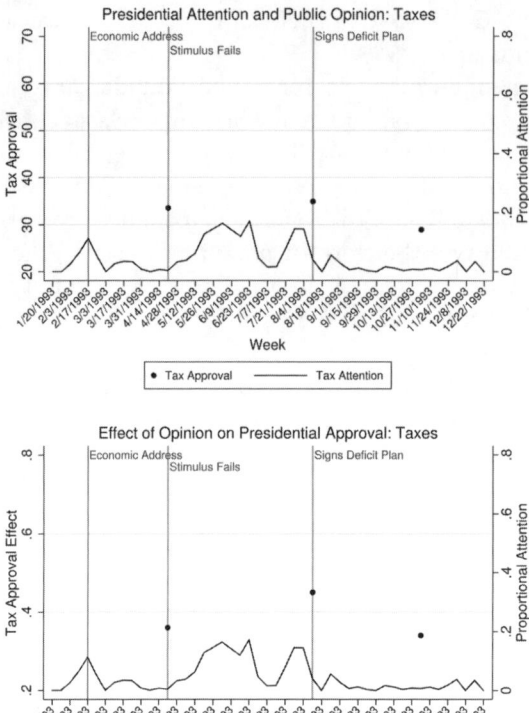

Figure 7.4 Clinton and Taxes

and Shapiro 2000). Clinton's intent, ultimately unsuccessful, was to sell the public on his plan in order to solidify the support of Congress rather than to secure the investment of legislators by letting them collaborate on the details or take the lead in drafting the legislation.

Clinton made his opening pitch for his health-care proposal in an address to the nation's governors on August 16. From here until the end of the year, he emphasized health care in his public remarks more than any other issue. Clinton's rhetorical attention to health care is provided in figure 7.5. His attention peaks again with his address to the nation on September 22 to detail and promote his plan, and once again when he submits the draft of the legislation to Congress on October 27.

Turning to the top panel of figure 7.5, Clinton's delay in addressing health care results in a drop in the public's approval of his handling of health care. Health-care approval, though, makes a noticeable improve-

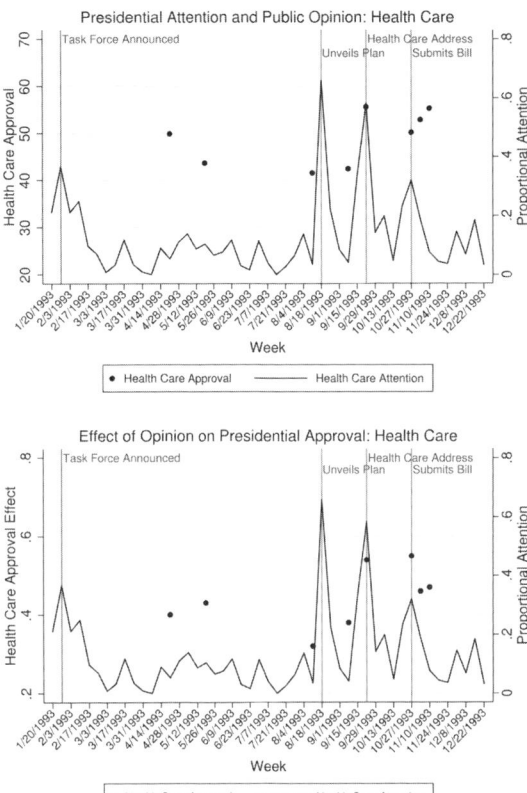

Figure 7.5 Clinton and Health Care

ment right after his address to the nation, once he starts attending to the issue, and remains strong in subsequent polls.

Additionally, and importantly, the effect of health-care approval on Clinton's overall approval, shown in the lower panel of figure 7.5, also increases markedly at this point. The mean effect before the address is .38 while the mean effect after the address is .51, a statistically significant increase ($F = 13.9$, $p < .01$). This is the first instance of a significant change in the impact of an issue consideration on presidential approval. While I anticipated that health care would be strongly connected to Clinton from the outset, it was only weakly related to evaluations of the president initially. Health care only becomes strongly reconnected to Clinton once he actively begins working on it, an example perhaps of how an issue primed repeatedly in the campaign can be more readily resurfaced later on. Nonetheless, given the centrality of the issue in his overall campaign, agenda accountability would predict a more consistent connection, one less dependent on this presidential nudge. In this sense, the effect of health care resembles that of the budget deficit: Both offer the possibility of malleability of the issue connections even after the campaign.

CLINTON AND TRADE: AGENDA INTERRUPTION

President Clinton inherited an already negotiated North American Free Trade Agreement from his predecessor, President George H. W. Bush. The pact established a barrier-free trading relationship with Mexico and Canada. As a candidate, Clinton had criticized the lack of labor and environmental protections in the agreement. As president, Clinton vowed not to submit NAFTA without additional side agreements to add these protections.

Clinton's U.S. trade representative, Mickey Kantor, successfully negotiated the side agreements and, on August 13, the administration announced the main elements of the accords to protect workers' rights and the environment. Clinton signed three side agreements—applying trade sanctions to any of the countries that failed to enforce their own environmental laws; ensuring Mexico enforced its worker health and safety laws, child labor laws, and minimum wage laws; and protecting domestic industries against unforeseen surges in exports from the other trading partners—on September 14 and forwarded the pact to Congress. Three former presidents—Gerald Ford, Jimmy Carter, and George Bush—attended the signing ceremony to support the effort. In Congress, he faced opposition from two thirds of the Democratic leadership in the House, Majority Leader Richard Gephardt, and Majority Whip David Bonior. Further complicating Clinton's push for NAFTA was Ross Perot, still a force after his remarkable third-party showing in the 1992 election, who was traveling the country hosting anti-NAFTA rallies.

In mid-October, Clinton unleashed a flurry of activity in support of NAFTA—announcing a program to retrain workers who lose their jobs to Mexico, detailing a plan to clean up pollution on the Mexican border, hosting a bazaar to highlight the benefits of free trade on the White House lawn, and most importantly, inviting groups of House members to the White House for a more personal touch (Cloud 1993).

After an uphill battle with the House, Clinton ultimately secured passage of NAFTA on November 17 by a vote of 234–200; the majority of the support, 132 votes, came from Republicans. The Senate followed suit on November 20, passing the bill by 61–38, again with the majority of support coming from Republicans (44 votes). On December 8, Clinton signed the trade agreement into law. Along with the budget deficit plan, NAFTA was the second big-ticket win of the Clinton presidency.

Clinton's burst of rhetorical effort on trade policy, particularly in October and November, is clearly visible in figure 7.6. Despite the significance of the legislative success for his administration, approval of Clinton's handling of trade policy is never especially high, generally hovering below 40 percent. This mirrors, in many respects, the public's response to the budget deficit, suggesting again the work the campaign repetition may be doing in setting up successful presidential credit-taking.

More pointedly, of the issues considered so far, Clinton's handling of trade is the least strongly related to his overall evaluations, averaging an effect size of .32. Given trade was not one of Clinton's key campaign issues, the limited impact it has on his performance ratings is not surprising. And in this case, at least, despite the brief prominence of trade on Clinton's legislative and rhetorical agenda, the salience of the issue never

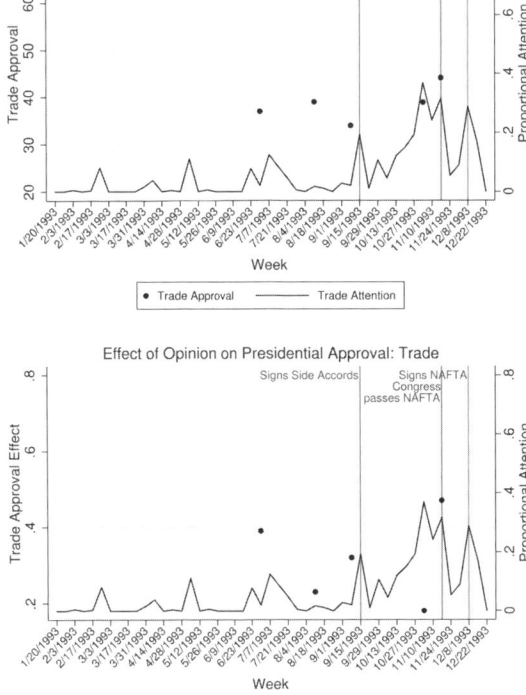

Figure 7.6 Clinton and Trade

discernibly increased, denying President Clinton a significant boost, on this basis, in his overall popularity.

CLINTON IN 1993: INTERRUPTED FOLLOW-THROUGH

The public responds to Clinton's efforts and neglect on his campaign issues—jobs and the economy, health care, and taxes—largely as expected. Clinton attempted to follow through by providing a short-term economic stimulus, and failed. The public's approval of Clinton's handling of the economy declines in response. After successfully seeing his deficit-reduction proposals become law, the public's evaluation of Clinton on the issue improves. And throughout, this key campaign agenda item remains strongly connected to evaluations of Clinton's overall performance.

Clinton dropped his middle-class tax-cut proposals in response to new economic forecasts. The public's evaluation of Clinton on taxes is, in response to this neglect, quite low. But this issue consideration only modestly impacts his performance ratings. Perhaps, like Gore in 2000 and as his team believed at the time, tax cuts did not become positively connected to evaluations of Clinton as a candidate. Surely he would be starting at a disadvantage on the issue, though without the appropriate survey data to ascertain the development of the connections in the campaign, we can only speculate.

Clinton's efforts on health care were repeatedly delayed as he prioritized other items in the agenda sequence, and the public's evaluation of his handling of the issue suffered as a result. But health-care approval picked up when he began to actively follow through on the issue. The public responded to his apparent efforts. For this issue, though, the strength of the connection to overall presidential popularity moves with presidential attention and effort. The trend in the impact of health care suggests the public needed to be nudged to remember the connection between Clinton and health care; but there's no question that once Clinton started acting on the issue, approval of health care becomes particularly strongly related to evaluations of Clinton's job performance. Given the relatively positive perception of Clinton's performance on the issue, the impact of health care worked to boost Clinton's evaluations in the latter half of 1993. Again, without knowing with certainty that the public connected the issue to Clinton in the campaign, interpretation must be speculative. At best, this seems to represent a more tentative connection in the public's mind and suggests that expectations of presidential problem-solving can move, at least on the margins, in the administration as well.

Clinton provides some enlightening examples of agenda interruption with the budget deficit and trade. On both issues, he met with success, but for neither did the public respond with higher levels of approval of his handling of these issues. For trade, the connection to his public support is weak; while he doesn't benefit from his policy success on NAFTA, he doesn't really suffer for it either. On the budget deficit, though, the connection to his public support is surprisingly strong. The deficit in Clinton's rhetoric and in the minds of citizens is closely tied to the economy.[5] In one sense, then, this isn't an entirely new issue for Clinton. But reducing the budget deficit was not any sort of priority for Clinton as a candidate. And the dynamics of the deficit's effect on approval of Clinton suggest the issue became a key factor in his evaluations only temporarily, while the issue was high on the government agenda. Again, the public's expectations and the president's dimensions of accountability may be open to some temporary influence. The lack of issue approval for the deficit, though, makes this connection disadvantageous for Clinton. What's most interesting about these cases of agenda interruption may well be the president's inability to attain credit via increased issue approval.

To help put the connection between these issues and President Clinton in a broader context, table 7.1 provides the average approval level and the average magnitude of the relationship between issue approval and Clinton's evaluations for a wider variety of the issues asked about in the surveys used above; the table demarcates the issues that were prominent in Clinton's campaign, those that were added to Clinton's

Table 7.1 Comparison across Issues: President Clinton

	Effect on Approval*	Approval of Issue	Rhetorical Effort (1993)
Campaign Issues			
Economy/Jobs	0.59	40.3	12.9
Health Care	0.44	48.9	12.9
Taxes	0.38	32.4	4.3
New Issues			
Budget Deficit	0.49	36.2	9.6
Trade	0.32	38.6	6.2
Nonissues			
Foreign Policy	0.38	44.1	6.5
Education	0.28	50.2	4.2
Environment	0.25	56.9	<2.0
Gay Rights	0.25	37.1	<2.0
Crime	0.25	37.3	4.1
Immigration	0.17	33.3	<2.0

*Effect of issue approval on presidential approval controlling for partisanship, education, age, and gender.

agenda during his first year in office, and issues that were never high on Clinton's priority list either in the campaign or his early administration. As well, the table provides the average percent of paragraphs (rhetorical effort) in the president's public remarks that referenced each issue during the first year.

The economy is the issue most strongly related to Clinton's evaluations, an important if not surprising confirmation of the enduring connection between the issue repeated most often in Clinton's campaign and his administration. The economy seems a likely candidate for a chronically accessible presidential consideration, but the stronger connection between the economy and Clinton, relative to Bush, also suggests there is room to create a stronger association between the issue and the president via the campaign emphasis. The budget deficit is the next most strongly connected issue to Clinton, followed closely by health care.

The fourth most important issue in evaluating Clinton was taxes, equal in effect with foreign policy. Despite his neglect of taxes, evident in the especially low approval of his handling of the issue, the issue remains modestly connected to him and more closely tied to Clinton than the remaining issues that were not a central part of his campaign. Still, this represents the weakest effect among the campaign issues.

The remaining issues have a weaker impact on Clinton's evaluations. Trade is slightly more closely connected to Clinton's overall approval than the issues that were not part of the campaign or the first year of his presidency, indicating some room for presidents to add agenda expectations while in office. Nevertheless, the broad pattern is one of stronger connections between issue approval and evaluations of Clinton for issues that were highlighted in Clinton's campaign agenda, and notably weaker connections between issue approval and evaluations of Clinton for noncampaign issues. The key exception is the deficit, an issue that rose in rhetorical prominence and in the impact on Clinton's evaluations over the summer of 1993. The deficit was more closely tied to economic evaluations than the Clinton team understood at the time; unfortunately, the public did not fully recognize the work Clinton was doing to bring the deficit under control.

These patterns of approval and connection do not appear to be purely a function of presidential success; if they were, Clinton would have received a greater reward for NAFTA and deficit reduction, his two notable policy wins. Instead, the campaign appears to be doing some important, and generally ignored, work in setting up the early problem-solving expectations of the president.

Obama's Campaign and Accountability

President Obama's first year contributes additional examples of agenda follow through, with his response to jobs, taxes, health care, and energy. While the first three were Obama's most repeated campaign themes, energy was evident in the campaign agenda but not as heavily emphasized, and thus, serves as an example of a midlevel agenda item. Obama also adds another case of agenda interruption with the banking crisis. Though this arose during the election and appeared to be a game-changing event, it did not receive the repeated attention by the candidates that the priority issues did, so is unlikely to be understood as a top goal of the president.

Barack Obama's campaign advertising most frequently referenced taxes (61 percent), in particular his support for middle-class tax cuts and McCain's support for tax cuts for the wealthy; the need to finally fix health care (36 percent); and rising unemployment (36 percent). The similarities between the campaign agendas of Clinton and Obama allow for additional useful comparisons.

Of course, without survey data on what citizens hear from the campaign and how their issue priorities connect to the candidates, we cannot say with certainty which issues became identified with Obama. Nevertheless, jobs and the economy are surely among the problems citizens most expected Obama to tackle, given the already established link between unemployment and Democrats and the tendency to prioritize economic issues during times of crisis. In addition, health-care reform is a likely candidate for the expectations of Obama developed during the campaign. Tax cuts, as before, may be harder for Democratic candidates to convince the public to take as seriously, though Clinton's experience suggests connections between a Democratic president and taxes can be made, if not strongly.

Another issue worth considering is energy, which Obama identified as an agenda item—creating green energy jobs, leading the world in the development of green technology. Though the issue was raised in only 13 percent of Obama's ad airings, it was an issue often paired with jobs and economic growth. Energy allows, as well, for another source of variation—the moderately emphasized campaign issue. The final issue dealt with here is the banking crisis. Because the financial crisis occurred so late in the campaign and did not receive sustained treatment by the candidates, solving the banking problem may not have become firmly identified with Obama. The severity of the crisis, the volume with which it was addressed in the media, and the novelty of the issue brought it to the public's agenda; the complexity of the issue and the candidate's decisions not to single it out in the campaign should have inhibited strong connections to the new president.

Obama's chief achievement in his first year was the passage of his economic stimulus package, the American Recovery and Reinvestment Act of 2009, signed into law on February 17, barely a month into his administration. The ARRA clearly followed through on his campaign focus on job creation and taxes. The White House reports that almost two million jobs were saved or created by the recovery package (Council of Economic Advisors 2010), an estimate about which independent economic experts agree (Leonhardt 2010). And $288 billion of the $787 billion package was targeted for tax cuts.

A week later, in his budget address to Congress on February 24, Obama laid out his agenda and its sequence: job creation, touting the promise of his recently passed recovery bill; resolving the credit crisis and restarting lending; and investments in clean energy, health-care reform, and expanding access to education. By the end of 2009, a version of health-care reform had passed both houses of Congress, and the prospects for passage seemed optimistic.

The trend in Obama's rhetorical attention on these themes—those on which he attempted to follow through (economic stimulus, tax cuts, and health care) and those that played less-prominent roles in the campaign (the financial crisis and energy conservation)—are shown in figure 7.7, again in order from the most frequently referenced to the least.

Health care stands out as one of the most prominent issues in President Obama's public remarks, particularly during the summer. The next most highly featured issue is unemployment and job creation, which receives a steady flow of attention. Energy and the bank crisis also receive a stable, though smaller, stream of rhetorical treatment, while tax cuts and taxes receive mostly passing reference, despite the record tax cuts passed as part of ARRA. How do these issues impact presidential approval, and what difference does presidential attention and achievement have on these effects? These are the questions to which we now turn.

OBAMA AND JOBS/ECONOMY: QUICK FOLLOW-THROUGH

On January 8, during the transition, Obama outlined some of the details of his American Recovery and Reinvestment Plan in a speech at George Mason University. He began meeting with lawmakers on the hill, Democrats and Republicans, the following week to push his proposals for infrastructure spending, tax cuts, and aid to the states (Clarke and Schatz

Beyond the Voting Booth: Clinton 1993 and Obama 2009 131

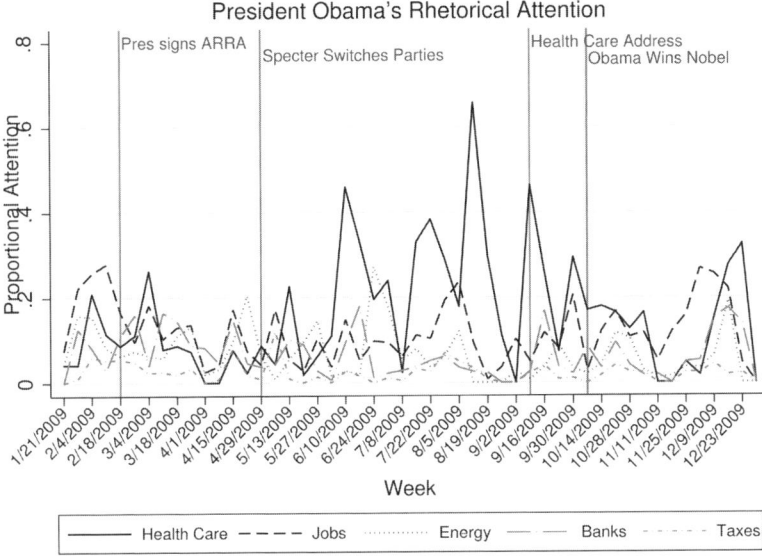

Figure 7.7 *Attention to Campaign Priorities: President Obama*

2009). In an effort to appeal to Republicans, the plan included expanded tax cuts for businesses. Nevertheless, only three Republicans voted for the plan,[6] which passed both houses of Congress on February 13, 2009. The bill, allocating $787 billion over the next two years to stimulate the flagging economy, was largely seen as a victory for Obama, despite criticism from the left that it was too small and criticism from the right that it was too big. Though he failed to secure the bipartisan support he had sought, he achieved significant short-term tax cuts targeted toward the middle class along with spending aimed at retaining and creating jobs.

Obama sought new solutions to the enduring problem of unemployment at the end of 2009, as unemployment rates hovered near 10 percent. Obama's proposals for additional tax breaks and spending, set forth in a December 8 address on the economy, largely built upon the February economic stimulus bill. The House narrowly passed a new jobs bill on December 16 (217–212), with all Republican members voting in opposition (Koss 2009).

Obama's attention to jobs and the economy, shown in figure 7.8, dips very slightly during the summer but never really stalls. Approval of his handling of the economy, shown in the top panel, however, drops below 50 percent in June, well before his overall evaluations do. Given his very early success in seeing his economic stimulus package become

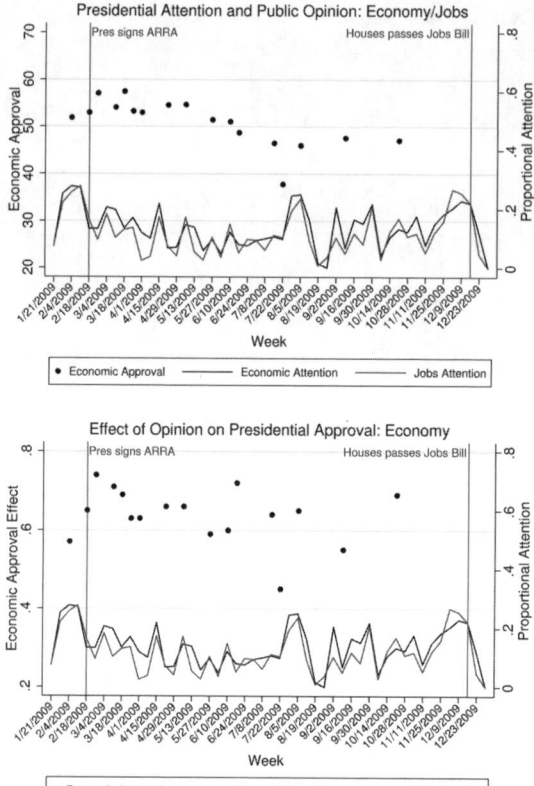

Figure 7.8 Obama and Jobs/Economy

law, perhaps the public expected equally rapid and drastic results. Certainly, the rising unemployment numbers did Obama no good. And the Republican criticism of the bill that continued throughout the year, in particular the claim that the bill had no effect on jobs (Milbank 2010), contrary to almost all independent economic assessments, made credit for staving off a worse economic crisis harder for Obama to attain.

The impact of economic evaluations on Obama's overall ratings, however, is considerably more stable. A glance at the lower panel of figure 7.8 suggests the impact of the economy could be declining, but there is no statistically discernible difference between the average effect before and after economic approval began to decline. Overall, the economy is very strongly tied to Obama's evaluations and does not move in accord with the president's rhetorical attention. Though economic approval begins to decline as the economic crisis lingers and unemployment rises, the *effect* of economic approval remains relatively constant; and it remains, throughout the year, the most strongly connected issue to the president of the issues polled.

OBAMA AND TAXES: QUICK FOLLOW-THROUGH

The ARRA provided Obama with his key success on tax cuts as well. The legislation allocated $288 billion for tax cuts; though considerably smaller than President Bush's $1.35 trillion tax-cutting package, the benefit of Obama's cuts went disproportionately to the middle-class. The stimulus tax cuts were temporary, though Obama proposed extending some of the stimulus cuts aimed at the middle class along with parts of the 2001 and 2003 tax cuts that primarily benefit the middle class in his 2010 budget (Rubin 2010).

Despite his efforts to win tax cuts in the recovery package, Obama expends very little rhetorical effort promoting them (figure 7.9). As the top panel of figure 7.9 shows, approval of his handling of taxes peaks right after passage of the recovery package and Obama's address to Congress, emphasizing economic issues. By July, his approval on taxes hovers around 40 percent. The president's failure to publicly promote the tax cuts may have aided in the public's failure to recognize his policy success.

The impact of tax approval on Obama's performance ratings, shown in the lower panel of figure 7.9, is comparatively stable. While the connection between taxes and Obama's performance ratings is notably weaker than the impact of economic approval, these still represent a strong connection with an average effect size of .50. Despite Obama's neglect of the issue in his public remarks, the public still uses the evaluations of his performance on tax cuts as a relatively strong consideration in evaluating Obama as president.

OBAMA AND HEALTH CARE:
SUSTAINED FOLLOW-THROUGH

The ARRA made some initial headway on health-care costs savings, with $19 billion to fund health-information technology. But the bulk of the health-care debate revolved around the legislative effort in Congress. Given the record time for passing ARRA, the public may have expected a smoother path for health-care reform. Instead, the health-care debate reverted to form with a long, drawn-out, partisan battle.

Mirroring Bush's legislative strategy, and in contrast to Clinton's, on health care Obama left the development of details to the legislators, outlining the broad principles he wanted reform to meet. Obama won

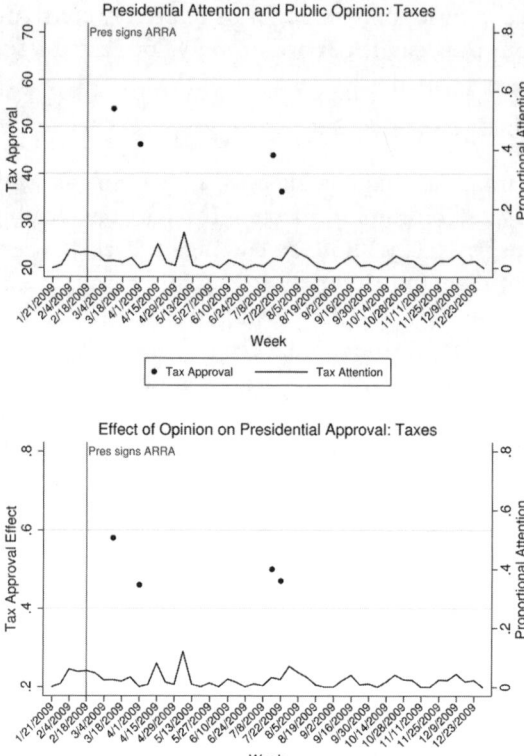

Figure 7.9 Obama and Taxes

a symbolic victory at the end of April when Congress passed a budget resolution that included reconciliation instructions to provide Obama's proposed health-care reforms protection from a Senate filibuster if bipartisan agreement could not be reached (Clarke 2009). Like much of the key legislation in Obama's first year, the budget resolution passed with no Republican votes in either house.

Consideration of the health-care reform proposals began in Congress in June but had yet to reach the floor of either house at the start of the August recess, missing a deadline repeatedly promoted by Obama. The raucous town halls and the rage of the right became a dominant news theme over the summer as congressional members returned to their districts and met with constituents regarding health care.[7] President Obama addressed a joint session of Congress and the nation on health care on

September 9 to rally congressional Democrats and to clear up public confusion about the health-care proposals in Congress. This address gave rise to the infamous heckling by Rep. Joe Wilson (R-S.C.). His shout, "You lie," garnered much of the attention of the press after the address, detracting from Obama's intended message.

Despite the negative tenor of the discourse on health care over the summer, the House passed a version of health-care reform on November 7, in a rare Saturday session. The vote was 220–215, with only one Republican member voting in support. The Senate followed suit, passing a health-care reform bill on Christmas Eve, where the strictly party-line vote ended twenty-five consecutive days of procedural battles and debate (Wayne 2009). Although Obama could not sign a bill before the year's end, his revised deadline, the most ambitious health-care plan in four decades had passed in both chambers. The outlook for a bill to expand coverage, rein in skyrocketing costs, and prohibit discrimination based on preexisting conditions and other unpopular practices of insurance companies looked promising at the close of 2009.[8]

Figure 7.10 shows the trend in Obama's rhetorical efforts on behalf of health-care reform. He referenced this issue more than any other during the first year, though his attention reveals more peaks and valleys than his attention on jobs, his second most frequently referenced issue.

Outside of the initial measure of approval of Obama's handling of health care, health-care approval hovers around 40 percent (see the top panel of figure 7.10). If anything, the trend in health-care approval improves during the summer, as the health-care battle begins in earnest, though the rise is not a statistically significant one. Nevertheless, the August town halls and the drawn-out process do not seem to have seriously eroded Obama's support on the issue below his already middling levels.

The impact of health-care approval on Obama's performance rating, too, remains stable with an effect size around .50, at least until the late August congressional recess (see the lower panel of figure 7.10). The already strong connection between health care and Obama approval remains elevated after the August recess. The average effect before and after the August recess, and the accompanying dominance of health care in the political discourse, is significantly different ($F = 13.23$, $p < .01$). The impact of health care on Obama's approval numbers was high from the beginning, generally on par with the effect of foreign policy approval, and by the end of the year the impact appears to have grown further. This suggests, again, that public expectations remain at least a little bit malleable.

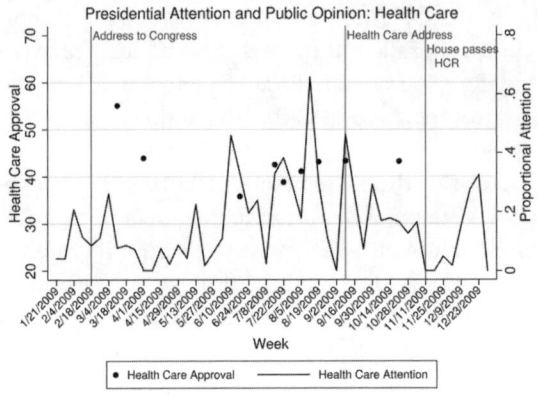
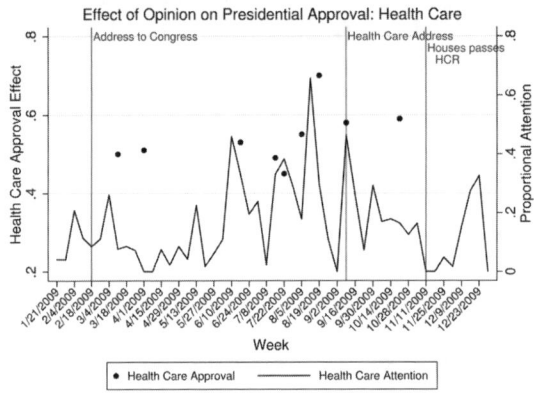

Figure 7.10 *Obama and Health Care*

OBAMA AND ENERGY: MIDLEVEL AGENDA FOLLOW-THROUGH

As president, Obama touted energy independence as a chief concern—one tied to the nation's security and economy as much as to the planet's protection. His emphasis on energy has been primarily about reducing dependence on foreign oil and promoting an energy economy—green technologies and green jobs—to create and revitalize American industry. Toward that end, on January 26, Obama signed two presidential memoranda, one directing the Department of Transportation to establish higher fuel-efficiency standards for model year 2011 vehicles, and the other allowing California to raise emissions standards above and beyond the national standards (Mufson and Eilperin 2009).

The ARRA also made headway on energy independence, providing tax credits for energy conservation and renewable-energy production and $70 billion for investments in green technologies, clean water, and other energy and environmental programs, though public awareness of this focus was likely reduced by the greater attention news reports paid to the size of the stimulus package and the party division that accompanied it.

A high-profile success on energy independence came in June when the House passed a comprehensive bill to overhaul energy policy and limit climate change. The bill, passed by a narrow 219–212 victory on June 26 after intense lobbying by Obama, would cap emissions of greenhouse gases and increase the production of alternative energy (Davenport and Palmer 2009). The success of the climate bill in the House was viewed as a significant legislative victory for President Obama, who characteristically portrayed the bill as an engine of job growth.

Also on June 26, Obama signed the Cash-for-Clunkers bill passed by the House and Senate earlier in the month. Though intended more as a stimulus to the automobile industry, the program also aimed to reduce fuel consumption by offering trade-in vouchers for consumers trading in an older gas-guzzling vehicle for a more fuel-efficient one. The program proved so popular that the initial $1 billion allocated to the program was nearly exhausted after the first week. Consequently, Congress passed a bill to replenish the program with another $2 billion. Obama signed this into law on August 7.

President Obama's steady stream of attention to the issue of energy independence is evident in figure 7.11. Obama generally couched his discussion of energy in the language of economic growth, and the trend in approval of Obama on energy, to the extent one can be discerned from the three instances in which it was asked, mirrors that for the economy (see the top panel of figure 7.11). Approval of Obama's handling of energy starts off high, right after the recovery act and his first address to Congress, and falls below the 50 percent mark by the summer.

The impact of energy approval on Obama's performance ratings, shown in the bottom panel of figure 7.11, remains relatively stable, and in this case, perhaps surprisingly strong, hovering between .40 and .50. Certainly the issue of energy was evident in Obama's campaign, though it was hardly the most prominent issue, and it remained strongly connected to Obama during his first year as president. It's possible that Obama successfully tied this issue to that of the economy or the public may simply have grown to expect this effort on energy independence from Obama following his modest attention to the issue in the campaign.

OBAMA AND FINANCE: AGENDA INTERRUPTION

The financial collapse that began in September 2008 brought a whole new set of issues to the front burner for the federal government. Obama

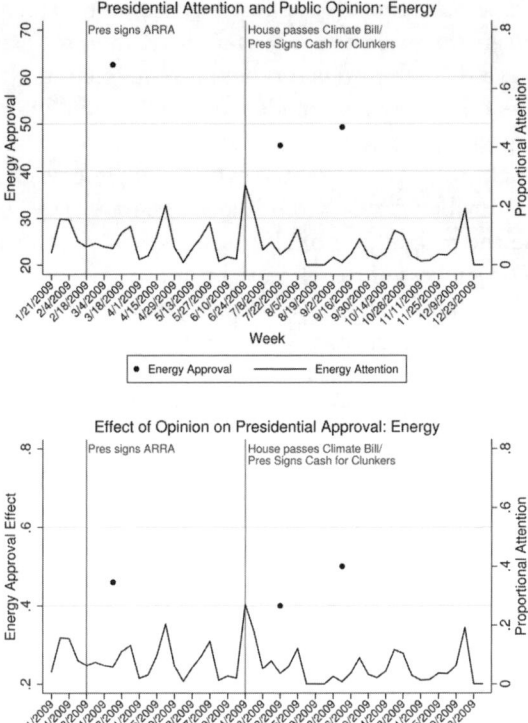

Figure 7.11 Obama and Energy

became the steward of Bush's bailout package, the Troubled Asset Relief Program (TARP), and of the popular outrage that would arise in 2009. In January 2009, Wall Street banks announced more than $18 billion in 2008 bonuses. Obama called the bonuses, coming on the heels of the $700 billion bailout, "shameful" and "the height of irresponsibility" (Obama 2009a). He followed up his public expression of outrage by announcing, on February 4, tougher executive compensation restrictions at some firms receiving federal aid.

In a February 9 press conference, Obama announced that his Treasury secretary, Timothy Geithner, would be releasing the administration's banking plan the following day, though the promise was premature as it became clear the plan was still a work in progress. Nevertheless, Secretary Geithner provided a sketch of his proposals, "a new Financial Stability Plan to stabilize and repair the financial system, and support the flow of credit necessary for recovery" (Geithner 2009). The centerpiece of the plan was the "stress tests" of nineteen big financial institutions, to determine whether the banks had enough money to withstand a deep recession and, if not, how much more capital was necessary for them to keep lending.

In March, after another announcement about seemingly excessive bonuses at a bailed-out firm (AIG), Obama tasked Secretary Geithner with pursuing "every single legal avenue to block these bonuses" (Obama 2009b). The bank "stress tests" were completed in early May and indicated the need for about $75 billion more in capital, to be achieved mostly through private recapitalization. The administration used the stress tests, in part, to reassure the public that the time for taxpayer bailouts was over. By the end of the year, as well, many of the big banks had begun repaying their bailout funds.

Also in May, on May 20, Obama signed legislation meant to respond to the growing foreclosure problem, including an overhaul of the Hope for Homeowners program that the Bush administration enacted in 2008. Two days later, the president signed credit card legislation that limited the credit card companies' ability to raise rates, charge late fees, or issue credit cards to people under the age of twenty-one, and requiring them to simplify the terms and conditions of contracts.

On October 22, the Treasury Department released new regulations on the compensation packages for the top executives at firms that received exceptional TARP assistance. The administration ordered seven firms to cut compensation to their highest-paid executives. And as the year came to an end, the House passed the Wall Street Reform and Consumer Protection Act, a sweeping reform of the financial regulatory system. The bill, passed on December 11 by 223–202 with no Republican votes, followed the blueprint of the Obama administration's June white paper on financial regulation. Coming more than a year after the financial crisis, the bill's fortunes in the Senate were uncertain.

Despite the administrative effort the financial problems demanded of his first year, Obama's rhetorical attention was contained relative to his attention to his top priorities of jobs and health care. Still, figure 7.12 suggests a steady attention to the issue. Indeed, banks and the financial crisis are among his five most frequently referenced issues in the first year (see table 7.2 in the following section), receiving more attention than other issues salient to the American public, such as the ongoing military efforts in Iraq and Afghanistan.

In return, he earns one the lowest approval ratings on this issue among the issues on which the public was queried (see the top panel of figure 7.12)—though, tellingly, pollsters did not see fit to ask the question very

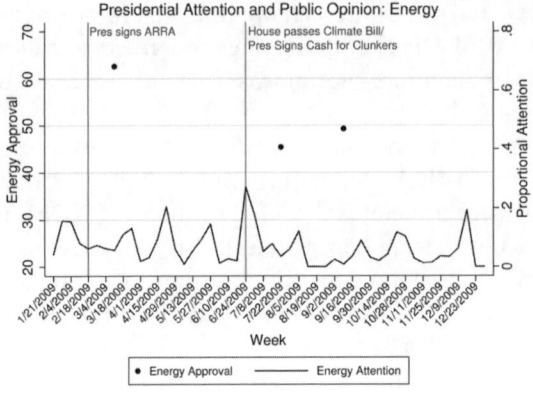

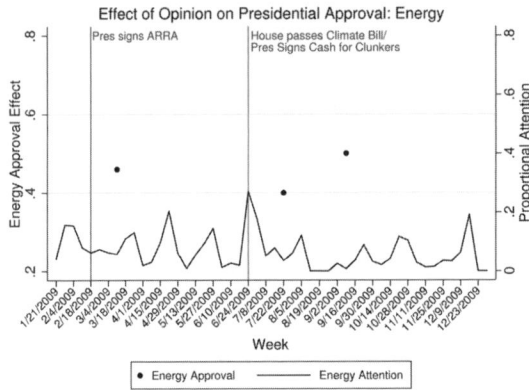

Figure 7.12 Obama and the Financial Crisis

often. And the bottom panel of figure 7.12 reveals one of the lowest issue connections, with approval of Obama's handling of the financial crisis and bank bailouts having only a relatively weak impact on performance ratings of the president. The final observation, occurring after the high-profile stress tests and passage of the mortgage and credit card bills, hints at a momentary increase in the connection between the issue and Obama's popularity. The potential increase is reminiscent of the temporarily stronger connection between deficits and President Clinton, reinforcing the pattern of a more transitory accountability for problems that interrupt the president's agenda.

OBAMA IN 2009: VARIATIONS ON FOLLOW-THROUGH

Obama's first year does not offer any examples of outright agenda neglect but does offer a sequencing of attention to the campaign priorities—the stimulus to create jobs and lower taxes, energy investment and progress on a comprehensive climate bill, and legislative progress on health-care reform. Also, the Obama presidency presents a borderline case of interruption; though the banking crisis began before the election and the Bush administration oversaw passage of the controversial TARP, much of the implementation of the program and the fallout from unpopular decisions by banks who had benefited from government assistance fell to Obama.

Whereas Clinton's attempt at economic stimulus failed and he punted on his expressed desire to cut middle-class taxes, Obama succeeded on both of these fronts. Approval of Obama's handling of these issues is correspondingly higher than it was for Clinton. While economic evaluations eventually fall for Obama, appraisals of his handling of the economy are noticeably higher at the beginning of his term than were Clinton's—despite the unquestionably worse economic conditions evident when Obama entered office—and these evaluation decline more slowly, never dropping as low as Clinton's. The public appears to be responding to President Obama's policy success, at least initially. And economic considerations remain the most strongly connected to evaluations of Obama's presidency throughout the year.

The case of taxes is more curious. Though the public begins with relatively high approval of Obama's handling of the issue, presumably in response to passage of the tax cuts in ARRA, by the end of summer, these evaluations fell markedly. Perhaps the depth of the tax cuts did not penetrate the public understanding; and the opposition party's repeated assertions that Obama's budget would raise taxes (through rescinding the Bush tax cuts for households with incomes over $250,000) obscured the administration's success. Underscoring how Obama's tax cuts may not have penetrated the public consciousness and the continued contestation over the stimulus bill at the end of the year, PolitiFact felt moved to fact-check Obama advisor David Axelrod's claim that "without, frankly, the help of the Republican caucus, we passed 25 tax cuts last year, mostly aimed at the middle class and small businesses." PolitiFact rated the claim true (PolitiFact.com 2010).[9] Approval of taxes for Obama did, however, remain higher than the analogous evaluations of Clinton. And taxes remained strongly tied to Obama's public support, suggesting the issue became associated with Obama during the campaign.

The public's response to Obama on health care looks quite similar to the response to Clinton on health care. Approval of his handling of the issue begins relatively high, drops in the spring, but begins to increase a bit as Obama's attention turns emphatically to the issue. Though evaluations of health care do not improve as noticeably for Obama as they did for Clinton, Obama sees more congressional success than Clinton did during the year. The legislative battles and the summer town halls dampen the public's response relative to that for Clinton, who had the stage largely to himself on this issue when it began. For Obama, though, the issue is always strongly tied to his evaluations.

On energy, Obama achieved at least partial policy success during his first year, winning new government investment in green energy and getting a climate bill passed in the House. Public appraisals of Obama's handling of the issue are relatively strong and moderately connected to Obama's overall performance ratings, consistent with the midlevel status the issue held on his campaign agenda. Though the evidence on energy is more limited, the president's and public's response to the issue is at least consistent with the expectations of agenda accountability.

The administration's response to the crisis in the financial system is the most complex issue considered here. Obama inherited the problem and the initial government response, dominated by TARP. A year-end audit of the program credits TARP and other financial programs for stabilizing the financial system and averting a more serious crisis, but faults it for failing to increase lending, remove toxic assets from the banks' balance sheets, or prevent home foreclosures (Congressional Oversight Panel 2009). It's not entirely clear what a reasonable public response to Obama's handling of the financial crisis should look like. Still, evaluations of Obama on the issue are relatively low, much like for Clinton's agenda interruptions. Like Clinton, as well, the connection between the issue and Obama's overall evaluations appears to increase in response to administration efforts and actions. While initially only very weakly connected to Obama's public support, by early summer the impact of approval of Obama's handing of the banking crisis jumps to a modest level. Issues that interrupt the administration's agenda appear to become at least temporarily tied to the president.

Table 7.2 briefly broadens the scope of issues considered to those beyond Obama's key issues to include issues that were high on neither his campaign agenda nor his administrative agenda during his first year. The table relays the average size of the relationship between each issue approval and overall approval, the average level of issue approval, and the percent of rhetorical attention Obama gave each issue in his public remarks in 2009.

As for Clinton and Bush, the economy is the issue most strongly related to Obama's performance ratings on average. For President Obama, the effect is especially strong, reflecting, perhaps, the particularly dire economic situation during Obama's first year in office. After economic

Table 7.2 Comparison across Issues: President Obama

	Effect on Approval*	Approval of Issue	Rhetorical Effort (2009)
Campaign Issues			
Economy/Jobs	0.64	51.4	11.7
Health Care	0.55	43.0	15.9
Taxes	0.50	45.1	2.4
Energy	0.46	52.4	6.8
New Issues			
Banks	0.33	40.5	6.5
Nonissues			
Foreign Policy	0.55	55.4	9.1
Education	0.36	57.7	5.3
Iraq	0.31	61.1	3.5
Afghanistan	0.24	57.0	3.5
Budget Deficit	0.46	40.8	3.3
Auto Industry	0.36	42.5	1.3

*Effect of issue approval on presidential approval controlling for partisanship, education, age, and gender.

approval, health-care approval and foreign-affairs approval are the next most strongly connected to Obama's evaluations. Health care was a more prominent issue in both his campaign and in his presidential rhetoric, and its continued connection to his evaluations during the year is supportive of the public's ability to engage in agenda accountability. Foreign policy considerations are, of course, thought to be chronically important in presidential evaluations, and that is borne out here: Foreign policy was attached to each of these presidents despite the small role foreign policy played in each of their initial campaigns.[10]

Tax approval also strongly shapes Obama's overall ratings, meaning that three of the four issues most strongly associated with Obama as president were issues he highlighted in his campaign. The issue with the next biggest impact on approval is energy, an issue that received real attention in Obama's campaign, though not as an obvious top priority. The strength of the energy connection speaks to the potential for even moderate campaign repetition to build agenda associations relevant to future accountability.

The banking crisis and perceptions of Obama's handling of the issue do not stand out as particularly tied to evaluations of Obama as president. The financial meltdown was not a prominent part of the presidential campaign, but given the sudden ascent of the issue on the public and governing agendas, it seemed reasonable to expect some connection driven by the sheer magnitude of the problem. In fact, the public—perhaps wisely—does not hold Obama excessively accountable for the state of the financial sector or the outrages provoked by the behavior of Wall Street after the historic bailout.

Of the remaining issues polled, only the budget deficit wields a notable impact on presidential approval. The approval of the president's handling of the deficit has been among the top five predictors of overall approval for each president considered, reinforcing the sense that the issue approval for this issue is in large part a function of broader economic approval.

The similar patterns for Obama and Clinton, particularly on issues where presidential success differed, like economic stimulus and tax cuts, speaks to the inability of policy success, or, indeed, policy popularity, to account for the dimensions underlying presidential approval.

Conclusion

Clinton campaigned on the economy and jobs, tax cuts for the middle class, and health care. He neglected tax cuts, citing the surprising growth in the deficit upon his election to office. He experienced an early failure on the economy with the defeat of the economic stimulus package, though the budget resolution passed by Congress accorded with some of his economic focus. And much of his public effort and certainly his biggest successes were on two issues that had not been strongly highlighted in his campaign—free trade and deficit cutting. Thus, Clinton offers examples of attempted follow-through (economic stimulus, health care), agenda neglect (taxes), and agenda interruption (deficit, trade).

Bush campaigned most heavily on education, Social Security, taxes, and Medicare modernization. He neglected Social Security and Medicare prescription coverage via delay, rather than retraction, but succeeded early on his tax agenda and made significant headway on his education proposals as well, ultimately signing a major education reform bill. Bush provides two cases of successful agenda follow-through and two cases of agenda neglect. Until the attacks of September 11, there was no other high-profile issue that Bush took on in his first year. Certainly Bush's early administration is an example of a narrower and more focused agenda.

Obama, like Clinton, campaigned on the economy and jobs, tax cuts for the middle class, and health-care reform. But unlike Clinton, he succeeded incredibly quickly in securing an economic stimulus package.

The ARRA included, in addition to spending and investments centered on saving and creating jobs, widely distributed tax cuts for 95 percent of working families. By the end of the year, health-care reform seemed closer to passage than any time in recent history. Obama, then, provides no cases of serious agenda neglect, though he does offer an example of effort on a midlevel campaign priority, one that may not have penetrated the public consciousness during the campaign but provokes consistent presidential effort in the administration—energy independence. The financial crisis, too, offers an illustration of an issue that was not central for most of the campaign but rose quickly and forcefully to the government agenda.

For both President Clinton and President Obama, who had strikingly similar campaign agendas, the top three campaign issues—the economy and jobs, health care, and middle-class tax cuts—were among the top four issues most connected to their evaluations.[11] For President Bush, the two issues that were actually connected to him in the campaign—taxes and Social Security—were also strongly connected to his job approval, but in his case these issues had the fourth and fifth strongest impact, after the economy, the budget deficit, and foreign policy. This pattern suggests some obvious constraints on the ability of presidential candidates to completely reorder public expectations. The economy appears to top the list regardless of what a candidate or a president does. Economic approval is always the most strongly related to overall approval, but the degree to which it rises above other issues appears to be related to the severity of the economic situation—the effect is most pronounced for Obama, then Clinton, and last Bush. But the severity of the economic situation is itself a key predictor of how much a candidate will emphasize the economy in the campaign. The consistent ranking of the issue lends credence to the argument that the economy is, via its frequency in the discourse surrounding the presidency, a chronically accessible consideration. The varying strength of the connection across these presidents suggests the consideration is nevertheless open to an increase (or decrease) in associational strength consistent with the preceding campaign. Foreign policy, too, ranks uniformly high in terms of effects on presidential approval. This is why the consistency of a heightened impact on approval across other issue dimensions is important—within the constraints of deeply held expectations—and the issues prioritized by the winning candidate prove some of the strongest predictors of presidential approval.

The general patterns of connections—the comparably strong connections between campaign agenda issue approval and overall job approval—

holds whether the president is a Democrat or a Republican. More significantly, it holds whether the president objectively accomplished something on the campaign issue or not. Obama, for instance, did objectively achieve some policy success on tax cuts, on economic stimulus, and at the end of 2009 appeared headed toward success on health-care reform; Clinton failed to achieve success on any of these issues in his first year, though health care still seemed like a possibility at the end of 1993. Bush offers perhaps a more convincing comparison, as the connection between campaign issue approval and presidential performance ratings held up for taxes, boosting overall approval, and Social Security, decreasing approval, despite their dramatically different fortunes.

Further, the pattern of results seems to hold regardless of whether the president continued to emphasize the issue in his early presidency or not. Although Obama did continue to emphasize the economy and jobs, and health care, he all but neglected tax cuts in his rhetoric. The same can be said of Clinton's presidential focus. And Bush, for his part, highlighted taxes in his remarks and neglected Social Security.

Finally, the patterns of connections early in the administration do not seem to depend on other advantages or disadvantages experienced by the president, like a bigger in-party congressional majority or the use of more obstructionist measures by the out-party in Congress. These things may well impact the level of approval—that is, whether the connection works in favor or against a president—as approval levels seem to move in accord with outcomes, at least some of the time. In particular, approval of Clinton's handling of the economy and health care appear to move up or down depending on his apparent successes or failures; but approval of Clinton's handling of the budget deficit and trade look less responsive to his objective policy successes. Meanwhile, evaluations of Obama's handling of the economy and taxes appear more dependent on continued economic crisis than on his success in getting his economic stimulus passed. The trend is less clear for approval of Obama's handling of health care, and given the paucity of data, it is even murkier on the issues of energy and the banking crisis. Approval of Bush's handling of education and taxes, though, do appear to increase modestly after key legislative successes. Perhaps the congressional context, particularly the cooperation or intransigence of the opposition party, makes it more or less likely for the president to gain credit for policy successes as reflected in the level of issue approval, but it does not strengthen or weaken the connection between the campaign issues and the president.

In this sense, then, the public does seem to continue to use expectations about presidential problem-solving reinforced during the campaign to make an ongoing judgment about presidential performance. Presidential performance is not judged on the same dimensions for all presidents, though certainly there are similarities. Rather, the campaign issues and the congruence of candidate and presidential priorities are strongly and consistently tied to presidential approval. Despite widespread misperceptions about the president as chief lawmaker rather than the prioritizer of a governing sequence, citizens regularly engage in a process resembling agenda accountability.

8 Campaign-Driven Accountability

> The ideas of economists and political philosophers, both when they are right and when they are wrong, are more powerful than is commonly understood. Indeed the world is ruled by little else.
> —John Maynard Keynes (1960, 383)

Our ideas of accountability, and the definitions of good campaigns and competent citizens that derive from them, shape what we demand from candidates and leaders and from the media and voters. And what we demand is not always realistic or wise.

Campaigns and elections offer an unrivaled opportunity for the public and leaders to interact. The operation of campaigns is important for the legitimacy of democratic government; the outcomes are important for the actions of government. We need campaigns and elections to work well. But what does it mean for a campaign to be good? What do we want campaigns to do? The answer to these questions should fundamentally depend on the answer to another question: What role does the leader in question play in governing? Yet the process of governing is mostly neglected by critics of campaigns—and so they provide standards for campaign quality that bear little relationship to the governing that might follow from the election. Campaigns, they tell us, should educate people about the candidates' policy stands, should provide clear and meaningful differences in the direction of future policy, and should highlight current conditions as the responsibility, for good or ill, of the incumbent party or administration. And these criteria for a good campaign seldom vary by office.

In the case of the presidency, the office with which I am concerned, the answer to the last question—What role does the leader play?—is something like this: Presidents can direct the attention of Congress and the public, can influence the sequencing of important legislative activity, can set the governing priorities. Presidents cannot dictate legislation—efforts to do so are met with resistance by Congress and mockery by the professional political "commentariat"; Bill Clinton's doomed health-care reform efforts stand as a useful reminder of this. What we then need to learn from presidential campaigns is, What will a candidate's priorities as president be? What problems does each candidate believe most require attention? What issues will earn his effort? On what legislative outcomes will he spend his political capital? In short, we should be asking not what will you do about a problem, but on what problems will you try to do something.

This focus, in addition to fitting better with the capacity of the presidency, fits well with the preferences of the public, a largely nonideological mass who wants government to do the work of fixing national problems. That citizens cannot always correctly identify the issue positions of major party candidates is not as dire as skeptics would have it. Citizens, voters and abstainers, hear the agenda emphasis in the campaign and understand what the candidates' priorities are. And even if campaigns don't move voters, they can still do this—disseminate priorities, establish expectations. This is not an apology for citizen ignorance but a call to reconsider what citizens need to know about a future leader in the context of the job the future leader seeks.[1]

It is not enough for citizens to understand competing issue agendas during the campaign, however; they must incorporate them into their understanding and expectations of the president. This is an outcome campaigns promote exceedingly well. The long, repetitive, nonspecific, sometimes tedious presidential campaign with its endless ads aired ad infinitum works to hammer the issue priorities home. While many bemoan these characteristics of the campaign—When will they say something new? Where are the policy details?—this, I contend, is a feature, not a bug. Campaigns could be improved, to be sure, but many of the reforms suggested for their improvement are misguided.

And it is not enough for citizens to incorporate the candidates' issue priorities into their understanding of the candidates, of the future president. Citizens must also continue to evaluate the president on the basis of his adherence to his own agenda. As new problems arise and new challenges unfold, his attention should adjust as well. But at the beginning of the presidential administration, particularly in the first year when a leader's ability to influence the agenda is at its peak, the campaign priorities should guide the president's efforts. The public should judge him accordingly. This is agenda accountability.

Improving Accountability

No model of accountability will capture the workings of democratic governance perfectly. Each contains kernels of truth; each is flawed. Yet the models we adopt, promote, and teach do inform what we expect from candidates, presidents, citizens, the media, and government more broadly. It is worth weighing the strengths and weaknesses of the alternatives, both empirically and normatively, keeping in mind that strengths and weaknesses often flow from the same well.

Prospective accountability, the party mandate model, provides the clearest standards and the most transparent understanding between the elected and the "electees." This model posits the most substantial role for citizens via issue voting. And the promissory representation embedded in the model infuses the interaction between citizens and candidates with the strongest moral obligation.

But the clarity of intentions and transparency of standards that prospective accountability presumes leave little leeway for presidents in a negotiated lawmaking process. And a negotiated process is what the American system requires. Calls for more policy specifics in presidential campaigns, by misunderstanding the role of the president, inadvertently ask a presidential candidate to box his future presidential self in by taking hard stands on points that ought to be part of deliberation within Congress and bargaining between Congress and the president. A president who has been overly specific in the campaign cannot engage in unencumbered negotiation. As Mansbridge notes while arguing against excessive transparency, "Negotiators need closed doors to try out potential solutions from which they may later back away, to acknowledge the needs of the other side in language that their constituents might consider betrayal, and to develop the mutual trust that forms one strand of a successful negotiation" (Mansbridge 2004, 12).[2]

Scholars have decried the rise in the permanent campaign, the presidential efforts to win policy battles by "going public" (Edwards 2008; Kernell 2007; Ornstein and Mann 2000). This strategy, the critics quite reasonably assert, is antithetical to governing. It pushes presidents to simplify the policy battle into black-and-white terms and to stake out firm positions; this impedes the bargaining necessary for governing. It encourages presidents to overplay their hand, to exaggerate their power. What goes largely unrecognized, however, is that similar position-taking and simplifying in the actual campaign can also frustrate later bargaining. Just as during the administration, the policy specifics called for in the campaign may inhibit the necessary compromise of legislation. A president tied to a hard policy position "may suffer significant opportunity costs as he overlooks less dramatic, but more realistic, chances for success" (Edwards 2008, 318), if for no other reason than to avoid appearing like he has reversed himself or betrayed some dearly held principles.

The strong role for citizens advanced by prospective accountability is matched by a corresponding insistence on their sustained political attention and awareness. Citizens need to make sense of and choose between competing issue platforms and policy positions. It is the practice of choice that provides citizens their key point of entry into the political sphere. The opportunity to choose is what makes the system democratic; the ability to choose is what makes people citizens (Lewin 2007). But the nature of the choice citizens are supposed to make has been conceived so as to write many individuals out of the running. Citizen choice need not be about policy specifics; citizens should not be expected to adjudicate between policy alternatives whose technical merits are understood only uncertainly, even by experts.

Concern with an informed electorate, by which advocates generally mean an electorate aware of the candidates' issue stands, is hardly new. It harkens back to Progressive Era reforms aimed at improving citizen knowledge but ultimately reducing the size of the electorate as many citizens were defined out of, or defined themselves out of, this informed citizenry (McGerr 1986). The policy details that the proponents of a more educational politics would like to see elevated and debated in campaigns is the sort of discourse that readily makes the majority of citizens feel ignorant and not a little defensive about their ignorance. When we judge campaigns (and the process of accountability more broadly) by the extent to which they produce an informed citizenry, we need to be more careful and explicit about what information is really required. The mass public has stubbornly refused to display the level of political sophistication required for prospective accountability. Elites use the lack of apparent political sophistication to argue against broader participation, sometimes explicitly (see, for example, Caplan 2007) though more often subtly.

Finally, just as the mass public fails to act according to the dictates of prospective accountability, candidates, not unwisely from the perspective of governing, stubbornly refrain from campaigning according to these standards. Presidential campaigns spend the bulk of their time highlighting a broader set of goals or outcomes. Clear policy specifics and programmatic proposals are not deemed a winning strategy. That we continue to expect this of them contributes to public cynicism toward politics and reinforces a belief in the inherent insincerity of politicians.

Because prospective accountability is not a reasonable expectation in a separated system with weak parties, the admirable standard the model defines is not realistic. The consequences for our understanding of and attitudes toward government are grave.

Retrospective accountability, to its credit, orients lawmakers toward big outcomes. And this model, in contrast to prospective accountability, provides leaders with a great deal of discretion in achieving those outcomes. At the same time, citizens are required to pay only minimal attention to the political realm—an arrangement with which citizens have shown themselves to be quite comfortable.

No doubt adherence to a retrospective accountability framework would push presidential attention to "maximize the general welfare." At the same time, by applying a collective accountability model to the unitary president, it reinforces a problematic understanding of the president. "Everybody now expects the man inside the White House to do something about everything" (Neustadt 1990, 7). This is clearly an untenable standard. Although holding presidents to such unrealistic expectations is unfair, fairness toward the president ought not, perhaps, be our primary concern. Rather, the unrealistic standard, in reinforcing the misconception that ours is a presidency-dominated system, encourages complacency about (if not an outright preference for) efforts to increase the reach and power of the president (Lowi 1985, 2009). The consequences of presidential overreach in the Bush administration will occupy scholars for years.

Similarly, the leeway granted to a president under the retrospective view goes too far. Presidents not only have leeway to negotiate policy solutions to problems but also to define the problems and outcomes of importance with little citizen input. The power to define the problem and the eventual outcomes offers elites an alarming opportunity to manipulate public perceptions. Even in the simpler terms of economic voting, the absence of some "objective state of the economy" means that economic facts, such as they are, are open to a great deal of interpretation (Keech 1995). The state of the nation in other regards—education, health, energy—is likely to be even murkier, though influencing citizens' perceptions of the state of the nation is not the only alternative at leaders' disposal. Officials at both ends of Pennsylvania Avenue, in the face of outcomes that cannot be spun positively, engage in efforts to camouflage responsibility, to shift blame onto opposing actors and institutions. The retrospective model, relying as it does on attributions of responsibility, invites such behavior by politicians.

Finally, citizens have no say in what outcomes are deemed important. Their participation in the campaign conversation isn't required. As a consequence, retrospective accountability provides citizens very little meaningful democratic control. Perhaps worse, it encourages the much-derided habit of citizens to demand their government meet contradictory goals. And why not? If citizens are not invited to consider or comment on the competing ends presidential contenders claim they will promote, why should we expect them to spend time on their own recognizing the tradeoffs or determining how they might rank a competing set of goals given limited resources? Though warranted, the critique of citizens for endorsing incompatible ends undermines the presence of a public voice by highlighting the apparent uselessness of that voice.

A retrospective accountability process has the virtue of being achievable within a separated system, if only under the right conditions—clear lines of responsibility, the presence of viable alternatives, alternatives clearly aligned on the outcome criteria at stake, and so forth (Anderson 2007). But it expects too much of presidents and reinforces misconceptions of the presidency in ways that seem to promote acceptance of greater presidential power. It provides only a modicum of control to accountability-holders while inadvertently promoting attitudes on the part of citizens that further undermine their involvement. Buchanan, in advocating for presidential standards of judgment that are "more sophisticated, informed, stable, equitable, and sensitive to the realities of presidential functioning," wisely warned that "Those who would preserve the power of the citizenry cannot afford to ignore this issue" (Buchanan 1987, 20).

Citizens have the capacity to hold leaders accountable in more meaningful ways. Agenda accountability, the process proposed in this book, retains some of the advantages of both of the dominant models. It promotes clear accountability standards while guarding leader discretion to engage in policy making. It promotes a focus on results but gives the public a hand in influencing the results of interest. It incorporates an element of promissory representation with the accompanying moral incentives for responsiveness this implies. And it posits a strong role for citizens, but one that defines an informed electorate in a manner attainable by the broadest swath of the public.

Agenda Accountability and Citizenship

An understanding and acceptance of agenda accountability could both inform the public and, at the same time, alter our conception of what an informed public looks like. The process of campaigning explicitly on a set of agenda priorities and goals conveys to the public that presidential attention and government resources are limited. It tells the public what problems the president will try to address without suggesting that he can dictate the legislative process. In this way, agenda accountability better aligns with and respects lawmaking in the American system. A campaign that reflects the realities of governing, in which a president details what priorities he will devote his resources to and what problems he will work to find solutions for, could ultimately make accountability more reasoned and fair. And anything that advances for the public a proper understanding of how our government works is more than worthwhile.[3]

Agenda accountability, by emphasizing attention to issue priorities, goes some way in addressing the distortions in the public's conception of the presidency. An emphasis on issue priorities in the presidential campaign, too, makes the tradeoffs among goals more explicit. The public and the president both receive criticism on this front, the public for demanding the government pursue conflicting goals—lower budget deficits and higher employment, lower taxes and better health care— and the president for feeding these inflated expectations in his campaign rhetoric and policy promises. Recognition of and attention to candidate issue priorities makes the necessary tradeoffs in desirable outcomes more explicit. We all want reduced unemployment, lower taxes, better quality air, secure retirements, and lower deficits, but we wouldn't all rank these desiderata similarly. Neither, of course, do presidential candidates. Greater clarity of agenda priorities and more appreciation of their value would serve to make the election a clearer exercise in priority setting with explicit tradeoffs.[4]

Agenda accountability occupies the ground between prospective and retrospective accountability with regard to the demands on and power of citizens. Like prospective accountability, it grants citizen choice more weight than simply choosing between elites. It acknowledges the important first step agenda setting plays in policy making. But like retrospective accountability, it posits a reasonable shortcut for that choice, one imbued with issue significance.[5] Citizens shape and choose among competing issue priorities and so influence presidential behavior. They needn't be policy experts to project a legitimate voice in the policy process.[6]

Our conceptions of accountability, what we teach in civics classes, define competence differently. In so doing, they privilege different kinds of knowledge and different configurations of power. The more specialized the knowledge required for competence, the more restrictive the definition of competence, and the more the less-educated and politically disadvantaged are squeezed out of the public sphere. Agenda accountability defines voter competence so as to invite the broadest possible set of citizens.

Prospective accountability defines competence as knowing the different policy solutions proffered by competing candidates on a range of issues, whether these are likely to be pursued by the candidates or not. The idea that citizens need to know the details of candidate positions to make an informed choice and to ultimately hold leaders accountable permeates much of the citizens' guilty understanding of themselves. The view that unless you understand the technical details you don't, and shouldn't, have a voice in politics is sadly widespread (Caplan 2007; Eliasoph 1998). Retrospective accountability defines competence as an understanding of how government action is translated into outcomes and who is most responsible for those actions, something the arrangement of government itself obscures. The alternative role offered to the public by retrospective accountability, that citizens need only hold leaders accountable in times of extreme lack of peace and prosperity, lets citizens off the hook, to some degree, and leaders off the hook to an even greater degree, but greatly limits the public's powers. Agenda accountability defines competence as understanding the competing priorities offered by the candidates, choosing a set of priorities most in line with one's own, and expecting the future president to follow through. Even busy citizens can recognize their priorities and goals as they relate to the direction of the nation. These priorities are based as much on their values as on any expert knowledge, and this is enough to grant them entrée into the democratic conversation.

Improving Agenda Accountability

There is no shortage of criticism of contemporary campaigns—too expensive, too negative, too trivial—or suggestions for reform. It often seems that we have inadvertently developed a process with which nobody is pleased. This is, in part, because we have separated evaluations of campaigns and their consequences from an understanding of governing. Most reforms are intended to promote greater prospective accountability in accord with a mandate view of elections. But this is not a view of democratic accountability most scholars put much stock in. What we need, instead, are reforms that will advance an achievable accountability. What could each of the central players do to promote greater clarity of the candidate agendas, greater understanding of these priorities by the public, and greater faithfulness by the president to the expectations established in the campaign?

THE MEDIA

Media coverage of presidential campaigns leaves much to be desired. Journalists focus too much on the hoopla of the campaign—the horse race, candidate missteps, and campaign tactics—at the expense of campaign substance. Reporters insert themselves too aggressively into campaign coverage, promulgating an attitude of detached cynicism (Farnsworth and Lichter 2002; Patterson 1993). From the perspective of agenda accountability, though, the key problems are the obfuscation of candidate issue priorities, the resistance to repetition of information, and the excessive attention to the presidency at the expense of Congress.

Campaign news coverage should, unquestionably, highlight more issue substance. But the nature of this substance needn't delve into policy details. Instead, news reports should clarify what goals or outcomes the candidates are promoting and provide some background to the problems candidates are talking about. This would require a different approach to achieving "balance" in news reports. Stories anchored by conflict around an issue, where the candidates' competing policy preferences are contrasted, serve to obscure the differences in the urgency and effort candidates would apply to an issue. Such stories, at a minimum, need to be supplemented with some sense of how each candidate is prioritizing the issue under discussion. Even better, journalists could provide some independent assessment of the scope of the problems the candidates are emphasizing. How serious is the problem, how far-ranging are the implications?

To further aid in agenda accountability and in the creation of an informed electorate, journalists must revise practices that inhibit repetition. Candidates spend a great deal of time on the stump giving some variant of the same speech. No doubt this feels tedious to campaign beat reporters. But most citizens haven't heard this speech and certainly haven't heard it more than once. News norms that emphasize the "new" serve to obscure the candidate's key priorities as it makes the geographic deviations in the stump speech more noteworthy than the central message.[7] This repetition might be achieved by simply providing more space or time for the candidate's own voice. Unfiltered reports of candidates' activities and speeches would help to convey the contenders' priorities in much the same way as campaign advertising does. When journalists and candidates are interacting, in interviews and debates, the press should consistently ask about the candidates' dominant agendas, prompting them to explain and defend these choices.

But coverage of the campaign is hardly the whole problem. Accountability operates after the inauguration and improved media practices should, as well. Media scholars are equally dissatisfied with media reporting on governance. For starters, the tone of presidential coverage has grown increasingly negative (Cohen 2008; Farnsworth and Lichter 2005). The actual coverage of the president, though, is not that problematic from the perspective of agenda accountability. Tone aside, news reports of the president tend to relay what the president is focusing on, what he's talking about, who he's meeting with. This is useful information for gauging presidential effort on his purported priorities. When a president achieves some step toward addressing a problem—shepherding legislation through a committee or one house of Congress—we tend to hear about it.

The most important defect in press accounts of governing is the imbalance in institutional coverage (Arnold 2006). The presidents get the bulk of media attention. This makes reporting simpler for the press, to be sure, but it reinforces an erroneous understanding of lawmaking for citizens. Media coverage of presidents belies a problematic belief in presidentialism. Political blogger Ezra Klein summed up this point well: "This endless op-ed alchemy in which anger at the hard, complicated thing (our relentlessly dysfunctional system of government) gets transformed into disappointment with the simple, easy thing (the single individual who occupies the White House) isn't just analytically lazy. It's actively damaging. It implies a solution that will not solve the problem. It implies the need for different presidents, or maybe better presidents. Presidents of the other party, or maybe no party at all (remember Unity 08?)" (Klein 2009). While it is clearly more difficult to summarize activity in Congress, journalists need to find a way to do this. Newscasts and newspapers have regular segments on economics, sports, and weather. Why not a regular report—daily or weekly—summarizing the top activities of the president and Congress? The understanding of the president as government means we not only ask the wrong thing of candidates and voters but we also finger the wrong culprit when the system doesn't operate as we wish. We search for solutions that will never fix the broader problem.

CAMPAIGNS

Proposals for more issue debates, more candidate dialogue, free air time for the candidates to speak unmediated to the public, and more and better distribution of voter information guides are primarily about pushing candidates to take clearer stands, sharpening issue differences between candidates, and clarifying the candidates' platforms for the public (see, for example, Bartels and Vavreck 2000; Maisel, West, and Clifton 2007). These are admirable goals, to be sure, but without a responsible party system and voters concerned to keep leaders accountable to campaign pledges, it is not clear what all this positive issue clarity and differentiation will produce. If the public does not attend to such details, at whom will this discourse be directed? If citizens primarily engage in retrospective accountability, rewarding and punishing leaders for broad economic outcomes, how do these reforms promote this behavior?

Fortunately, some features of campaigns already serve the ends of agenda accountability reasonably well. The ubiquitous 30-second ads highlight the candidates' agendas, the repetition of campaign themes helps make these stick, and the long campaign contributes to greater learning (Stevenson and Vavreck 2000).

From the perspective of agenda accountability, the most useful reforms would increase the odds that candidates are reaching a broader geographic electorate. The targeted nature of much of the presidential campaign, where candidates concentrate their efforts selectively as part of their overall Electoral College strategy, means that many citizens don't receive the full, or any, campaign. People in states not considered up for grabs are not likely to hear the candidates' priorities as clearly, at least not through the campaign ads and speeches. Meanwhile, people in swing states are inundated with messages, almost certainly beyond what is necessary to convey the candidate's key issue themes. Anything that would serve to equalize accessibility to the campaign message would also serve to promote broader agenda accountability, as more of the public would have the opportunity to learn the candidate priorities and develop appropriate expectations. Certainly the elimination of the Electoral College would do this, but so too would changes in how electoral votes are allocated. Moving away from a statewide winner-take-all allocation of electoral votes to a more proportional allocation method, whether allocating votes by the congressional district winner (as Maine and Nebraska currently do) or a fully proportional system, would encourage candidates to reach out to a wider national audience.[8]

Additionally, the more money candidates and campaigns spend, the more likely they are to reach more people with their key issue themes. The 2002 Bipartisan Campaign Reform Act (BCRA), while not specifically altering the amount of money spent in the campaign, may have inadvertently helped. To the extent it encourages candidates to opt out of public financing, as Obama did in the 2008 general election, and the accompanying spending limits, that's probably a good thing. Not only was Obama's spending unconstrained by law in 2008, he maintained more strategic control over how his funds would be used. This allows his message both to remain relatively clear and to reach a broader audience.

There is little question that BCRA, by banning party soft money, encouraged presidential candidates and parties to invest in recruiting a greater number of small donors (Corrado and Mann 2004). The growth in individual campaign contributors in 2004 and again in 2008 has been striking (Magleby 2008). In addition to weakening the links between policy makers and large donors in ways that ease bargaining in the legislative process, expanding the donor base means more citizens increase their stake in the political process. In addition, one of the most remarked-upon changes post-BCRA was the implementation of the "Stand by Your Ad" provision—the requirement that candidates appear in their ads while stating their approval of the message. While intended to discourage attacks on one's opponent, the strong visible association of the candidate with the message in the ad is a boon to agenda accountability as well.

Conclusion

Jones asks, "What happens to accountability in a system of separate institutions competing for shared powers? The answer is that accountability is highly diffused by dint of the dispersal that is characteristic of separationism. As it happens, something has to give in any effort to achieve multiple goals, such as prevention of tyranny, preservation of liberty, popular sovereignty, and public accountability" (1999, 13). But accountability as a whole is not missing, though the forms of collective accountability presumed or desired by theorists are not often found in our system. Rather, we have substantial individual accountability. Our task here has been to theorize and examine the operation of some of this individual accountability—that of the president—and, along the way, to argue for a more nuanced understanding of presidential accountability.

With decades of research to rely on, we've come to know a great deal about voting, campaigns, and elections. But we have not always situated the study of elections firmly within a broader understanding of American politics (Bartels 2010). Studies of campaigns, for instance, have recognized that campaigns help citizens to associate the candidates with particular considerations but have often emphasized associations—Gore with Clinton, Bush with compassion—that have little governing consequence. How are citizens to hold presidents accountable for image and style? I have emphasized here a particular kind of learning in the campaign—learning what problems citizens can expect a president to engage—that I contend has clear consequences for governing and the working of accountability.

Schattschneider once wrote, "The most legitimate question to be asked in a democracy is: how can people get control of the government?" (1960, xi). This is the point of accountability. Agendas are a key source of citizen control—both in selecting among competing agendas and holding leaders accountable to these. And here, the public proves more capable than her detractors have understood. Beyond the impact that campaigns have on who governs, the discourse of the campaign provides the yardstick of subsequent presidential performance for citizens, elites, and even the president himself. The quality of this discourse should, in part, be judged by the ability of citizens to understand the agenda priorities of the candidates and to choose a preferred agenda. If the campaign bewilders the public with policy specifics, detailed numbers, and debate on competing proposals that talk past each other, it can serve to intimidate individuals and convey that citizenship is much too hard. If campaigns simply ask citizens to assess their satisfaction with the current state of the country (or of their own situation), they can reinforce a passive and narrowly conceived idea of citizenship. If, instead, the campaign takes public concerns seriously, it can help to reveal to individuals their power as citizens and to legitimate citizen ability to prioritize the problems. In this way, the presidential campaign matters beyond the voting booth.

APPENDIX A
Most Frequently Aired Ads in 2000

The following tables show the most frequently aired ads by Gore and Bush with their respective national committees, the DNC and the RNC, in the 2000 presidential campaign. These ads, aired more than 2,500 times, are broadly representative of the candidates' advertising campaigns overall. The names, number of airings, and issues mentioned in each ad are provided.

Table A.1 Bush/RNC Most Aired Ads

Campaign Title	CMAG* title	Issues	Airings
Trust	I trust you (60,30)**	Social Security, Education, Budget	10,536
Expect More	Bush raised standards	Record, Education	9,380
Solvent	Gore say one thing	Integrity, Spending, Budget	8,249
This Generation	Bush new solutions	Social Security	8,059
Notebook	Gore Rx for disaster	Medicare/Drug plan	8,019
Compare	Real results	Medicare/Drug plan, Education, Taxes	7,728
Hard Things	A moment in history	Education, Social Security, Budget	7,603
No Changes, No Reductions	Rx plan	Social Security, Medicare/Drug plan	6,197
58%	58 percent	Education	5,881
Really	Reinventing Al Gore	Campaign finance, Integrity	5,508
Education Recession	Education recession	Education	5,296
Priority	AG Rx plan	Medicare/Drug plan	4,599
Agenda	Bush is cleaning up Texas	Integrity, Environment	4,276
Nonsense	Gore mother-in-law Rx	Medicare/Drug plan, Social Security, Integrity	3,903
Big Relief vs. Big Spending	Whose economic plan is best	Taxes, Budget, Spending	3,605
Tools	Children grow too fast	Families/Children	3,558
Gore-gantuan	2.2 trillion	Budget, Spending	3,299
Expect More	Hard things	Education	2,968
Phyllis	Phyllis Hunter	Education, Record	2,507

*Campaign Media Analysis Group
**The "Trust" ad aired 4,986 times in a thirty-second version and 5,550 times in a sixty-second version.

Table A.2 Gore/DNC Most Aired Ads

Campaign Title	CMAG* title	Issues	Airings
Impact	Fatherhood	Background, Taxes	5,351
Veteran	Veteran	Background, Record, Taxes, Education, Welfare, Crime, Children	5,206
Bean Counter	Play God	Health Care	4,760
Environment**	Environment	Environment, Special interest	4,467
Starts	Education	Education	4,098
Patients	PBR	Health Care	3,892
Question	Question SS	Record, Taxes, Budget, Health care	3,819
Why	Bush can't keep promises SS	Social Security, Integrity	3,774
Protect	Victim's rights	Crime	3,595
Cover	Cover	Medicare/Drug plan, Health care	3,564
Sign**	Bush got to be kidding	Environment, Special interest	3,293
Prescription Drugs	The Gore plan	Health care, Medicare/Drug plan	3,215
Accountability	Education plan	Education, Taxes	3,084
Doesn't Add	8 Nobel Laureates	Social Security, Taxes, Budget	2,927
Down	Trickle	Taxes, National debt, Social Security, Medicare/Drug plan, Education	2,858
Super	Prosperity	Economy, National debt, Education, Medicare/Drug plan, Taxes	2,777
Judge	Texas health care	Health Care, Children	2,595
NA***	Big oil tax break	Taxes, Health Care, Minimum wage, Environment	2,551

*Campaign Media Analysis Group
**The CMAG storyboards were unavailable for these ads. Based on the information coded in the WiscAds data, I've made an educated guess about what available campaign ads each most likely represents.
***I was unable to find a copy of this ad elsewhere for viewing so could not find the campaign's title.

APPENDIX B
Estimated Models for Chapter 4

The full-ordered probit models used to generate the figures presented in chapter 4 are reported below. Note that party identification was centered at the midpoint, so 0 represents Independents, –3 represents strong Republicans, and 3 represents strong Democrats. Issue priority was also centered at the midpoint, so 0 represents a respondent who gives the issue a "medium" priority, 2 represents a "very high" priority, and –2 represents a respondent who said the issue was not a priority at all. The estimates on the interaction between issue priority and party indicate whether partisans who prioritize an issue highly are more likely to hear their party's candidate talking about the issue (projection). The estimates for candidate emphasis represent the effect of increasing attention to an issue on the probability that an Independent who places a medium priority on the issue accurately hears the candidate talking about the issue. The estimates on the interaction between candidate emphasis and party indicate whether campaign emphasis has a stronger or weaker effect on the probability that a partisan accurately recognizes the emphasis (selective exposure). None of these interactions achieve conventional levels of significance.

The model can be summarized as (Equation 1)

$$\text{Hear Cand Issue}_{im} = \beta_0 + \beta_1 \text{Cand Issue Emphasis}_m + \beta_2 \text{Issue Priority}_i + \beta_3 \text{Party}_i + (\beta_4 \text{Issue Priority}_i \cdot \text{Party}_i) + (\beta_5 \text{Issue Emphasis}_m \cdot \text{Party}_i) + \mathbf{X}_j \beta_j + u_i$$

where i indexes individual respondents, m denotes the information environment, designated by a respondent's media market and time of interview, and $\mathbf{X}_j$ includes the individual-level control variables.

Table B.1 Hearing Education Talk

	Gore		Bush	
	Coefficient	SE	Coefficient	SE
Candidate Ad Emphasis	0.045**	0.019	0.022*	0.012
Issue Priority	0.056	0.040	0.030	0.040
Party ID	0.087***	0.032	−0.124***	0.034
Issue Priority × Party ID	0.009	0.018	0.021	0.019
Ad Emphasis × Party ID	0.004***	0.008	0.004	0.005
Political Awareness	0.571***	0.046	0.540***	0.045
Education	0.027***	0.032	−0.055*	0.032
Age	0.007	0.002	0.007***	0.002
Female	−0.029***	0.067	0.080	0.067
Minority	0.340*	0.089	0.163*	0.088
Days to Election	0.001	0.000	0.000	0.000
T_1	−0.897	0.116	−1.135	0.125
T_2	−0.410	0.114	−0.493	0.122
T_3	0.576	0.114	0.651	0.122
T_4	1.351	0.117	1.338	0.125
N	1065		1067	
Log Likelihood	−1520.01		−1502.24	
Model chi²	256.629		214.042	

***$p < .01$, **$p < .05$, *$p < .10$.

Table B.2 Hearing Health Care Talk

	Gore		Bush	
	Coefficient	SE	Coefficient	SE
Candidate Ad Emphasis	0.023	0.017	0.005	0.013
Issue Priority	0.014	0.038	0.022	0.038
Party ID	0.019	0.028	−0.039	0.029
Issue Priority × Party ID	0.058***	0.017	−0.018	0.017
Ad Emphasis × Party ID	0.005	0.007	−0.002	0.006
Political Awareness	0.494***	0.045	0.363***	0.045
Education	0.045	0.032	−0.072**	0.032
Age	0.009***	0.002	0.010***	0.002
Female	−0.058	0.067	0.109	0.067
Minority	0.397***	0.089	0.273***	0.088
Days to Election	0.001***	0.000	0.000	0.000
T_1	−0.786	0.116	−0.892	0.115
T_2	−0.277	0.115	−0.136	0.113
T_3	0.628	0.115	1.042	0.115
T_4	1.443	0.119	1.776	0.124
N	1059		1061	
Log Likelihood	−1531.69		−1461	
Model chi²	244.152		124.615	

Notes: ***$p < .01$, **$p < .05$, *$p < .10$.

Table B.3 Hearing Social Security Talk

	Gore		Bush	
	Coefficient	SE	Coefficient	SE
Candidate Ad Emphasis	0.061**	0.024	0.044***	0.014
Issue Priority	0.078*	0.042	–0.019	0.041
Party ID	0.013	0.031	–0.087***	0.032
Issue Priority × Party ID	0.048**	0.019	–0.018	0.019
Ad Emphasis × Party ID	–0.007	0.011	0.002	0.006
Political Awareness	0.586***	0.046	0.422***	0.045
Education	0.042	0.032	–0.027	0.032
Age	0.010***	0.002	0.013***	0.002
Female	–0.016	0.068	0.102	0.067
Minority	0.358***	0.089	0.195**	0.089
Days to Election	0.000	0.000	0.001	0.000
T_1	–0.845	0.110	–0.831	0.119
T_2	–0.291	0.108	–0.098	0.116
T_3	0.656	0.109	1.025	0.119
T_4	1.408	0.113	1.848	0.128
N	1062		1062	
Log Likelihood	–1520.29		–1470.18	
Model chi^2	282.021		206.419	

Notes: ***$p < .01$, **$p < .05$, *$p < .10$.

Table B.4 Hearing Tax Talk

	Gore		Bush	
	Coefficient	SE	Coefficient	SE
Candidate Ad Emphasis	0.054**	0.022	0.014	0.012
Issue Priority	–0.013	0.034	–0.052	0.034
Party ID	0.033	0.023	0.029	0.025
Issue Priority × Party ID	0.060***	0.016	–0.089***	0.016
Ad Emphasis × Party ID	0.004	0.009	–0.002	0.005
Political Awareness	0.322***	0.045	0.560***	0.046
Education	–0.070**	0.032	0.020	0.032
Age	0.007***	0.002	0.007***	0.002
Female	0.178***	0.067	–0.117*	0.067
Minority	0.367***	0.089	0.208**	0.089
Days to Election	0.001	0.000	0.000	0.000
T_1	–0.526	0.106	–1.138	0.109
T_2	0.190	0.105	–0.502	0.106
T_3	1.277	0.110	0.486	0.106
T_4	1.935	0.118	1.251	0.109
N	1064		1068	
Log Likelihood	–1489.3		–1527.64	
Model chi^2	137.582		269.378	

Notes: ***$p < .01$, **$p < .05$, *$p < .10$.

APPENDIX C
Estimated Models for Chapter 5

The regression models used to generate the figures presented in chapter 5 are reported below. Note that party identification was centered at the midpoint, so 0 represents Independents, −3 represents strong Republicans, and 3 represents strong Democrats. Issue priority was also centered at the midpoint, so 0 represents a respondent who gives the issue a "medium" priority, 2 represents a "very high" priority, and −2 represents a respondent who said the issue was not a priority at all. Consequently, the estimates for issue priority represent the effect of prioritizing the issue on the candidate evaluation for an Independent who is situated in a place that has received no candidate advertising on the issue. The estimates on the interactions between candidate emphasis and issue importance, between candidate emphasis and party, and between candidate emphasis, issue importance, and party indicate whether campaign emphasis strengthens the weight given to issue priority in candidate evaluations overall or for supporting partisans.

The model can be summarized as (Equation 2):

$$\text{Cand Eval}_{im} = \beta_{om} + \beta_{1m}\text{Issue Priority}_i + \beta_{2m}\ln(\text{Issue Emphasis}_m) + \beta_3 \text{Party}_i + \mathbf{X}_j \beta_j + u_{im}$$

where i indexes individual respondents, m denotes the information environment, designated by a respondent's media market and time of interview, and $\mathbf{X}_j$ includes the individual-level control variables. β_{1m} captures the primary relationship of interest, the relationship between how a citizen prioritizes an issue and her evaluation of the candidate. The weight given to issue priorities, though, is itself modeled as a function of the citizens' campaign environments. The weight citizens give to a particular issue in producing their evaluations of each candidate is allowed to vary as a function of the attention a candidate has paid to a particular issue within a respondent's media market, individual partisanship, and the interaction between partisanship and the respondent's campaign environment (Equation 3):

$$\beta_{1m} = \gamma_{10} + \gamma_{11}\ln(\text{Issue Emphasis}_m) + \gamma_{12}\text{Party}_i + \gamma_{13}[\ln(\text{Issue Emphasis}_m) \cdot \text{Party}_i]$$

Substituting Equation 3 into Equation 2 produces the estimated interactive model. The interaction between candidate issue emphasis and individual partisanship is included as well to adhere to the principle of marginality.

Table C.1 Tax Priority and Candidate Evaluations

	Gore Evaluations	Bush Evaluations
Tax Priority	−4.902***	1.354
	(0.845)	(0.988)
Tax Ads × Tax Priority	−0.028	0.493*
	(0.465)	(0.274)
Tax Ads × Partisanship × Tax Priority	0.139	0.084
	(0.218)	(0.131)
Tax Ads	0.968*	−0.385
	(0.544)	(0.353)
Partisanship × Tax Priority	0.340	0.378
	(0.402)	(0.470)
Tax Ads × Partisanship	−0.011	−0.108
	(0.269)	(0.173)
Partisanship	7.099***	−6.497***
	(0.557)	(0.639)
Ideology	−0.798**	2.801***
	(0.369)	(0.370)
Economic Perceptions	1.304***	1.214***
	(0.376)	(0.376)
Education	−0.202	−1.554**
	(0.738)	(0.740)
Political Awareness	1.669*	1.326
	(1.007)	(1.014)
Female	1.934	−2.476
	(1.533)	(1.538)
Age	0.014	0.004
	(0.047)	(0.047)
Minority	7.026***	−2.046
	(2.040)	(2.049)
Constant	38.751***	28.419***
	(6.257)	(6.309)
R^2	0.393	0.359
N	1023	1019

***$p < .01$; **$p < .05$; *$p < .10$. Standard errors in parentheses.

Table C.2 Education Priority and Candidate Evaluations

	Gore Evaluations	Bush Evaluations
Education Priority	2.927***	-2.810**
	(1.007)	(1.253)
Education Priority × Education Ads	0.020	0.266
	(0.522)	(0.302)
Education Priority × Education Ads × Partisanship	0.202	0.062
	(0.250)	(0.141)
Education Ads	0.635	-0.430
	(0.880)	(0.518)
Education Priority × Partisanship	-1.153**	-0.515
	(0.458)	(0.586)
Education Ads × Partisanship	-0.030	-0.272
	(0.416)	(0.239)
Partisanship	9.171***	-5.108***
	(0.795)	(1.001)
Ideology	-0.858**	2.929***
	(0.373)	(0.371)
Economic Perceptions	1.058***	1.388***
	(0.382)	(0.380)
Education	0.134	-1.814**
	(0.739)	(0.737)
Political Awareness	1.745*	1.257
	(1.011)	(1.009)
Female	0.488	-1.867
	(1.550)	(1.544)
Age	0.047	-0.013
	(0.048)	(0.047)
Minority	6.145***	-0.870
	(2.038)	(2.043)
Constant	32.261***	31.947***
	(6.401)	(6.459)
R^2	0.381	0.353
N	1025	1021

***$p < .01$; **$p < .05$; *$p < .10$. Standard errors in parentheses.

Table C.3 Health Care Priority and Candidate Evaluations

	Gore Evaluations	Bush Evaluations
Health Care Priority	2.717***	−1.678
	(0.992)	(1.103)
Health Care Priority × Health Care Ads	−0.205	0.251
	(0.378)	(0.321)
Health Care Priority × Health Care Ads × Partisanship	0.013	0.111
	(0.175)	(0.148)
Health Care Ads	1.109*	−0.355
	(0.577)	(0.494)
Health Care Priority × Partisanship	−0.784*	−0.186
	(0.436)	(0.489)
Health Care Ads × Partisanship	0.161	−0.304
	(0.265)	(0.225)
Partisanship	8.469***	−5.704***
	(0.704)	(0.793)
Ideology	−0.839**	2.958***
	(0.371)	(0.372)
Economic Perceptions	1.217***	1.321***
	(0.379)	(0.380)
Education	0.208	−1.895**
	(0.741)	(0.743)
Political Awareness	1.396	1.014
	(1.019)	(1.020)
Female	0.551	−2.080
	(1.545)	(1.547)
Age	0.021	0.006
	(0.048)	(0.048)
Minority	5.542***	−0.959
	(2.031)	(2.048)
Constant	32.036***	29.831***
	(6.348)	(6.408)
R^2	0.385	0.347
N	1019	1015

***$p < .01$; **$p < .05$; *$p < .10$. Standard errors in parentheses.

Table C.4 Social Security Priority and Candidate Evaluations

	Gore Evaluations	Bush Evaluations
Social Security Priority	−0.839	−0.852
	(1.009)	(1.174)
Social Security Priority × Social Security Ads	−0.387	0.922***
	(0.678)	(0.356)
Social Security Priority × Social Security Ads × Partisanship	0.733**	0.004
	(0.304)	(0.170)
Social Security Ads	1.416	−0.993*
	(1.066)	(0.574)
Social Security Priority × Partisanship	−0.693	−0.566
	(0.460)	(0.527)
Social Security Ads × Partisanship	−0.650	−0.287
	(0.483)	(0.276)
Partisanship	8.765***	−5.234***
	(0.769)	(0.877)
Ideology	−1.040***	3.016***
	(0.375)	(0.368)
Economic Perceptions	1.296***	1.261***
	(0.384)	(0.379)
Education	0.062	−1.758**
	(0.749)	(0.743)
Political Awareness	1.543	1.253
	(1.023)	(1.009)
Female	1.317	−2.446
	(1.573)	(1.558)
Age	0.049	−0.019
	(0.049)	(0.048)
Minority	5.779***	−1.096
	(2.062)	(2.047)
Constant	35.691***	29.849***
	(6.454)	(6.419)
R^2	0.371	0.356
N	1019	1015

***$p < .01$; **$p < .05$; *$p < .10$. Standard errors in parentheses.

NOTES

Introduction

1. Figure 1.1 includes the marginal approval rates from all polls referenced in the Roper Center's collection of Job Performance Ratings during each president's first year in office. Overlaid on these points is a lowess regression line that estimates the trend in approval rating, smoothing over the sampling error across the many polls and polling organizations.

Chapter 1. The Meaning of Presidential Accountability

1. Accountability requires the ability to sanction and is distinct from responsiveness (Manin, Przeworski, and Stokes 1999). A responsive government is one that adopts policies preferred by its citizens; an accountable government is one whose citizens can punish or reward it for outcomes and actions. Though both promote better representation, responsiveness depends on what leaders do and accountability depends, in large measure, on what citizens do.

2. Issue voting does occur, but empirical examinations increasingly strive to identify which limited segments of the public are more likely to engage in it. Political sophisticates (Lau and Redlawsk 2006) and the most certain (Alvarez 1997) are some of the primary suspects. As Fiorina (1981) rightly points out, though, many of the measures used to gauge issue voting seldom allow us, or require survey respondents, to distinguish between policy instruments and policy outcomes. Other work suggests that the congruence between individual attitudes, attitudinal agreement with candidates, and vote choice is, at least partly, a function of persuasion and projection (Rahn, Krosnick, and Breuning 1994; Ray 1999; Visser 1994); but see Markus and Converse (1979).

3. Out of a scale from 0 to 100, where 100 represents the same level of attention across all issues, Sigelman and Buell (2004) find presidential campaigns average about 71 percent overlap in issue attention profiles from 1960 to 2000. Relying on advertising, rather than Sigelman and Buell's record of campaign statements in the *New York Times*, Kaplan, Park, and Ridout (2006) find a similar level of issue convergence in the 2000 presidential election, 68 percent.

4. In a penetrating legal analysis, Gardner (2006) further argues that what current election law presupposes is election campaigns intended merely to tabulate already-held preferences, and it does not provide for the more deliberative or persuasive process embodied in the prospective view.

5. Senators elected with the president will never again share a ballot with him.
6. This was, for the founders, a feature of the American system, not a bug.
7. Manin, Przeworski, and Stokes (1999), among others, label this the electoral accountability perspective, implying that accountability is not part of the responsible party/mandate model. As Mansbridge (2003) insightfully explains, however, the promissory representation assumed by the party mandate model provides the most thoroughgoing foundation for accountability by delineating an explicit set of standards to which those in power will be held to account. The coherence imposed by parties and mandates is what makes accountability meaningful, in this view.
8. We might be tempted by the compromise position that voters exercise both forward-looking and backward-looking accountability, that elections may promote both promissory and anticipatory representation, but this is not a tenable position. While some voters may rely more on retrospective considerations, others on prospective considerations, this heterogeneity of voter calculus serves to muddy both signals. These two forms of citizen power are at odds. Voters sacrifice their ability to signal to governments what to do when they use their vote to render a judgment about what government has done (Manin, Przeworski, and Stokes 1999). This poses a fundamental problem for the prospective view, as reelection cannot clearly endorse a new platform while simultaneously rendering a judgment on fulfillment of the old platform.
9. An extreme example highlighted by Fiorina is provided by the war in Vietnam: "By the early 1970s, majority opinion favored the policy outcome of an end to the war. A significant part of the citizenry—and its size was often commented on—didn't much care how. Unilateral withdrawal or nuking the North appeared to be equally efficacious and acceptable means of bringing the boys home" (1981, 13).
10. Politicians are not, of course, entirely unconstrained. Presumably they will respond to the exogenous shocks of crises, scandals, or tragedies in anticipation of future voters' satisfaction with outcomes. But retrospective accountability provides no means for citizens to direct or constrain government attention.
11. Rudolph (2003) finds that the president is not considered the most responsible for economic outcomes by a plurality of citizens. In 1998, 32 percent said businesspeople were the most responsible for economic conditions, 31 percent claimed Congress as the most responsible, and 22 percent perceived the president as the actor most responsible.
12. Though the retrospective accountability model is largely a response to the failure of prospective accountability due to the absence of a responsible party system, work focusing on clarity of responsibility, ironically, promotes a more responsible party model as the only institutional context that accommodates a reasonable retrospective accountability (see, for example, Powell 2000).
13. Absent this, and with greater separation of the presidential and congressional electoral arenas (evidenced by the weak effect of presidential approval on congressional votes), "we should expect only a politics of imagery and deceit, a politics of claiming credit for positive events and conditions and shirking blame for negative events and conditions, neither of which the powerless executive had much to do with" (Fiorina 1981, 203).
14. Fiorina's more nuanced view still focuses on policy content, not priorities,

as I will here, though he rightly notes that these are often conflated for ideologues: A particular policy becomes the only way to achieve an end.

15. Citizens should, perhaps, be forgiven for not always knowing to which of these measures they ought to respond. The emphasis on objective economic outcomes elides the confusing multiplicity of outcomes about which we might care.

16. That scholars have seldom asked citizens about their perceptions of presidential policy fulfillment is, perhaps, testament to the unlikelihood that they hold for this possibility.

17. Achen and Bartels (2002), in particular, highlight the possibility of "blind retrospection," finding evidence that incumbent President Woodrow Wilson lost votes in New Jersey in response to the numerous and unprecedented shark attacks on the New Jersey coastline in the summer of 1916.

18. As Bartels (2008) notes, the government's ability to time growth in economic indicators, like income growth, strategically is a problem primarily because voters are so myopic.

19. The president, as "chief economist," may reasonably include the economy as a priority along with other goals and concerns.

20. Donald Stokes (1963) labeled these "valence" issues, a name that has stuck in political science. Valence issues are those on which the public generally agrees on the ends. Fiorina (1981) notes that some issues on which there is broad consensus on ends, such as reducing dependence on foreign oil, have come to be defined in terms of more controversial means, such as offshore drilling or an increase in the gas tax.

21. A handful of other studies have highlighted the role of issue importance over issue position in vote choice with reference to Congress (Abbe et al. 2003) and presidential primaries (Aldrich and Alvarez 1994).

22. Riker's work (see, for example, 1996), building on social choice theory, similarly argues that to the degree that leaders can shape the agenda, they can arrange the decision-making process to their advantage. Agendas are not wholly separate from alternatives but are fundamental to achieving, from a leader's point of view, a desirable outcome.

23. The adoption of super-citizen standards seems deeply embedded in the minds of the American public in ways that are quite damaging. Less politically involved citizens frequently don't believe their voice belongs in the public discourse unless they have considerable policy knowledge (Eliasoph 1998). Unfortunately, more politically involved citizens often agree (for instance, Caplan 2007).

24. Too much specificity also invites easy attacks by the opposition.

25. But see Sulkin (2005) for an examination of how the behavior of members of Congress responds to the campaigns of their recent challengers.

26. Political scientists have not ignored the link between presidential campaigning and governing entirely. At least three research agendas touch directly on the intersection of these activities and thus could prove instructive here. Work on candidate-centered campaigns credits the distancing of candidates from their parties with decreased coattails, more divided government, and the absence of any unifying philosophy within the party, all of which reduces the influence of the president on members of his party in Congress (Polsby 1983). The candidate-centered campaign also complicates presidential transitions, which can keep a new president from hitting the ground running (Jones 1998; Pfiffner 1996). Work

on "the permanent campaign," where presidents govern through a continual campaign for their policies, provides another point of intersection (Blumenthal 1980; Ornstein and Mann 2000). Curiously, while this work emphasizes the continued operation and strategy of the campaign, it neglects the content. Still, the retention of key campaign staff may serve to keep the campaign agenda in the mix. Finally, work on the fulfillment of campaign promises consistently concludes that presidents act on most of their promises (Fishel 1985; Krukones 1984; Pomper 1980). The rhetoric of the campaign is largely sincere, not simply politically expedient.

27. Presidency scholars acknowledge that the campaign agenda does influence the governing agenda on occasion, when a president expresses a high level of commitment to the issue (Kingdon 1995; Light 1999).

28. It also assumes it is desirable for the "ephemeral or weakly held policy preferences" of the public to be translated into policy, an assumption increasingly called into question by work on public opinion (for example, Bartels 2003; Geer 1996).

Chapter 2. Agenda Accountability in Action

1. Of course, a similar criticism has been leveled at the message communicated through the vote (Dahl 1990; Kelley 1983).

2. Erikson, MacKuen, and Stimson (2002) suggest policy liberalism does not appear related to approval in the aggregate because it improves approval among co-partisans and decreases approval among opposing partisans in countervailing ways. In my formulation, though, it is not the direction of policy but the selection of priorities that matters. Brody (1992) argues something similar.

3. Further, individuals in these models not only base their evaluations of presidents on the same criteria for all presidents, they also necessarily base their evaluations of a particular president on the same criterion as one another. There is no room for individual heterogeneity.

4. Brody's (1992) explanation relies on the more traditional notion of mass media priming, the transitory change in evaluative standards that result from recent news coverage. I argue, instead, that the presidential campaign is one of the events that regularly and predictably attempts to establish different, more favorable, criteria in an enduring way.

5. As an empirical matter, any analysis of aggregate approval will pick up precisely the evaluative considerations presidents have in common, not the variations on those considerations that individual candidates induce.

6. From political consultant James Carville's famous war-room haiku: "Change vs. more of the same; The economy, stupid; Don't forget health care."

7. The 1992 advertising data come from Just et al.'s study of the 1992 campaign (1996). While the television advertising data for 2000 and 2008 incorporate information about how often ads were aired to construct measures of issue emphasis, the 1992 data codes a representative sample of ads actually aired but contains no weighting for how frequently an ad was used.

8. Based on author analysis of the 1992 National Election Study survey. Respondents could list up to three problems in response to the open-ended question.

9. Clinton was caught off-guard when he learned that the budget resolution had endorsed spending caps that effectively slashed his investment proposals, later noting, "I don't have a goddamn Democratic budget until 1996. None of the investments, none of the things I campaigned on" (Woodward 1994, 161, 165).

10. ABC News/Washington Post Poll, February 25–February 28, 1993; ABC News Poll, July 30, 1993. This and subsequent data provided by the Roper Center for Public Opinion Research, University of Connecticut, unless otherwise noted.

11. Time/CNN/Yankelovich Partners Poll, February 10–February 11, 1993; Time/CNN/Yankelovich Partners Poll, May 12–May 13, 1993; Time/CNN/Yankelovich Partners Poll, January 17–January 18, 1994.

12. Newsweek/Princeton Survey Research Associates Poll, April 22–April 23, 1993; Gallup/CNN/USA Today Poll, August 8–August 10, 1993; Gallup/CNN/USA Today Poll, November 2–November 4, 1993.

13. Gallup/CNN/USA Today Poll, April 20–April 22, 2001; Gallup/CNN/USA Today Poll, August 10–August 12, 2001.

14. Time/CNN/Harris Interactive Poll, July 10–July 11, 2002.

15. CNN/Opinion Research Corporation Poll, August 23–August 24, 2008. Data obtained from PollingReport.com.

16. USA Today/Gallup Poll, August 21–August 23, 2008. Data obtained from PollingReport.com.

17. CNN/Opinion Research Corporation Poll, August 23–August 24.

18. At least some conservatives were assuaged when McCain appointed the conservative governor of Alaska, Sarah Palin, as his running mate.

19. Based on trial heats reported at PollingReport.com.

20. Iraq played a more modest role in the general election as it was overshadowed by the floundering economy. It has been deemed central, though, to Obama's primary victory (Saldin 2008).

21. Al Franken, a Democratic senator from Minnesota, was not sworn in until July 7, 2009, after a prolonged court battle.

22. Though the Bush tax cuts of 2001 and 2003 were larger, the impact of cuts in the first two years for each of these was smaller—totaling $174 billion in 2002–2003 and $231 billion in 2004–2005. Obama's tax cuts, in comparison, totaled $288 billion in the two years for which they were in effect (Weisman and Bendavid 2009).

23. Congress, though, has inhibited Obama's ability to close Guantánamo. In June, Congress denied Obama's request for $80 million in a fiscal 2009 supplemental spending measure to help finance the closing of the prison. The fiscal 2010 Defense appropriations bill, passed in December, continued to deny funds requested by Obama to initiate the prison's closure (Oliveri 2009). In October, Congress passed a Homeland Security spending measure prohibiting the transfer of detainees from Guantánamo Bay, Cuba, to the United States except for prosecution (Anderson 2009).

24. When Senator Franken was seated in July, Democrats had their sixty seats.

25. In the midst of all of this, Obama was awarded, unexpectedly and controversially, the Nobel Peace Prize, underscoring his remarkable first year.

26. Marist Poll, April 1–April 3. Obama received high marks regardless of how the question was asked. Sixty-six percent said he has been keeping the promises

he made during the campaign (Gallup/USA Today Poll, April 20–April 21), 60 percent agreed he is keeping his major campaign promises (ABC News/Washington Post Poll, April 21–April 24), and 68 percent said he is doing a good job of keeping the important promises he made during the campaign (CNN/Opinion Research Corporation Poll, April 23–April 26, 2009).

27. Gallup/USA Today Poll, October 16–October 19.
28. ABC News/Washington Post Poll, January 12–January 15.

Chapter 3. Campaigning on Issues

1. Geer analyzes each appeal made in an ad (on average, twelve separate appeals per ad), so the percent of all *ads* in his analysis that reference issues is much higher—92 percent.

2. Some presidential candidates did attempt to speak more directly to the people prior to the widespread use of radio and other communication technologies to transmit candidate messages—most notably, Williams Jennings Bryan in his 1896 campaign. But only with the development of a national communications network could candidates be assured that their messages would be disseminated both broadly and accurately.

3. In the absence of campaign dialogue, though, such issue specificity will not make the contrasts between the candidates especially clear.

4. Page's findings regarding ambiguity in campaign rhetoric are similar, as well, to the findings of Pomper (1980) and Fishel (1985) regarding the specificity of campaign pledges.

5. Indeed, shared priorities and concerns is a key way that candidates convey "character" and emphasizing a problem conveys that a candidate cares about people "like us." In this way, candidate issue priorities work to bridge the divide between candidate image and substance.

6. Candidate commitment is universally neglected in models of voting. Spatial models, concerned with the proximity of voter issue positions to candidate issue positions, have tried to account for personal or national issue salience, that is, how important an issue is to an individual or in the aggregate. But these models do not acknowledge that commitment on the part of a candidate also varies.

7. An update of Fishel's approach applied to Clinton produces a comparable estimate of 69 percent of promises fully or partially fulfilled (Shaw 1998).

8. These records were broken in subsequent presidential election cycles.

9. The 1992 campaign generated the most interest in this period, with 83 percent responding they were somewhat or very interested. The 1972 campaign was a low point, with only 72 percent expressing interest.

10. Analysis of the "Most Important Problem" question asked in National Election Studies surveys demonstrates that the economy was named by a plurality of respondents in 1976, 1980, 1988, and 1992. The economy tied for the top spot in 1984, along with foreign affairs. Foreign affairs ranks the highest in 1960, 1964, 1968, and 1972. And social welfare issues (such as education, housing, health care, welfare) are at the top of the list in 1996 and 2000.

11. 1976, 1980, 1984, 1988, and 1992.

12. Some of these limitations are overcome by examining part of this process for presidents Clinton and Obama in chapter 7.

13. At the end of the 1998–1999 season, *NBC Nightly News* ranked first in the Nielsen ratings for overall viewers, households, and adults 25–54. Campaign coverage across different networks tends to be highly correlated (Hofstetter 1976; Patterson 1980; Williams, Shapiro, and Cutbirth 1983), and local network and newspaper coverage resemble national network coverage (Just et al. 1996). Consequently, the coverage of the campaign on *NBC Nightly News* serves as a reasonable measure of the information available to most citizens.

14. These issues were also the most frequently mentioned in the candidates' national press releases (Marschall and McKee 2002). Among Bush's national campaign press releases, education received the most attention, mentioned in 38 percent of the press releases, followed by taxes (35.5 percent), health care (33.7 percent), and Social Security (27.1 percent). Gore's press releases most frequently mentioned taxes (54 percent), health care (50.1 percent), education (40.6 percent), and Social Security (35.9 percent).

15. These are the four issues asked about in the survey.

16. I focus on the most frequently aired ads by each candidate, those aired more than 2,500 times. These ads are broadly representative of the candidates' advertising campaigns overall, based on a viewing of the ads and storyboards for the majority of ads aired. The names, number of airings, and issues mentioned in each ad are provided in the appendix.

Chapter 4. Hearing the Campaign

1. These thoughts about candidates, though, need not involve issue positions.

2. We might well expect, however, that learning issue positions implies having heard the candidates emphasize an issue.

3. While it is generally taken for granted that citizens pick up the campaign agenda, the studies often cited in favor of this conclusion (for example, Just et al. 1996; West 1997) do not actually demonstrate this conventional wisdom.

4. The University of Wisconsin Survey Center administered the survey component. The UWSC conducted a daily national telephone survey from November 1999 to November 2000 of the forty-eight contiguous states, with sampling carried out on a daily basis. Thus, each day's interviews represent a very small sample that is independent of each other day's sample, allowing for respondents to be aggregated to any desired time point or split on any day to produce larger independent samples. Approximately thirty interviews were completed each week, producing a total of 1,528 respondents through Election Day.

5. These measures are used to construct an index of political awareness for the analyses that follow.

6. More so, of course, in times of peace.

7. Although the 2000 campaign saw the arrival of several massive and innovative election surveys—the National Annenberg Election Survey and the Vanishing Voter Project—these studies, unfortunately, do not contain questions on what citizens heard, used here, or on how citizens prioritized the key issues, used in the next chapter.

8. I will use the variation in campaign time and contexts to compare the responses of citizens inhabiting different information environments. Given the general correspondence between the issue emphasis in advertising and in na-

tional news coverage and the growing attention to advertising by both voters and scholars, I will focus primarily on the advertising campaign as a measure of campaign discourse.

9. While I cannot ascertain whether individuals actually saw the ads aired in their media markets, I can produce measures of how available candidate campaign themes were in their geographic and temporal contexts. Since much campaign information is transmitted via other sources—opinion leaders, social networks, or the mass media—the impact of such advertising does not rest solely on observation of the spots by individuals. Nonetheless, a measure of exposure to the ads would be preferable. Lacking this, the ad measure contains error and the resulting estimates of the effects based on the ads should be attenuated. While controlling for political attentiveness should help soak up some of the noise in the ad measure, thereby increasing the signal-to-noise ratio and reducing the bias, unquestionably some attenuation bias remains. In addition, the bulk of real-world, campaign-effects studies do not directly link the campaign *content* with public opinion, instead looking for outcomes like differences in evaluations or differences in the predictors of evaluations across different campaigns. Thus, even an imperfect link between campaign content and citizen opinion constitutes a worthwhile improvement.

10. In addition, these counts of issue mentions are logged. A candidate cannot continually increase the reception of his issue message simply by talking about an issue continuously. As an attempt at recognizing this constraint, I use the natural log of the ad count to reflect the decreasing marginal impact of more and more ad airings on the same issue.

11. The values for the histogram are represented along the right y axis. The histogram does not represent the overall distribution of a candidate's advertising on an issue but the distribution of the respondents' media environments as they vary over both time and location. So the peak at zero is a combination of folks living in media markets that the candidates ignored as well as folks interviewed before the candidates started advertising in earnest.

12. These results do not demonstrate that projection is occurring but are consistent with such a process. It is also consistent with issue publics—those most concerned about an issue—managing to pick up agenda emphases from other venues.

Chapter 5. Candidate Messages and Citizen Expectations

1. This distinction between recency and frequency priming is key, I suspect, to resolving the debate about whether the most informed (Krosnick and Brannon 1993; Miller and Krosnick 2000) or the least informed (Iyengar et al. 1984; Krosnick and Kinder 1990) are more susceptible to priming. For example, recency priming may be greater for individuals with low levels of knowledge due to their reliance on considerations to which they have been recently exposed. Frequency priming may be more effective for the most knowledgeable, however, because a more organized knowledge structure makes it easier for these individuals to make sense of new information, find an appropriate place to incorporate it into memory, and retrieve it at a later date.

2. Altering what goes into an evaluation, or the weight given to particular con-

siderations, has the potential to alter the evaluation itself. Changing the weights citizens give to particular issues, however, need not necessarily alter the aggregate evaluations or the distribution of public issue priorities.

3. The authors don't pursue the suggestive differences produced from repetition over five days and repetition in the same day in any detail. In comparing one-day experiments that include three or six priming messages, however, Iyengar and Kinder find no discernible difference.

4. This interpretation reminds us that economic voting, Key's (1966) reward–punishment process, is not automatic. Further, if the campaign can make the economy more or less salient, it can make other issues more or less salient.

5. This is largely a function of the type of data that has been widely available to date, most of which is not especially well suited to capturing spatial or temporal dynamics in public responses to a campaign that varies over time and space.

6. I also tried a third measure using the previous seven days. The results with this measure consistently fell somewhere between the accumulated and three-day measures.

7. The key coefficients in the models are two- and three-way interactions, and the coefficients in interactive models don't convey everything we want to know. In particular, it is not always clear from these coefficients when the marginal effect of the variable of interest is significant. The three-way interactions with continuous variables can make interpretation especially difficult to convey clearly, as marginal effects depend on the summation of three coefficients. For instance, even if none of the constitutive coefficients are individually significant, the marginal effect of an issue priority may be significant if the covariance terms comprising the standard errors are negative. For a cogent discussion of these issues, see Brambor, Clark, and Golder (2006).

8. Because the inclusion of confidence intervals for all three lines would overwhelm the figures, I follow Brambor et al.'s (2006) recommendation and use stars to indicate at what points on the graph the marginal effects are statistically significant.

9. As in chapter 4, the spike at zero represents both places that never received any advertising attention to the issue along with places that hadn't received any advertising attention to the issue by the time the respondent was interviewed.

10. The marginal effect of education priority on evaluations for Bush among independents is about -3. So the difference between an Independent who prioritizes education the most highly (a 2 on the education priority measure) and an Independent who doesn't prioritize education at all (a -2 on the priority measure) would be $(-3 \cdot 2) - (-3 \cdot -2) = -12$ in overall evaluations of Bush, all else equal.

Chapter 6. Campaign Connections and Presidential Evaluations

1. The president's unitary powers have, perhaps, been undersold (Mayer 2002; Howell 2003), but Pomper's seminal study on party platform promise-keeping found only about 10 percent of platform promises were enacted via executive powers (1980). Rudalevige, too, demonstrates that the president's legislative program is a cornerstone of the administration, representing the core of his policy agenda (2002). Consequently, most of the campaign priorities with which we're concerned will require congressional cooperation.

Notes to Chapter 6

2. Scholarship on the concept of mandates demonstrates how presidents use the mandate argument strategically to influence lawmakers (Conley 2001); but strategic presidents must base their mandate claims on the agenda put forward in their campaigns. These claims are most valid when candidates have talked about an issue, citizens understand that a candidate has talked about an issue, and citizens agree with the assessment of the candidate that the issue is worthy of a high level of national attention.

3. Similarly, Edwards and Barrett (2000) find that presidential initiatives make up 41 percent of potentially significant bills on the congressional agenda in the first two years of a president's term. In the second half of a presidential term, presidential initiatives make up 30 percent of the potentially significant bills on the congressional agenda.

4. Media practices reinforce the influence of first-term activity. Rozell notes that the media's early evaluations of presidential leadership "provide the touchstone to which journalists return throughout the term" (1996, 168). Early legislative success or failure colors impressions in ways that tend to stick. Carter's persistent bad reputation on this front despite his increased success during his administration, and Reagan's enduring positive reputation based on his first-year success despite his weakening prowess, are testament to this endurance.

5. Peterson notes that 43 percent of the president's lowest priority proposals are ignored in Congress, while neglect is the outcome for only 20 percent of the president's highest priority proposals (1993, 170–71).

6. These connections, once established, need not persist on their own to wield influence. The development of associations between candidates and issues in the minds of citizens means that these issues and ideas are more easily processed and incorporated when later mentioned by the president, the media, the opposing party, or future challengers. In short, citizens are more readily reminded of these links by elites with an interest in persuading a president to be accountable.

7. In comparison, Bush's much vaunted faith-based initiative received only four paragraphs of attention.

8. From the author's content analysis of the president's spoken remarks in the *Public Papers of the President of the United States: George W. Bush*, 2001.

9. During the campaign, the tax-cut proposal was generally justified in terms of the record budget surplus.

10. The president initiates the annual federal budget process with a detailed proposal, usually in February. Congress then develops a blueprint, a budget resolution, that sets limits on how much each committee can spend or reduce revenues over the course of the year. The budget resolution is not law and does not require the president's signature but is enforced against individual appropriations, entitlement bills, and tax bills on the House and Senate floors.

11. Bush would not seriously revisit the issue until his second term, though Social Security played little role in his 2004 campaign (only 7 percent of Bush's aired ads in 2004 mentioned the issue).

12. In March of 2002, the administration began the process of creating the required regulation, finally issuing a regulation in August. In December 2003, after making it one of his top legislative priorities that year, Bush signed a law that added a prescription drug benefit to Medicare and included the discount cards (Connolly 2003).

13. Issue approvals of education, taxes, Social Security, or prescription drug coverage were not asked again in 2001 after September 11.

14. More specifically, plotted in the lower panel are the coefficients from a regression of presidential approval on the approval rating of education, controlling for party identification, educational achievement, age, and gender. This and all subsequent graphs are drawn on the same scale for comparability.

15. The July Gallup poll, though, was completed the day before Bush began talking about his Medicare reform principles and his discount drug card proposal.

16. Recall that he had not successfully seen education reform become law by September 2001.

Chapter 7. Beyond the Voting Booth: Clinton 1993 and Obama 2009

1. From the author's content analysis of the president's spoken remarks in the *Public Papers of the President of the United States: William J. Clinton,* 1993.

2. Clinton was caught off-guard when he learned that the budget resolution had endorsed spending caps that effectively slashed his investment proposals, later noting, "I don't have a goddamn Democratic budget until 1996. None of the investments, none of the things I campaigned on" (Woodward 1994, 161, 165).

3. The issue approval data pulls together polls sponsored by Gallup, ABC/the *Washington Post*, NBC/the *Wall Street Journal*, CBS/the *New York Times,* and *Time/CNN* from January to December 1993. Only organizations that asked about approval of the relevant issues more than once during this period were included. The polls were provided by the Roper Center for Public Opinion Research, University of Connecticut.

4. As in chapter 6, the effects of issue approval on job performance represent the magnitude of the coefficient of performance ratings regressed on each issue approval while controlling for partisan identification, education, gender, and race.

5. Approval of Clinton's handling of the economy and of the budget deficit are the most highly correlated issue approvals in the nine surveys in which they both occur. Given the view of economists that large deficits slow economic growth, this is reasonable correlation.

6. Moderate Republicans Arlen Specter (Penn.), Olympia Snowe (Maine), and Susan Collins (Maine) were the only Republicans to support the bill.

7. Some media commentators contend that the media misrepresented public opinion by highlighting the minority of rowdy gatherings at the expense of the mostly civil sessions encountered by members of both parties (see, for example, Dionne 2009).

8. After the death of Senator Edward M. Kennedy, D-Mass., and the election of Republican Scott Brown on January 19, 2010, to fill his seat, Senate Democrats lost their filibuster-proof majority. The fate of health care became more precarious. Nevertheless, Congress passed comprehensive health-care reform and on March 23, 2010, Obama signed into law the Patient Protection and Affordable Care Act. A week later, Obama signed the Health Care and Education Reconciliation Act of 2010 enacting the House and Senate negotiated amendments to the initial legislation.

9. Nevertheless, conservative writer Conrad Black asserted that Obama's claim, from his January 27, 2010, State of the Union Address, of having cut taxes for 95 percent of working families "strained credibility" (Black 2010).

10. Foreign policy has the fourth biggest effect on job approval, on average, for both President Clinton and President Bush.

11. For Clinton, the budget deficit was also in the top four. For Obama, foreign policy rounded out the top four.

Chapter 8. Campaign-Driven Accountability

1. It is worth keeping in mind that all decision makers use shortcuts. Indeed, members of Congress, even with access to policy briefings, expert testimony at committee hearings, and staffers employed to keep them informed on everything from the economy to foreign policy to constitutional law, use decision-making shortcuts (Kingdon 1989). How could we expect citizens to do more with less? Of course, the more relevant to future behavior the shortcut is, the better. Issue priorities are strongly related to future presidential behavior.

2. Hard positions may also occur in the form of attacks against an opponent's proposals. Obama, for instance, consistently attacked McCain's support for lifting the tax deduction for health-care benefits in the 2008 campaign. Consequently, it was harder for the president or Democrats in Congress to consider lifting the deduction as a source of funding their own health-care reform efforts.

3. Popular misunderstanding of how governing is supposed to work, in particular a belief in presidentialism, would seem to justify distrust in government and dissatisfaction with politicians when faced with how government actually operates.

4. In addition, an explicit focus on priorities would serve to remind citizens that the priorities—and values—of others differ from their own, something people do not always recognize (Hibbing and Theiss-Morse 2002).

5. Voters have always used information shortcuts to inform their choices. Sometimes these have been understood in terms of individual characteristics, as when demographics are presumed to signal interests. Sometimes these have been understood in terms of party identification. But these interests are clearly related to issue priorities. In the candidate-centered era, candidates may have to establish or renew these shared priorities more explicitly.

6. The more politically knowledgeable may still contact their congressional representative regarding votes and policy stands, of course.

7. Reducing the traveling campaign press corps might improve things, as the candidate's themes quickly become old news, boring and tedious, to reporters following a given candidate around (Bartels and Vavreck 2000).

8. Media coverage, if it provided more repetition and clarity of issue agendas, could help compensate for the regional neglect experienced by many voters.

REFERENCES

Abbe, Owen G., Jay Goodliffe, Paul S. Herrnson, and Kelly D. Patterson. 2003. Agenda Setting in Congressional Elections: The Impact of Issues and Campaigns on Voting Behavior. *Political Research Quarterly* 56 (4): 419–30.

Achen, Christopher H., and Larry M. Bartels. 2002, August 28. Blind Retrospection: Electoral Responses to Drought, Flu, and Shark Attacks. Presented at the annual meeting of the American Political Science Association, Boston, Mass.

Aldrich, John H., and R. Michael Alvarez. 1994. Issues and the Presidential Primary Voter. *Political Behavior* 16 (3): 289–317.

Aldrich, John H., John L. Sullivan, and Eugene Borgida. 1989. Foreign Affairs and Issue Voting: Do Presidential Candidates "Waltz before a Blind Audience?" *American Political Science Review* 83 (1): 123–41.

Allen, Mike. 2001. Bush Will Seek Big Hill Victories; Education Is First Priority in Ambitious Legislative Push. *Washington Post*, January 20, A1.

Althaus, Scott L., and Young Mie Kim. 2006. Priming Effects in Complex Information Environments: Reassessing the Impact of News Discourse on Presidential Approval. *Journal of Politics* 68 (4): 960–76.

Alvarez, R. Michael. 1997. *Information and Elections*. Ann Arbor: University of Michigan Press.

Anderson, Christopher J. 2007. The End of Economic Voting? Contingency Dilemmas and the Limits of Democratic Accountability. *Annual Review of Political Science* 10:271–96.

Anderson, Joanna. 2009. Senate Clears Bill That Would Limit Moving Detainees from Guantánamo. *CQ Weekly*, October 26, 2461.

Anderson, John R. 1983. *The Architecture of Cognition*. Cambridge, Mass.: Harvard University Press.

Arnold, R. Douglas. 1990. *The Logic of Congressional Action*. New Haven: Yale University Press.

———. 2006. *Congress, the Press, and Political Accountability*. Princeton: Princeton University Press.

Bai, Matt. 2009. Taking the Hill. *New York Times*, June 7, MM30.

Balz, Dan. 1992. Setting Priorities and Tone; Clinton Signals Governing Style. *Washington Post*, November 13, A1.

Balz, Dan, and Eric Pianin. 1992. Clinton Promises Open Door to Hill; Economic Plan Pledged Next Month. *Washington Post*, November 20, A1.

Bargh, John A., Ronald N. Bond, Wendy J. Lombardi, and Mary E. Tota. 1986. The Additive Nature of Chronic and Temporary Sources of Construct Accessibility. *Journal of Personality and Social Psychology* 50 (5): 869–78.

Bartels, Larry M. 2003. Is "Popular Rule" Possible? Polls, Political Psychology, and Democracy. *Brookings Review* 21 (3): 12–15.

———. 2005. Homer Gets a Tax Cut: Inequality and Public Policy in the American Mind. *Perspectives on Politics* 3 (1): 15–31.

———. 2008. *Unequal Democracy: The Political Economy of the New Gilded Age.* Princeton: Princeton University Press.

———. 2010. The Study of Electoral Behavior. In *The Oxford Handbook of American Elections and Political Behavior,* edited by Jan E. Leighley, 239–61. New York: Oxford University Press.

Bartels, Larry M., and Lynn Vavreck, eds. 2000. *Report of the Task Force on Campaign Reform.* Ann Arbor: University of Michigan Press.

Berelson, Bernard R., Paul F. Lazarsfeld, and William N. McPhee. 1954. *Voting: A Study of Opinion Formation in a Presidential Campaign.* Chicago: University of Chicago Press.

Bettelheim, Adriel. 2001. Senate Democrats' Priorities Drafted with an Eye on 2002. *CQ Weekly,* June 9, 1344–45.

———. 2009. Obama Reverses Bush Policies. *CQ Weekly,* January 26, 184–85.

Black, Conrad. 2010. The Obama Economy. *National Review Online,* February 4. http://article.nationalreview.com/423767/the-obama-economy/conrad-black (accessed April 26, 2010).

Blitzer, Wolf. 2009. Economy Tops Obama's List of '09 Priorities. *CNN,* October 31.

Blumenthal, Sidney. 1980. *The Permanent Campaign: Inside the World of Elite Political Operatives.* Boston: Beacon Press.

Bond, Jon R., and Richard Fleisher. 1992. *The President in the Legislative Arena.* Chicago: University of Chicago Press.

Brace, Paul, and Barbara Hinckley. 1992. *Follow the Leader: Opinion Polls and the Modern Presidents.* New York: Basic Books.

Brambor, Thomas, William Roberts Clark, and Matt Golder. 2006. Understanding Interaction Models: Improving Empirical Analyses. *Political Analysis* 14: 63–82.

Brehm, John O. 1993. *The Phantom Respondents: Opinion Surveys and Political Representation.* Ann Arbor: University of Michigan Press.

Brody, Richard A. 1992. *Assessing the President: The Media, Elite Opinion, and Public Support.* Stanford, Calif.: Stanford University Press.

Buchanan, Bruce. 1987. *The Citizen's Presidency: Standards of Choice and Judgment.* Washington, D.C.: CQ Press.

Budge, Ian, and Richard I. Hofferbert. 1990. Mandates and Policy Outputs: U.S. Party Platforms and Federal Expenditures. *American Political Science Review* 84 (1): 111–31.

Bush, George W. 2001a. *Address before a Joint Session of the Congress on Administration Goals.* Washington, D.C.: Government Printing Office.

———. 2001b. *Statement on Senate Action on Education Reform Legislation.* Washington, D.C.: Government Printing Office.

Campbell, Angus, Philip E. Converse, Warren E. Miller, and Donald E. Stokes. 1960. *American Voter.* Chicago: University of Chicago Press.

Campbell, James E. 2001. The Referendum That Didn't Happen: The Forecasts of the 2000 Presidential Election. *PS: Political Science and Politics* 34 (1): 33–38.

Canes-Wrone, Brandice, and Scott de Marchi. 2002. Presidential Approval and Legislative Success. *Journal of Politics* 64 (2): 491–509.

Canes-Wrone, Brandice, and Kenneth W. Shotts. 2004. The Conditional Nature of Presidential Responsiveness to Public Opinion. *American Journal of Political Science* 48 (4): 690–706.

Caplan, Bryan. 2007. *The Myth of the Rational Voter: Why Democracies Choose Bad Policies*. Princeton: Princeton University Press.

Carey, Mary Agnes. 2001a. Bush Proposes Drug Discount Card as Key Element of His Medicare Plan. *CQ Weekly*, July 14, 1690–91.

———. 2001b. Drug Plan's Low-Key Launch Signals Bush May Be Open to Deal. *CQ Weekly*, February 3, 281–82.

Carsey, Thomas M. 2000. *Campaign Dynamics: The Race for Governor*. Ann Arbor: University of Michigan Press.

Cheibub, Jose Antonio, and Adam Przeworski. 1999. Democracy, Elections, and Accountability for Economic Outcomes. In *Democracy, Accountability, and Representation*, edited by Adam Przeworski, Susan C. Stokes, and Bernard Manin, 222–49. Cambridge: Cambridge University Press.

Clarke, David. 2009. Budget Moves on Hard Party Lines. *CQ Weekly*, May 4, 1036–37.

Clarke, David, and Joseph J. Schatz. 2009. The Devil's in the Stimulus Plan Details. *CQ Weekly*, January 12, 77–78.

Clarke, Kevin. 2003. Nonparametric Model Discrimination in International Relations. *Journal of Conflict Resolution* 47 (1): 72–93.

Cloud, David S. 1993. Trade: Clinton Turns Up Volume on NAFTA Sales Pitch. *CQ Weekly*, October 23, 2863–64.

Cohen, Jeffrey E. 2008. *The Presidency in the Era of 24-Hour News*. Princeton: Princeton University Press.

Congressional Oversight Panel. 2009. Taking Stock: What Has the Troubled Asset Relief Program Achieved? December 9. http://cop.senate.gov/documents/cop-120909-report.pdf (accessed April 26, 2010).

Conley, Patricia Heidotting. 2001. *Presidential Mandates: How Elections Shape the National Agenda*. Chicago: University of Chicago Press.

Connolly, Ceci. 2003. Medicare Prepares to Cut the Cards; U.S. Issues Rules for Drug Discounts. *Washington Post*, December 11.

Connolly, Ceci, and R. Jeffrey Smith. 2008. Obama Positioned to Quickly Reverse Bush Actions; Stem Cell, Climate Rules among Targets of President-Elect's Team. *Washington Post*, November 9, A16.

Conover, Pamela Johnston, and Stanley Feldman. 1989. Candidate Perception in an Ambiguous World: Campaigns, Cues, and Inference Processes. *American Journal of Political Science* 33 (4): 912–40.

Converse, Philip E. 1964. The Nature of Belief Systems in Mass Publics. In *Ideology and Discontent*, edited by David Apter, 206–61. New York: Free Press.

Corrado, Anthony, and Thomas E. Mann. 2004. In the Wake of BCRA: An Early Report on Campaign Finance in the 2004 Elections. *Forum* 2 (2). http://www.bepress.com/forum/vol2/iss2/art3/ (accessed April 26, 2010).

Council of Economic Advisors. 2010. The Economic Impact of the American Recovery and Reinvestment Act of 2009. January 13. http://www.whitehouse.gov/administration/eop/cea (accessed April 26, 2010).

CQ Staff. 2001. Agency by Agency: Where the Money Would Go. *CQ Weekly*, March 3, 456.
Dahl, Robert A. 1990. Myth of the Presidential Mandate. *Political Science Quarterly* 105 (3): 355–72.
Dalager, Jon K. 1996. Voters, Issues, and Elections: Are the Candidates' Messages Getting Through? *Journal of Politics* 58 (2): 486–515.
Davenport, Coral, and Avery Palmer. 2009. A Landmark Climate Bill Passes. *CQ Weekly*, June 29, 1516–17.
Delli Carpini, Michael X., and Scott Keeter. 1997. *What Americans Know about Politics and Why It Matters*. New Haven: Yale University Press.
Dentzer, Susan. 2001. Securing a Commission. *PBS NewsHour*, May 2.
Devroy, Ann. 1993. Clinton Cancels Abortion Restrictions of Reagan-Bush Era; "Gag Rule" on Clinics, Federal Ban on Fetal Tissue Research Are Lifted. *Washington Post*, January 23, A1.
Dionne, E. J., Jr. 2009. The Real Town Hall Story. *Washington Post*, September 3, A19.
Drehle, David Von. 1992. Clinton Outlines His Economic Agenda; Short-Term Upturns Can Mask Long-Term Trends, Student Group Told. *Washington Post*, December 8, A6.
Druckman, James N. 2004. Priming the Vote: Campaign Effects in a U.S. Senate Election. *Political Psychology* 25 (4): 577–94.
Editorial. 1992. A Monumental, Fragile Mandate. *New York Times*, November 4, A30.
Edwards, George C., III. 2003. *On Deaf Ears: The Limits of the Bully Pulpit*. New Haven: Yale University Press.
———. 2008. *Governing by Campaigning: The Politics of the Bush Presidency*. New York: Pearson Longman.
Edwards, George C., III, and Andrew Barrett. 2000. Presidential Agenda Setting in Congress. In *Polarized Politics: Congress and the President in a Partisan Era*, edited by Jon R. Bond and Richard Fleisher, 109–33. Washington, D.C.: CQ Press.
Edwards, George C. III, William Mitchell, and Reed Welch. 1995. Explaining Presidential Approval: The Significance of Issue Salience. *American Journal of Political Science* 39 (1): 108–34.
Eggen, Dan, and Michael A. Fletcher. 2008. Obama Offers Recovery Proposals; He Announces Two More Officials on Economic Team. *Washington Post*, November 26, A3.
Eliasoph, Nina. 1998. *Avoiding Politics: How Americans Produce Apathy in Everyday Life*. New York: Cambridge University Press.
Enda, Jodi. 2001. Bush Reaches Out to Liberal Kennedy on Education. *Philadelphia Inquirer*, January 26, A12.
Erikson, Robert S., Michael B. MacKuen, and James A. Stimson. 2002. *The Macro Polity*. New York: Cambridge University Press.
Farnsworth, Stephen J., and S. Robert Lichter. 2002. *The Nightly News Nightmare: Network Television's Coverage of U.S. Presidential Elections, 1988–2000*. Lanham, MD: Rowman and Littlefield.
———. 2005. *Mediated Presidency: Television News and Presidential Governance*. Lanham, MD: Rowman & Littlefield.

Ferejohn, John. 1986. Incumbent Performance and Electoral Control. *Public Choice* 50 (1–3): 5–25.

Finn, Peter. 2008. Guantanamo Closure Called Obama Priority. *Washington Post*, November 12, A1.

Fiorina, Morris P. 1981. *Retrospective Voting in American National Elections*. New Haven: Yale University Press.

Fishel, Jeff. 1985. *Presidents and Promises: From Campaign Pledge to Presidential Performance*. Washington, D.C.: CQ Press.

Fletcher, Michael A. 2008. Aide: Middle-Class Tax Cut a Priority; Emanuel Hints That Increase for Upper Incomes Also Won't Be Postponed. *Washington Post*, November 10, A1.

Franz, Michael M., Paul B. Freedman, Kenneth M. Goldstein, and Travis N. Ridout. 2007. *Campaign Advertising and American Democracy*. Philadelphia: Temple University Press.

Frey, Dieter. 1986. Recent Research on Selective Exposure to Information. In *Advances in Experimental Social Psychology*, edited by Leonard Berkowitz, vol. 19, 41–80. New York: Academic Press.

Gardner, James A. 2006. Deliberation or Tabulation? The Self-Undermining Constitutional Architecture of Election Campaigns. Buffalo Legal Studies Research Paper No. 2006-013.

Geer, John G. 1996. *From Tea Leaves to Opinion Polls*. New York: Columbia University Press.

———. 2006. *In Defense of Negativity: Attack Ads in Presidential Campaigns*. Chicago: University of Chicago Press.

Geithner, Timothy. 2009, February 10. Secretary Geithner Introduces Financial Stability Plan. http://www.ustreas.gov/press/releases/tg18.htm (accessed April 26, 2010).

Gelman, Andrew, and Gary King. 1993. Why Are American Presidential Election Campaign Polls So Variable When Votes Are So Predictable? *British Journal of Political Science* 23 (4): 409–51.

Gilens, Martin, Lynn Vavreck, and Martin Cohen. 2007. The Mass Media and the Public's Assessments of Presidential Candidates, 1952–2000. *Journal of Politics* 69 (4): 1160–75.

Goldreich, Samuel. 2001. CBO Numbers on Steep Cost of Prescription Drugs for Seniors Fuels Medicare Overhaul Debate. *CQ Weekly*, March 24, 664.

Goldstein, Amy. 2001. Judge Blocks Prescription Discount Plan. *Washington Post*, September 7, A1.

Goldstein, Kenneth, Michael Franz, and Travis Ridout. 2002. Political Advertising in 2000. Combined File [dataset]. Final release. Madison: Department of Political Science at the University of Wisconsin-Madison and the Brennan Center for Justice at New York University.

Gorman, Siobhan. 2001. Schooled in Survival. *National Journal*, December 15, 3854–55.

Grant, Ruth W., and Robert O. Keohane. 2005. Accountability and Abuses of Power in World Politics. *American Political Science Review* 99 (1): 29–43.

Gronke, Paul. 1999. Policies, Prototypes, and Presidential Approval. Working Paper.

Gronke, Paul, Jeffrey Koch, and J. Matthew Wilson. 2003. Follow the Leader?

Presidential Approval, Presidential Support, and Representatives' Electoral Fortunes. *Journal of Politics* 65 (3): 785–808.

Hager, George. 1993. President Throws Down Gauntlet. *CQ Weekly*, February 20, 355–59.

Hall, Richard L. 1996. *Participation in Congress.* New Haven: Yale University Press.

Harris, John F. 2005. *The Survivor: Bill Clinton in the White House.* New York: Random House.

Hastie, Reid. 1986. A Primer on Information-Processing Theory for the Political Scientist. In *Political Cognition*, edited by Richard R. Lau and David O. Sears, 11–39. Hillsdale, N.J.: Erlbaum.

Heith, Diane. 2004. *Polling to Govern: Public Opinion and Presidential Leadership.* Stanford, Calif.: Stanford University Press.

Hershey, Marjorie Randon. 2001. The Campaign and the Media. In *The Election of 2000: Reports and Interpretations*, edited by Gerald M Pomper, 46–72. New York: Chatham House.

Hetherington, Marc J. 1996. The Media's Role in Forming Voters' National Economic Evaluations in 1992. *American Journal of Political Science* 40 (2): 372–95.

Hibbing, John R., and Elizabeth Theiss-Morse. 2002. *Stealth Democracy: American's Beliefs about How Government Should Work.* New York: Cambridge University Press.

Higgins, E. Tory. 1996. Knowledge Activation: Accessibility, Applicability, and Salience. In *Social Psychology: Handbook of Basic Principles*, edited by E. Tory Higgins and Arie W. Kruglanski, 133–68. New York: Guilford Press.

Higgins, E. Tory, and C. Miguel Brendl. 1995. Accessibility and Applicability: Some Activation Rules Influencing Judgment. *Journal of Experimental Social Psychology* 31 (3): 218–43.

Hodgson, Godrey. 1980. *All Things to All Men, The False Promise of the Modern American Presidency.* New York: Simon and Schuster.

Hofstetter, C. Richard. 1976. *Bias in the News: Network Television Coverage of the 1972 Election Campaign.* Columbus: Ohio State University Press.

Holman, Craig B., and Luke P. McLoughlin. 2001. *Buying Time 2000: Television Advertising in the 2000 Federal Elections.* New York: Brennan Center for Justice, New York University School of Law.

Howell, William G. 2003, July. *Power without Persuasion: The Politics of Direct Presidential Action.* Princeton: Princeton University Press.

Ifill, Gwen. 1992. Clinton, Gazing beyond Nov. 3, Outlines Vision. *New York Times*, October 28, A1.

Iyengar, Shanto. 1991. *Is Anyone Responsible? How Television Frames Political Issues.* Chicago: University of Chicago Press.

Iyengar, Shanto, and Donald R. Kinder. 1987. *News That Matters: Television and American Opinion.* Chicago: University of Chicago Press.

Iyengar, Shanto, Donald R. Kinder, Mark D. Peters, and Jon A. Krosnick. 1984. The Evening News and Presidential Evaluations. *Journal of Personality and Social Psychology* 46 (4): 778–87.

Iyengar, Shanto, and Adam F. Simon. 2000. New Perspectives and Evidence on

Political Communication and Campaign Effects. *Annual Review of Psychology* 51:149–69.

Jacobs, Lawrence R., and Robert Y. Shapiro. 1994. Issues, Candidate Image, and Priming: The Use of Private Polls in Kennedy's 1960 Presidential Campaign. *American Political Science Review* 88 (3): 527–40.

———. 1995. The Rise of Presidential Polling: The Nixon White House in Historical Perspective. *Public Opinion Quarterly* 59 (2): 163–95.

———. 2000. *Politicians Don't Pander: Political Manipulation and the Loss of Democratic Responsiveness*. Chicago: University of Chicago Press.

Jamieson, Kathleen Hall, and Paul Waldman, eds. 2001. *Electing the President, 2000: The Insiders' View*. Philadelphia: University of Pennsylvania Press.

Johnston, Richard, Andre Blais, Henry Brady, and Jean Crete. 1992. *Letting the People Decide: Dynamics of a Canadian Election*. Stanford, Calif.: Stanford University Press.

Johnston, Richard, Michael G. Hagen, and Kathleen Hall Jamieson. 2004. *The 2000 Presidential Election and the Foundations of Party Politics*. Cambridge: Cambridge University Press.

Jones, Bryan D., and Frank R. Baumgartner. 2005. *The Politics of Attention: How Government Prioritizes Problems*. Chicago: University of Chicago Press.

Jones, Charles O. 1998. *Passages to the Presidency: From Campaigning to Governing*. Washington, D.C.: Brookings Institution Press.

———. 1999. *Clinton and Congress, 1993–1996: Risk, Restoration, and Reelection*. Norman: University of Oklahoma Press.

———. 2000. Reinventing Leeway: The President and Agenda Certification. *Presidential Studies Quarterly* 30 (1): 6–26.

———. 2005. *The Presidency in a Separated System*. 2nd ed. Washington, D.C.: Brookings Institution Press.

Just, Marion R., Ann N. Crigler, Dean E. Alger, and Timothy E. Cook. 1996. *Crosstalk: Citizens, Candidates, and the Media in a Presidential Campaign*. Chicago: University of Chicago Press.

Kahn, Kim Fridkin, and Patrick J. Kenney. 2001. The Importance of Issues in Senate Campaigns: Citizens' Reception of Issue Messages. *Legislative Studies Quarterly* 26 (4): 573–97.

Kaplan, Noah, David K. Park, and Travis N. Ridout. 2006. Dialogue in American Political Campaigns? An Examination of Issue Convergence in Candidate Television Advertising. *American Journal of Political Science* 50 (3): 724–36 (July).

Keech, William R. 1995. *Economic Politics: The Costs of Democracy*. New York: Cambridge University Press.

Kelley, Stanley Jr. 1960. *Political Campaigning; Problems in Creating an Informed Electorate*. Washington, D.C.: Brookings Institution Press.

———. 1983. *Interpreting Elections*. Princeton: Princeton University Press.

Kelly, Michael. 1993. Gambling That a Tax-Cut Promise Was Not Taken Seriously. *New York Times*, February 17, A16.

Kernell, Samuel. 1978. Explaining Presidential Popularity. *American Political Science Review* 72 (2): 506–22.

———. 2007. *Going Public: New Strategies for Presidential Leadership*. 4th ed. Washington, D.C.: CQ Press.

Key, V. O. 1961. *Public Opinion and American Democracy*. New York: Alfred A. Knopf.

———. 1966. *The Responsible Electorate: Rationality in Presidential Voting, 1936–1960*. Cambridge, Mass.: Harvard University Press.

Keynes, John Maynard. 1960. *The General Theory of Employment, Interest and Money*. New York: Harcourt, Brace.

Kinder, Donald R. 1998. Communication and Opinion. *Annual Review of Political Science* 1:167–97.

King, John. 2001. President Bush Interviewed by CNN. *CNN*, April 25.

Kingdon, John W. 1989. *Congressmen's Voting Decisions*. 3rd ed. Ann Arbor: University of Michigan Press.

———. 1995. *Agendas, Alternatives and Public Policies*. 2nd ed. New York: HarperCollins.

Klapper, Joseph T. 1960. *The Effects of Mass Communication*. Glencoe, Ill.: Free Press.

Klein, Ezra. 2009. It's the System, Stupid. *Washington Post*, July 2. http://voices.washingtonpost.com/ezra-klein/2009/07/its_the_system_stupid.html (accessed April 26, 2010).

Kornblut, Anne E. 2001. Bush Tries to Build Ties with Kennedy. *Boston Globe*, January 11, A1.

Koss, Geoff. 2009. House-Passed Jobs Measure Will Wait. *CQ Weekly*, December 28, 2950–51.

Krosnick, Jon A. 1990. American's Perceptions of Presidential Candidates: A Test of the Projection Hypothesis. *Journal of Social Issues* 46 (2): 159–82.

Krosnick, Jon A., and Laura A. Brannon. 1993. The Impact of the Gulf War on the Ingredients of Presidential Evaluations: Multidimensional Effects of Political Involvement. *American Political Science Review* 87 (4): 963–75.

Krosnick, Jon A., and Donald R. Kinder. 1990. Altering the Foundations of Support for the President through Priming. *American Political Science Review* 84 (2): 497–512.

Krugman, Paul. 2008. The Obama Agenda. *New York Times*, November 7, A35.

Krukones, Michael G. 1984. *Promises and Performance: Presidential Campaigns as Policy Predictors*. Lanham, MD: University Press of America.

Lau, Richard R., and David P. Redlawsk. 2006. *How Voters Decide: Information Processing in Election Campaigns*. New York: Cambridge University Press.

Lazarsfeld, Paul F., Bernard R. Berelson, and Hazel Gaudet. 1944. *The People's Choice: How the Voter Makes Up His Mind in a Presidential Campaign*. New York: Duell, Sloan and Pearce.

Leonhardt, David. 2010. Judging Stimulus by Job Data Reveals Success. *New York Times*, February 17, B1.

Lewin, Leif. 2007. *Democratic Accountability: Why Choice in Politics Is Both Possible and Necessary*. Cambridge, Mass.: Harvard University Press.

Lewis-Beck, Michael S., and Martin Paldam. 2000. Economic Voting: An Introduction. *Electoral Studies* 19 (2–3): 113–21.

Lewis-Beck, Michael S., and Tom W. Rice. 1992. *Forecasting Elections*. Washington, D.C.: CQ Press.

Light, Paul C. 1999. *The President's Agenda: Domestic Policy Choice from Kennedy to Clinton*. 3rd ed. Baltimore, Md.: Johns Hopkins University Press.

Lowi, Theodore J. 1985. *The Personal President: Power Invested, Promise Unfulfilled*. Ithaca, N.Y.: Cornell University Press.
———. 2009. Bend Sinister: How the Constitution Saved the Republic and Lost Itself. *PS: Political Science & Politics* 42 (1): 3–9.
Lupia, Arthur, and Matthew D. McCubbins. 1998. *The Democratic Dilemma: Can Citizens Learn What They Need to Know?* New York: Cambridge University Press.
MacKuen, Michael B. 1983. Political Drama, Economic Conditions, and the Dynamics of Presidential Popularity. *American Journal of Political Science* 27 (2): 165–92.
MacKuen, Michael B., Robert S. Erikson, and James A. Stimson. 1992. Peasants or Bankers? The American Electorate and the U.S. Economy. *American Political Science Review* 86 (3): 597–611.
Magleby, David B. 2008. Rolling in the Dough: The Continued Surge in Individual Contributions to Presidential Candidates and Party Committees. *Forum* 6 (1). http://www.bepress.com/forum/vol6/iss1/art5/ (accessed April 26, 2010).
Maisel, L. Sandy, Darrell M. West, and Brett M. Clifton. 2007. *Evaluating Campaign Quality: Can the Electoral Process Be Improved?* New York: Cambridge University Press.
Manin, Bernard, Adam Przeworski, and Susan C. Stokes. 1999. Introduction. In *Democracy, Accountability, and Representation*, edited by Adam Przeworski, Susan C. Stokes, and Bernard Manin, 1–26. Cambridge: Cambridge University Press.
Mansbridge, Jane. 2003. Rethinking Representation. *American Political Science Review* 97 (4): 515–28.
———. 2004. Representation Revisited: Introduction to the Case against Electoral Accountability. *Democracy and Society* 2 (1): 1, 12–13.
Marcus, Ruth. 1992. Clinton Vows Fast Economic Action; Shifts on Abortion, Haitians Promised. *Washington Post*, November 13, A1.
Markus, Gregory B., and Philip E. Converse. 1979. A Dynamic Simultaneous Equation Model of Electoral Choice. *American Political Science Review* 73 (4): 1055–70.
Marschall, Melissa J., and Robert J. McKee. 2002. From Campaign Promises to Presidential Policy: Education Reform in the 2000 Election. *Educational Policy* 16 (1): 96–117.
Mayer, Kenneth. 2002. *With the Stroke of a Pen: Executive Orders and Presidential Power*. Princeton: Princeton University Press.
McGerr, Michael E. 1986. *The Decline of Popular Politics: The American North, 1865–1928*. New York: Oxford University Press.
McGraw, Kathleen M., and Milton Lodge. 1996. Political Information Processing: A Review Essay. *Political Communication* 13 (1): 131–42.
McGraw, Kathleen M., Neil Pinney, and David Neumann. 1991. Memory for Political Actors: Contrasting the Use of Semantic and Evaluative Organizational Strategies. *Political Behavior* 13 (2): 165–89.
McGraw, Kathleen M., and Marco Steenbergen. 1995. Pictures in the Head: Memory Representations of Political Candidates. In *Political Judgment: Structure and Process*, edited by Milton Lodge and Kathleen M. McGraw, 15–41. Ann Arbor: University of Michigan Press.

McGuinn, Patrick J. 2006. *No Child Left Behind and the Transformation of Federal Education Policy, 1965–2005.* Lawrence: University Press of Kansas.
McWilliams, Wilson Carey. 2001. The Meaning of the Election. In *The Election of 2000: Reports and Interpretations*, edited by Gerald M. Pomper, 177–201. New York: Chatham House.
Mendelsohn, Matthew. 1996. The Media and Interpersonal Communications: The Priming of Issues, Leaders, and Party Identification. *Journal of Politics* 58 (1): 112–25.
Milbank, Dana. 2001. Bush Likely to Drop Vouchers; Education Policy to Focus on Testing, States' Flexibility. *Washington Post*, January 2, A1.
———. 2010. Stimulus Criticism: It's the Gift that Keeps on Giving. *Washington Post*, February 18.
Milburn, Michael A. 1979. A Longitudinal Test of the Selective Exposure Hypothesis. *Public Opinion Quarterly* 43 (4): 507–17.
Miller, Joanne M., and Jon A. Krosnick. 1996. News Media Impact on the Ingredients of Presidential Evaluations: A Program of Research on the Priming Hypothesis. In *Political Persuasion and Attitude Change*, edited by Diana C. Mutz, Paul M. Sniderman, and Richard A. Brody, 79–99. Ann Arbor: University of Michigan Press.
———. 2000. News Media Impact on the Ingredients of Presidential Evaluations: Politically Knowledgeable Citizens Are Guided by a Trusted Source. *American Journal of Political Science* 44 (2): 301–15.
Montgomery, Lori. 2008. For Obama, White House Keys Could Come with License to Spend. *Washington Post*, November 6, A30.
Mueller, John E. 1973. *War, Presidents, and Public Opinion.* New York: Wiley.
Mufson, Steven, and Juliet Eilperin. 2009. Obama Issues Orders toward More Fuel-Efficient Cars. *Washington Post*, January 27.
Mufson, Steven, and Eric Pianin. 1993. Worried Clinton Aides Plot Strategy in Wake of Legislative Defeat. *Washington Post*, April 23, F1.
Mutz, Diana C., and Paul S. Martin. 2001. Facilitating Communication across Lines of Political Difference: The Role of Mass Media. *American Political Science Review* 95 (1): 97–114.
Nadeau, Richard, Richard G. Niemi, David P. Fan, and Timothy Amato. 1999. Elite Economic Forecasts, Economic News, Mass Economic Judgments, and Presidential Approval. *Journal of Politics* 61 (1): 109–35.
Nather, David. 2001a. Broad Support Is No Guarantee for Bush's Legislative Lead-off. *CQ Weekly*, January 27, 221–25.
———. 2001b. Democrats Leaving Their Stamp on Bush's Education Bill. *CQ Weekly*, May 12, 1079–81.
———. 2001c. Despite Senate's Plan to Cut a Deal, ESEA Bill Bogs Down in Details. *CQ Weekly*, April 28, 917–18.
———. 2001d. Education Bill May Create Senate Logjam. *CQ Weekly*, September 8, 2072.
———. 2001e. Education Bill Passes in House with Strong Bipartisan Support. *CQ Weekly*, May 26, 1256–57.
———. 2001f. Freed of Election-Year Pressures, Education Debate Begins in Earnest. *CQ Weekly*, April 21, 871–73.

Neustadt, Richard E. 1990. *Presidential Power and the Modern Presidents: The Politics of Leadership from Roosevelt to Reagan*. New York: Free Press.
Nicholson, Stephen P., and Gary M. Segura. 1999. Midterm Elections and Divided Government: An Information-Driven Theory of Electoral Volatility. *Political Research Quarterly* 52 (3): 609–29.
Nitschke, Lori. 2001a. Proposals to Alter Bush's Tax Plan Multiply despite White House Appeals for Unity. *CQ Weekly*, February 17, 377–79.
———. 2001b. Senate Tax Bill Trade-offs Leave a Fragile Coalition. *CQ Weekly*, May 19, 1145–49.
———. 2001c. Tax-Cut Bipartisanship Down to One Chamber. *CQ Weekly*, March 10, 529–33.
———. 2001d. Tax Cut Deal Reached Quickly as Appetite for Battle Fades. *CQ Weekly*, May 26, 1251–55.
———. 2001e. Writing Size of a Cut in the Budget Looms as Tax Turning Point. *CQ Weekly*, January 27, 218–20.
Obama, Barack. 2009a. Remarks Following a Meeting with Economic Advisers and an Exchange with Reporters. January 29. *Daily Compilation of Presidential Documents*, DCPD No. 00034.
———. 2009b. Remarks to Small-Business Owners and Community Lenders. March 16. *Daily Compilation of Presidential Documents*, DCPD No. 00157.
Oliveri, Frank. 2009. Congress Clears $636 Billion Defense Bill. *CQ Weekly*, December 28, 2948–49.
Ornstein, Norman J., and Thomas E. Mann, eds. 2000. *The Permanent Campaign and Its Future*. Washington, D.C.: Brookings Institution Press.
Ostrom, Charles W., and Dennis M. Simon. 1985. Promise and Performance: A Dynamic Model of Presidential Popularity. *American Political Science Review* 79 (2): 334–58.
———. 1989. The Man in the Teflon Suit? The Environmental Connection, Political Drama, and Popular Support in the Reagan Presidency. *Public Opinion Quarterly* 53 (3): 353–87.
Ostrom, Charles W., and Renée M. Smith. 1992. Error Correction, Attitude Persistence, and Executive Rewards and Punishments: A Behavioral Theory of Presidential Approval. *Political Analysis* (1): 127–83.
Page, Benjamin I. 1978. *Choices and Echoes in Presidential Elections: Rational Man and Electoral Democracy*. Chicago: University of Chicago Press.
Pan, Zhongdang, and Gerald M Kosicki. 1997. Priming and Media Impact on the Evaluations of the President's Performance. *Communication Research* 24 (1): 3–30.
Parks, Daniel J. 2001a. Bush's Budget Now before the Senate, Where Moderates Wield the Critical Votes. *CQ Weekly*, March 31, 711–13.
———. 2001b. GOP Budget Resolution Squeaks By, but Implementation Will Be Tougher. *CQ Weekly*, May 12, 1066–68.
———. 2001c. It's the Day of the Centrist as Bush Tax Cut Takes a Hit. *CQ Weekly*, April 7, 768–74.
Parks, Daniel J., and Lori Nitschke. 2001. CBO Update Bolsters Tax-Cut Plans. *CQ Weekly*, February 3, 276–77.
Patterson, Thomas E. 1980. *The Mass Media Election: How Americans Choose Their President*. New York: Praeger.

———. 1993. *Out of Order*. New York: Alfred A. Knopf.
———. 2002. *The Vanishing Voter: Public Involvement in an Age of Uncertainty*. New York: Alfred A. Knopf.
Pearlstein, Steven. 1992. Clinton Advisers Still Stress New Economic Tack. *Washington Post*, December 9, A14.
Peterson, Mark A. 1993. *Legislating Together: The White House and Capitol Hill from Eisenhower to Reagan*. Cambridge, Mass.: Harvard University Press.
Petrocik, John R. 1996. Issue Ownership in Presidential Elections, with a 1980 Case Study. *American Journal of Political Science* 40 (3): 825–50.
Petrocik, John R., William L. Benoit, and Glenn J. Hansen. 2003. Issue Ownership and Presidential Campaigning, 1952–2000. *Political Science Quarterly* 118 (4): 599–626.
Pfiffner, James P. 1996. *The Strategic Presidency: Hitting the Ground Running*. 2nd ed. Lawrence: University Press of Kansas.
Pianin, Eric. 1993a. Clinton to Press Major Deficit Cut; Short-Term Stimulus, Tax Reduction Fade. *Washington Post*, January 12, A1.
———. 1993b. House Passes Clinton Plan, Economic Stimulus Package. *Washington Post*, March 19, A1.
———. 1993c. Senate Endorses Clinton's Budget; GOP Thwarted in Moves against Plan. *Washington Post*, March 26, A1.
PolitiFact.com. 2010, February 2. Axelrod Claims Democrats Passed 25 Tax Cuts Last Year. http://www.politifact.com/truth-o-meter/statements/2010/feb/02/david-axelrod/axelrod-claims-democrats-passed-25-tax-cuts-last-y/ (accessed April 26, 2010).
Polsby, Nelson W. 1983. *Consequences of Party Reform*. New York: Oxford University Press.
Pomper, Gerald M. 1980. *Elections in America: Control and Influence in Democratic Politics*. 2nd ed. New York: Longman.
———. 2001. The Presidential Election. In *The Election of 2000: Reports and Interpretations*, edited by Gerald M. Pomper, 125–54. New York: Chatham House.
Popkin, Samuel L. 1991. *The Reasoning Voter: Communication and Persuasion in Presidential Campaigns*. Chicago: University of Chicago Press.
Powell, G. Bingham. 2000. *Elections as Instruments of Democracy: Majoritarian and Proportional Visions*. New Haven: Yale University Press.
Powell, G. Bingham, and Guy D. Whitten. 1993. A Cross-national Analysis of Economic Voting: Taking Account of the Political Context. *American Journal of Political Science* 37 (2): 391–414.
Price, Vincent, and David Tewksbury. 1997. News Values and Public Opinion: A Theoretical Account of Media Priming and Framing. In *Progress in Communication Sciences*, edited by George A. Barnett and Franklin J. Boster, vol. 13, 172–212. Norwood, N.J.: Ablex.
Quirk, Paul J., and Sean C. Matheson. 2001. The Presidency: The Election and the Prospects for Leadership. In *The Elections of 2000*, edited by Michael Nelson, 161–84. Washington, D.C.: CQ Press.
Rahn, Wendy M., Jon A. Krosnick, and Marijke Breuning. 1994. Rationalization and Derivation Processes in Survey Studies of Political Candidate Evaluation. *American Journal of Political Science* 38 (3): 582–600.

Ray, Leonard. 1999. Conversion, Acquiescence, or Delusion: The Contingent Nature of the Party-Voter Connection. *Political Behavior* 21 (4): 325–47.

Riker, William H. 1996. *The Strategy of Rhetoric: Campaigning for the American Constitution*. New Haven: Yale University Press.

Rivers, Douglas, and Nancy L. Rose. 1985. Passing the President's Program: Public Opinion and Presidential Influence in Congress. *American Journal of Political Science* 29 (2): 183–96.

Rozell, Mark J. 1996. *The Press and the Bush Presidency*. Santa Barbara, Calif.: Praeger.

Rubin, Richard. 2010. High Hopes, High Deficits. *CQ Weekly*, February 18.

Rudalevige, Andrew. 2002. *Managing the President's Program: Presidential Leadership and Legislative Policy Formulation*. Princeton: Princeton University Press.

Rudolph, Thomas J. 2003. Who's Responsible for the Economy? The Formation and Consequences of Responsibility Attributions. *American Journal of Political Science* 47 (4): 698–713.

Rudolph, Thomas J. and J. Tobin Grant. 2002. An Attributional Model of Economic Voting: Evidence from the 2000 Presidential Election. *Political Research Quarterly* 55 (4): 805–23.

Saldin, Robert P. 2008. Foreign Affairs and the 2008 Election. *Forum* 6 (4). http://www.bepress.com/forum/vol6/iss4/art5 (accessed April 26, 2010).

Schattschneider, E. E. 1960. *The Semisovereign People*. New York: Holt, Rinehart and Winston.

Sedikides, Constantine, and Thomas M. Ostrom. 1988. Are Person Categories Used When Organizing Information about Unfamiliar Sets of Persons? *Social Cognition* 6 (3): 252–67.

Shaw, Carolyn M. 1998. President Clinton's First Term: Matching Campaign Promises with Presidential Performance. *Congress and the Presidency* 25 (1): 43–65.

Shepsle, Kenneth A. 1972. The Strategy of Ambiguity: Uncertainty and Electoral Competition. *American Political Science Review* 66 (2): 555–68.

Shiller, Robert J. 2008. The Real Mandate Is to Bridge the Wealth Gap. *New York Times*, November 9, B6.

Shoemaker, Pamela J., and Stephen D. Reese. 1996. *Mediating the Message: Theories of Influences on Mass Media Content*. 2nd ed. White Plains, N.Y.: Longman.

Sides, John. 2006. The Origins of Campaign Agendas. *British Journal of Political Science* 36 (3): 407–36.

Sigelman, Lee, and Emmett H. Buell. 2004. Avoidance or Engagement? Issue Convergence in U.S. Presidential Campaigns, 1960–2000. *American Journal of Political Science* 48 (4): 650–61.

Simon, Adam F. 2002. *The Winning Message: Candidate Behavior, Campaign Discourse, and Democracy*. New York: Cambridge University Press.

Stevenson, Randolph T., and Lynn Vavreck. 2000. Does Campaign Length Matter? Testing for Cross-national Effects. *British Journal of Political Science* 30 (2): 217–35.

Stimson, James A. 2004. *Tides of Consent: How Public Opinion Shapes American Politics*. New York: Cambridge University Press.

Stokes, Donald E. 1963. Spatial Models of Party Competition. *American Political Science Review* 57 (2): 368–77.

Sulkin, Tracy. 2005. *Issue Politics in Congress*. New York: Cambridge University Press.

———. 2009. Campaign Appeals and Legislative Action. *Journal of Politics* 71 (3): 1093–1108.

Tufte, Edward R. 1978. *Political Control of the Economy*. Princeton: Princeton University Press.

Tyler, Tom R. 1982. Personalization in Attributing Responsibility for National Problems to the President. *Political Behavior* 4 (4): 379–99.

Visser, Max. 1994. Policy Voting, Projection, and Persuasion: An Application of Balance Theory to Electoral Behavior. *Political Psychology* 15 (4): 699–711.

Wayne, Alex. 2009. Senate Passes Sweeping Health Overhaul. *CQ Weekly*, December 28, 2944–47.

Weaver, R. Kent. 1986. The Politics of Blame Avoidance. *Journal of Public Policy* 6 (4): 371–98.

Weisman, Jonathan, and Naftali Bendavid. 2009. Obama Eyes $300 Billion Tax Cut. *Wall Street Journal*, January 5, A1.

West, Darrell M. 1997. *Air Wars: Television Advertising in Election Campaigns, 1952–1996*. 2nd ed. Washington, D.C.: CQ Press.

Westen, Drew. 2007. *The Political Brain: The Role of Emotion in Deciding the Fate of the Nation*. Cambridge, Mass.: Public Affairs.

Wilgoren, Jodi. 2001. In Reconciling School Bills, 2 Chambers Agree on Tests. *New York Times*, June 15, A34.

Williams, Wenmouth, Jr., Mitchell Shapiro, and Craig Cutbirth. 1983. The Impact of Campaign Agendas on Perceptions of Issues in the 1980 Campaign. *Journalism Quarterly* 60 (2): 226–31.

Wlezien, Christopher. 2001. On Forecasting the Presidential Vote. *PS: Political Science and Politics* 34 (1): 24–31.

Wood, B. Dan. 2007. *The Politics of Economic Leadership*. Princeton: Princeton University Press.

Woodward, Bob. 1994. *The Agenda: Inside the Clinton White House*. New York: Simon and Schuster.

Zaller, John. 1992. *The Nature and Origins of Mass Opinion*. New York: Cambridge University Press.

Zhao, Xinshu, and Steven H. Chaffee. 1995. Campaign Advertisements versus Television News as Sources of Political Issue Information. *Public Opinion Quarterly* 59 (1): 41–65.

INDEX

accessibility, 73–74, 88
accountability: agenda, 4–6, 20–22, 153–60; agenda neglect and, 120–21; campaign, 94–96, 114–15, 129–30, 144–47, 157–59; defined, 9–10; economic outcomes and, 15–16; improving, 150–53, 155–60; late follow-through and, 121–24; media, 156–57; practiced by citizens, 17–22, 23, 176nn7–11; prospective, 10–12, 17, 150–51, 155; reconsidered, 17–22; responsive government and, 175n1; retrospective, 12–16, 17, 152–53, 176n12; theory of agenda, 4–6
ads, election year: agendas of, 48–52; citizen perception effects of, 68; cumulative attention and, 81–87; focused on issues, 41; 1992, 29; 2000, 33, 45, 48–52, 92–93, 161, 162–63; 2008, 36
agendas: accountability, 4–6, 20–22, 120–26, 153–60; citizen control and, 160; during campaigns of Bush and Gore, 48–52, 54–55, 78, 112–13; interrupted, 124–28; midlevel follow-through of, 136–37; neglect, 120–21; priming, 72–73; priorities, 44–45, 58–59, 71, 92–94; sustained follow-through of, 133–35; variations on follow-through in, 140–44
Aldrich, John H., 77
American Recovery and Reinvestment Act (ARRA), 2, 38, 39, 130, 133, 136, 141
AmeriCorps, 32
anticipatory representation, 13
approval ratings, 2, 3, 39–40; of Barack Obama, 35–39, 130–44; based on wide variety of issues, 26–27; of Bill Clinton, 28–33, 118–28; citizen expectation variances and, 27; compared across issues, 109–12; evaluated at the individual level, 27–28; of George W. Bush, 33–35, 103–12; interrupted agendas an, 124–28; political significance of, 25–26; presidential focus and, 30–31; quick follow-through and, 133; understanding, 26–28; variation in standards of, 19–20. *See also* presidents
Aspin, Lee, 31; attention, citizen, 58–60; cumulative, 81–87
Axelrod, David, 141

Benoit, William L., 46
Bipartisan Campaign Reform Act (BCRA), 158–59
Blitzer, Wolf, 37
Bonior, David, 124
Borgida, Eugene, 77
Brody, Richard A., 27, 43
Brown, Scott, 185n8
Budge, Ian, 44
Bush, George H. W., 28–30, 33, 124
Bush, George W., 2, 40; ads, 33, 45, 48, 92–93, 161, 162–63; agenda of, 48–52, 54–55, 78, 92–94, 112–13; approval ratings of, 33–35, 103–12; campaign and accountability, 94–96, 144–47; citizen hearing and, 61, 62–70; cumulative attention and, 81–87; economic policies, 34–35, 99–101, 105–7; education legislation and, 95, 96–99, 105; inferences about, 61; issues in 2000 campaign of, 45–52; media coverage of, 52–53; Medicare prescription

201

coverage and, 102–3, *104*, 109; most frequently aired ads by, 161, *162–63*; person node of, 75; repetition used by, 81–83, 93; Social Security legislation, 102, *104*, 107–8; tax legislation and, 99–101, 105–7; victory over Al Gore, 11, 33–34, 77

Bush v. Gore, 33–34

Campaign Media Analysis Group, 47
campaigns and candidates: accessibility, 73–74, 88; accountability of, 94–96, 114–15, 129–30, 144–47, 157–59; agendas of, 20–21, 29, 34, 36, 48–52, 54–55; citizens interest in, 46, 56–57, 148–49; criticism of, 1–2; goals, 44; impact on governing, 22–24; inferences about, 60; media priming and, 76–79; policy making power of presidents and, 11–12; projection and, 60; promises made by, 1–2, 177–78n26; public ignorance about, 11; repetition used by, 78–79, 81–87, 93; research on citizen view of, 23–24; theory of agenda accountability applied to, 4–6. *See also* issues; priming
candidates. *See* campaigns and candidates
Carter, Jimmy, 30, 124
Cash-for-Clunkers, 137
Chafee, Lincoln, 100, 101
Cheney, Dick, 111
citizens: attention, 58–60, 81–87; control and agendas, 160; distortions in hearing messages, 60–70, 154; expectations of presidents, 27; hearing over time, 62–64; interest in campaigns, 46, 56–57, 148–49; message heard by, 57–60; perception and hearing, 64–70; practice of accountability, 17–22, 23, 176nn7–11; predispositions and hearing, 61
climate change, 39
Clinton, Bill, 2, 28–33, 40, 45, 149; approval ratings of, 118–20; campaign and accountability, 114–15, 144–47; economic agenda of, 30–32, 116–20; health care legislation and, 115–16, 121–24; interrupted agenda of, 124–28; NAFTA and, 29, 32, 115, 116, 124–26; tax legislation and, 120–21
Clinton, Hillary, 35, 115, 121
Congress: American Recovery and Reinvestment Act (ARRA) and, 2, 38, 39, 130, 133, 136, 141; Bipartisan Campaign Reform Act and, 158–59; legislative negotiations with Barack Obama, 130–31, 185n8; legislative negotiations with Bill Clinton, 117–18; legislative negotiations with George W. Bush, 96–99, 100–101; NAFTA and, 29, 32, 115, 116, 124–26; separation of powers and, 11–12; Troubled Asset Relief Program (TARP) and, 138–40
Conover, Pamela Johnston, 60, 61
Conrad, Kent, 100
cumulative attention, 81–87

Dalager, Jon K., 57
Democratic National Committee (DNC), 48

Economic Growth and Tax Relief Reconciliation Act, 101
economic policies: Barack Obama and, 39, 130–33, 137–40, 142; Bill Clinton and, 30–32, 116–20; George W. Bush and, 34–35, 99–101, 105–7; outcomes and approval ratings, 15–16, 176n11
education: ads, 49–50; citizen hearing over time and, 62; citizen perception and, 66–67; cumulative attention and, 84–85, 86; George W. Bush's presidency and, 95, 96–99, 105; priority, 92–93, *171*
Electoral College, 158
Elementary and Secondary Education Act of 1965, 96
Emanual, Rahm, 39
energy policies, 136–37, 142

Feldman, Stanley, 60, 61
Fiorina, Morris P., 12, 14, 175n2
Fishel, Jeff, 44–45
Ford, Gerald, 124
frequency priming, 182n1

Geer, John G., 41, 43, 46
Geithner, Timothy, 138, 139
Gephardt, Richard, 124
Gore, Al: ads, 33, 45, 161, *162–63*; agenda of, 48–52, 54–55; citizen hearing and, 60, 61, 62–70; Clinton's budget vote and, 32, 117, 118; cumulative attention and, 81–87; inferences about, 61; issues in 2000 campaign of, 45–52; loss to George W. Bush, 11, 33–34, 77; media coverage of, 52–53; most frequently aired ads by, 161, *162–63*; projection of issues and, 60; repetition versus recency priming and, 81–83
Grassley, Charles E., 100
Greenberg, Stanley, 31
Gronke, Paul, 27
Guantánamo Bay, 38, 179n23
Gulf War, 76

Hansen, Glenn J., 46
health care: ads, 48–49; Barack Obama and, 38–39, 133–35, 141–42, 185n8; Bill Clinton and, 115–16, 121–24; citizen hearing over time and, 63; citizen perception and, 68–69; cumulative attention and, 85, 86–87; George W. Bush and, 102–3, *104*, 109; priority, 92, *172*
hearing, message: citizen attention and, 57–60; distortions in, 60–70, 154; estimated models of, 165, *166–67*; explaining, 64–70; over time, 62–64
Hofferbert, Richard I., 44
Human Intelligence Collector Operations, 38

inferences about candidates, 61
Iran-Contra scandal, 76
Iraq War, 35, 38
issues: accessibility, 73–74; ads addressing, 41; approval ratings compared across, 109–12; citizen perception and, 64–70; messages heard by citizens, 57–60; overlap, 175n3; political parties and "ownership" of, 20, 46–47, 64; priorities, 43–44, 79–81, 165, *166–67*; projection, 60, 70; repetition

of, 78–79; specificity, 42–43; valence, 43, 177n20. *See also* priming
Iyengar, Shanto, 73, 76

Jeffords, James M., 34, 98, 100, 101
Johnson, Lyndon, 1
Jones, Charles O., 10, 11, 26, 159

Kahn, Kim Fridkin, 57
Kennedy, Edward, 96, 185n8
Kennedy, John F., 42
Kenney, Patrick J., 57
Key, V. O., 12, 14, 15
Keynes, John Maynard, 148
Kinder, Donald R., 73, 76
King, John, 98
Kingdon, John W., 21
Klein, Ezra, 157
Krosnick, Jon A., 60
Krukones, Michael G., 45

Light, Paul C., 1

Mansbridge, Jane, 16, 150
McCain, John, 35, 36–37, 129
McGraw, Kathleen M., 75
media coverage, 47, 52–53, 181n13; improving accountability of, 156–57; priming and, 76–79
Medicare, 37, 50, 70, 93; George W. Bush's presidency and, 102–3, *104*, 109
Milbank, Dana, 97
Miller, Zell, 100

National Defense Authorization Act, 32
National Election Studies survey, 46
NBC Nightly News, 47, 52–53, 181n13
Neumann, David, 75
Neustadt, Richard E., 12
Nixon, Richard M., 42
No Child Left Behind, 34, 96–99
node, person, 75
North American Free Trade Agreement (NAFTA), 29, 32, 115, 116, 124–26

Obama, Barack, 2, 40; accessibility of, 74; approval ratings of, 35–39, 130–44;

Index

campaign and accountability, 129–30, 144–47; economic agenda, 39, 130–33; energy legislation and, 136–37, 142; health care legislation and, 38–39, 133–35, 141–42, 185n8; tax legislation and, 133, 141; Troubled Asset Relief Program (TARP) and, 138–40; variations on agenda follow-through by, 140–44
"ownership" of issues, 20, 46–47, 64

Page, Benjamin I., 11, 16, 42–43
Panetta, Leon, 30
Patient's Bill of Rights, 50, 70
Patterson, Thomas E., 42
perceptions, citizen, 64–70
Perot, Ross, 29, 30
person node, 75
Petrocik, John R., 46
Pinney, Neil, 75
political parties: agendas and, 48; approval ratings and, 103–5; negotiation on legislation, 96–99; "owning" issues, 20, 46–47, 64; regression models and, 169–70, 171–73
PolitiFact, 141
Pomper, Gerald M., 44
presidents: limited powers of, 11–12, 90–92; role in policy making, 90–92; transition from campaigning to governing, 92–94. *See also* approval ratings; Bush, George W.; Clinton, Bill; Obama, Barack
priming, 72–73, 89; candidate-issue priority and, 80–81; components of, 73–76; media, 76–79; recency, 81–83, 182n1. *See also* issues
priorities: campaign, 44–45, 58–59, 71, 154; presidential powers and, 91–92
projection, 60, 70
prospective accountability, 10–12, 17, 150–51, 155

recency priming, 81–83, 182n1
regression models, 169–70, 171–73
repetition, 78–79, 93; representation, anticipatory, 13; versus recency priming, 81–83
Republican National Committee (RNC), 48
Republican Party. *See* political parties
retrospective accountability, 12–16, 17, 152–53, 176n12
Retrospective Voting, 12

Sasser, Jim, 32
Schattschneider, E. E., 20–21, 160
separation of powers, 11–12
September 11, 2001 terrorist attacks, 35, 47, 99
Sides, John, 11
social security: ads, 50–51; citizen hearing over time and, 63; citizen perception and, 67, 69; cumulative attention and, 85, 86–87; George W. Bush's presidency and, 102, 104, 107–8; priority, 92–93, 173
specificity, issue, 42–43
Specter, Arlen, 39, 101
Stokes, Donald E., 42
Sullivan, John L., 77

Tauzin, Billy, 102
taxes: Barack Obama and, 133, 141; Bill Clinton and, 120–21; as a campaign priority, 92–93, 170; citizen hearing and, 63; citizen perception and, 67–68; cumulative attention and, 85–86; George W. Bush and, 99–101, 104, 105–7
trade agreements, 29, 32, 115, 116, 124–26
Troubled Asset Relief Program (TARP), 138–40, 142

valence issues, 43, 177n20

Washington Post, 97
Wilson, Joe, 135
Wilson, Woodrow, 177n17
Wisconsin Advertising Project, 49

MICHELE P. CLAIBOURN is an assistant professor of political science at the University of Virginia.

The University of Illinois Press
is a founding member of the
Association of American University Presses.

Composed in 9.5/12.5 Trump Mediaeval
by Celia Shapland
at the University of Illinois Press
Manufactured by Cushing-Malloy, Inc.

University of Illinois Press
1325 South Oak Street
Champaign, IL 61820–6903
www.press.uillinois.edu